A Grim Almanac of
Sussex

D1638810

A Grim Almanac of

SUSSEX

W.H. JOHNSON

The Grim Almanacs
are from an original idea by Neil R. Storey

First published 2007
by Sutton Publishing

This edition published 2011

The History Press
The Mill, Brimscombe Port
Stroud, Gloucestershire, GL5 2QG
www.thehistorypress.co.uk

British Library Cataloguing in Publication Data.
A catalogue record for this book is available from the British Library.

isbn 978 0 7524 6509 8

Typesetting and origination by The History Press
Printed in Great Britain

Title page photograph: An
eighteenth-century public
execution. *(Kevin Turton)*

CONTENTS

Acknowledgements

I am very grateful to all those who have helped me with this book. Tony Spencer and Alan Skinner have accompanied me on photographing jaunts while Bob Harvey, a complete stranger, has given me access to the mugshots of long-dead convicts. Yet another stranger, Neil Storey, has generously permitted me to use pictures from his archive. As on previous occasions, researcher Viv Burgess has scoured the National Newspaper Library for illustrative material while Peter Longstaff-Tyrrell and David Arscott, both of them knowledgeable about our county, have readily answered plaintive pleas for help. And once more, I am grateful to graphic designer Andy Gammon for his response, as well as to Brian Allchorn. My thanks, too, go to artists Ted Shipsey and David Taylor and to Helen Wilson of Pentrich Historical Society for their generous help. John Dibley, former Assistant Chief Constable of Sussex, has also rallied to my appeals for information, as has Bev Baker of the National Galleries of Justice.

The museums and library services of East and West Sussex have as ever been helpful. May I therefore thank in no particular order Sue Sutton of Seaford Museum; Paul Bailey of Newhaven Museum; Alan Hibbs of Lewes Reference Library; Martin Hayes and Morwenna Peters of Worthing Reference Library; Roger Bristow of Hastings Reference Library; Dhimati Acharya and Sian Taylor of Eastbourne Reference Library and the staffs of Sussex Police Library, of Arundel Museum and Heritage Centre, of Weald and Downland Open Air Museum and of Steyning Museum.

But perhaps my greatest thanks ought to go to all those long-gone journalists who have furnished such dramatic and full accounts of past events, both minor and major, and to the contributors, most of them amateur, to the now sadly defunct *Sussex County Magazine (SCM)* whose volumes are a rich mine for all who seek information on this county's past.

Not least, my thanks yet again go to my wife Anne for her sorely tried patience and for her invaluable commentary on every item in the book. As a consequence of her input there are fewer infelicities of language, fewer gross solecisms, and less unnecessary verbiage.

Every effort has been made to trace copyright holders. Although working through so much material does present occasional problems I hope that they have for the most part been overcome. If any unintentional omissions have occurred the publishers will be pleased to add an appropriate acknowledgement in future editions.

And once more, to each and all, my grateful thanks for all of your help.

INTRODUCTION

I suppose that digging into the past ought to reveal something, ought to give new insights into our own situation. But this book makes no high-sounding claims. It is a record of criminality and vice, of wretched living conditions and of blind fate which could lead to the most appalling consequences. It offers simply what the title proposes. It is an almanac and it is certainly grim.

There are graphic accounts of the wretchedness of the poor and the squalor they lived in; of lawlessness, sometimes frightening, sometimes understandable; of the harshness of the sentences handed down to hapless small-time thieves and even young boys and girls. Nor do the entries from the first half of the twentieth century suggest that better living conditions had raised the aspirations of many.

One change is apparent. There is less poisoning in the twenty-first century than in times past. Some of what might be described as among the great classic poisonings took place in the county: meet in these pages lovelorn Sarah French, the serial killer Mary Geering, the demented Christiana Edmunds and Ann Whale and Sarah Pledge acting in concert, and all of them driven to poison. Forensic science and easier divorce have pretty well put an end to that kind of dispatch. And mercifully, there is no longer any spectacle at the gallows or indeed at the stake on Broadbridge Heath. At one time people turned up in their thousands to watch these obscene rites. So perhaps we have made some advances.

I have included extracts from official reports, letters and diary entries which give some savour of the concerns of the 200 years covered in this book. Most interesting is how the newspapers once reported catastrophes with a frankness that even the brashest tabloid of today would shun. Yet the idea of newspaper sales promoted through shock was not in the minds of any of the editors. They knew their readers did not wish to be spared the awful details of some or other calamity but they express a righteous anger and horror at the wickedness of criminals and some kind of awe at cataclysmic events. It is then for their sometimes startling intensity that I have quoted frequently from the earlier newspapers, especially from the *Sussex Weekly Advertiser*, at one time the only local newspaper. The newspaper columns from the early twentieth century onwards are milk and water compared to the strong brews of the past. Nevertheless, despite its dour promise, there is room in these pages for acts of kindness, undoubted courage and honourable behaviour in the face of the disasters and dangers which spring from the most awful occasions.

So, as they consider their fellow men, readers may find themselves hovering somewhere in a web of uncertainty, swinging from optimistic illusion to deepest despair about the past and the people who inhabited it. But it should always be remembered that the darkest deeds are carried out by a minority and that the darkest times almost always pass.

JANUARY

Horsham Stocks, *c.* 1859. *(West Sussex Library Service)*

1 JANUARY **1841** 'Moven wagrunce out of my district.' So wrote PC Sheather of Boreham Street in his notebook, referring to the constant battle to keep vagrants on the move. Sheather was a member of the recently formed East Sussex Constabulary and throughout his dozen or so years as a constable he recorded his daily struggle to maintain the law. Thus we learn that he went 'To Lewes for witness gants thomas and steven turrner For sheep steling Steven turrner was found gilty and his sintance to transported for ten years.' On another occasion Sheather announced: 'Haprehend George Biggs of West Chilton Labourer Seen stealing Broom in the Parsh of Ashburnham The property of the Earl of Ashburnham tock Him before the magistrate and He was Committed to Battle house of Corraction for fortiteane days.'

Some years earlier Robert Peel, as Home Secretary, had expressed the view that even senior police officers should not be drawn from the educated middle class as they would find the work beneath them. It is no surprise to learn that constables were generally poorly educated.

2 JANUARY **1851** The last robbery of the notorious Isaacs gang was at Downland House, Uckfield. At 3 a.m. eight of the gang forced entry through the dairy window and got into the kitchen. Here they found some clothes. To disguise themselves Joseph Carter and William Brooks put on women's bonnets, and the others pulled on coats belonging to the butler.

Wood, the butler, who was bustled downstairs to the pantry, watched as the thieves threw food and silver plate into an apron. Eventually the gang left with property estimated at £300 (£25,000 at today's value).

Returning to Crowborough the men stopped in a wood for a substantial breakfast – hare, veal, roast mutton, ham, pork, bread and cheese – after which they settled down to divide the money.

'We all shared this after breakfast,' James Hamilton told the court, 'a sovereign and 7s each but there was a deal more money smuggled among themselves.' Then he gave a revealing account of how criminal gangs determined the always knotty problem of sharing their loot. 'After the breakfast and after the sharing of the money we looked the plate over and broke up what we thought was not silver. There were two gold watches and two silver ones. The two gold watches were along with the plate, and the silver plate which came from the Old Pie public house was put along with it. The two silver watches were put up among us for those who would give most for them. Carter was the highest bidder at 11s for the small watches; and the other one, a double-cased one, was taken by Morgan for 25s. John Isaacs took all the plate etc in a flag basket . . . Hillyer took the cutlass.' At this point the party divided, agreeing to meet some days later at Warlingham in Surrey.

But within days they were rounded up by the police.

3 JANUARY **1942** At 7 p.m, a former Brighton and Hove footballer, Thomas Turnbrill, and now licensee of the Jolly Sailors public house at Portslade, and William Rothwell, a 57-year-old widower, began their twelve-hour firewatching duty at Hole's and Davigdor Dairies premises in North Street. The following morning, when her husband had not returned home, Mrs Turnbrill went to the firewatchers' room and found it filled with gas. Her husband was sitting in a chair, dead. Rothwell, lying on a bed, was also dead. Witnesses said the men had turned on both gas heaters as it had been a cold night. It was thought perhaps that one of the heaters had been turned off later as the small room became too hot. Although the gas tap functioned properly there was the possibility that it had not been fully turned off. The fact that there was no flue also made for potential danger in such a small room.

1798   4 JANUARY

GEESE STOLEN. Whereas on the night of the 4th inst, Three Geese were stolen from the premises of Mr Hickes, at Laughton, in the county of Sussex – A reward of FIVE GUINEAS will be paid by Mr Hickes, to any person or persons giving information of the offender or offenders, so that he or they may be convicted, over and above a reward of TWO GUINEAS to be paid by Mr ATTREE, Attorney, Brighton, Treasurer to the Laughton Society for prosecuting Thieves, on conviction of the offender or offenders. January 12, 1798.

STOLEN.

From the lands, called Branns, of Mr. John King, of Ninfield, in the county of Suffex, in the night of the 31ft of July laft,

TWO fat WETHER SHEEP; and in the night of the 20th of December laft, from the fame lands, alfo, another fat WETHER SHEEP.

Whoever fhall give information of the offender or offenders will be intitled to a reward of FIVE GUINEAS, on a conviction, for each offence, from the Members of the Ninfield Society for profecuting thieves, &c.——and will moreover receive of Mr. KING, a reward of TEN GUINEAS, on a conviction for the firft offence, and FIVE GUINEAS for the laft.

JAS. MARTIN,
Clerk to the faid Society.
Battle, Jan. 3, 1798.

GEESE STOLEN.

WHEREAS on the night of the 4th inft. Three Geefe were ftolen from the premifes of Mr. Hickes, at Laughton, in the county of Suffex.—— A reward of FIVE GUINEAS will be paid by Mr. Hickes, to any perfon or perfons giving information of the offender or offenders, fo that he or they may be convicted, over and above a reward of TWO GUINEAS to be paid by Mr. ATTREE, Attorney, Brighton, Treafurer to the Laughton Society for profecuting Thieves, on conviction of the offender or offenders.

January 12, 1798.

'Stolen': the original advertisements from the *Sussex Advertiser* detailing the theft of geese and sheep. (*Sussex Advertiser*)

1822 The sloop *Lark*, Captain Burrows in command, was on the way from   5 JANUARY
Whitstable to its home port, Newhaven, when it was almost overcome by huge winds and towering seas. The captain attempted to turn and make a run back to Whitstable but in the storm the boat snagged against some hidden rocks, lost its rudder and was consequently unmanageable. Some help came from Whitstable and the *Lark* was attached by a cable to another boat. But so ferocious was the weather, the winds hurricane force, that they lost touch and the thought now was to abandon ship. Captain Burrows went below to bring away some important bags just at the time when a monstrous wave hit the Lark and all of the crew – most of them Newhaven men – were lost overboard. Alone on his vessel the captain decided to climb into the rigging and hang on there in the hope that his plight might be seen. When finally the *Lark* was sighted Burrows

was still there, dead now, hanging upside down, his legs entangled in the rigging. He left a widow and four children.

6 JANUARY **1881** In the afternoon William Friend was killed on the line just above Plumpton station. Friend, aged about 45, was walking down the siding on the Up side of the rails with a bundle of briar sticks on his shoulder. Seeing a goods train approaching on the Up line, he waited to let it pass. As soon as it was gone he started to cross the line, unaware that the 1.30 p.m. fast train from London to Hastings was approaching. The fireman was the first to see Friend and he immediately alerted the driver, who blew his whistle and tried to stop the train, but it was too late. Before the man was aware of the situation the train was upon him, and he was instantaneously killed – literally cut to pieces, his face frightfully disfigured, his brains scattered in all directions. . . . The remains were removed to a shed where the dead man's sister later identified him by his clothes, the features being unrecognisable.

7 JANUARY **1823** *The Times* observes: 'It is said that in future, poachers (of whom there are generally a large number in the Lewes House of Correction) are to work during their time of imprisonment at the treadmill.'

8 JANUARY **1832** Mrs Ann Marchant, in a letter to her sister Mrs Sophie Peskett, wrote of how many in the area were alarmed at the outbreak of arson. There had been fires in recent months at Berwick Court farm, at the Parsonage Barn on the Tye, in the Alfriston tannery and at Milton Court farm. She was glad to report that two of the arsonists had been caught.

'We were dreadfully alarmed with the fires and have no doubt but the greater part of Alfriston would have been consumed before the winter had ended had they not been arrested in their progress as they seemed bent on destruction.'

9 JANUARY **1836** At Petworth Quarter Sessions it was decided that Edward Mills 'be committed to the House of Correction for six weeks, enter into his own recognizances in £20, and find two sureties in £10 each, for his good behaviour for two years, and that he be further imprisoned till such recognizances, as those be entered into and sureties given'.

Appearing previously before the Horsham Bench for a misdemeanour, he had angrily told the magistrates, who had ordered him to find sureties for his good behaviour, that 'It [their judgment] is a rascally thing.' To Percy Burrell, the Chairman, he had said, 'You are a pretty sort of gentleman,' adding to the court in general, 'Mr Percy Burrell would hang any man.'

Mills had fallen foul of the law when he had criticised conditions at Shipley workhouse. When his daughter died, leaving seven children, Mills had taken two of them under his wing and his son had taken two others as apprentices, but it was impossible for the three youngest to be cared for. In consequence they had been taken to the workhouse at Warnham. Later they went to Shipley workhouse which accommodated up to 100 occupants, including about 40 children. Mills learnt of the bad conditions at Shipley and went

there himself to find out how things were. He took the children away. They
had had no food on the day of their arrival and since then they had been
fed gruel and small quantities of bread. Mills said that they slept on straw
mattresses on the floor and that the room in which two of his grandchildren
were accommodated was so cold that he feared for their lives. He told the
court that some of the other children had lice and spoke of others who had
absconded.

Shipley Workhouse,
1830. *(Weald and
Downland Open Air
Museum)*

The evidence brought before the court, however, told of happy, well-fed
paupers; of larders bulging with beef, beer and bread; of double beds, each with
sheets and three blankets (even the soldiers at Woolwich barracks had only
two blankets). So Mills was disbelieved, condemned as a troublemaker and
sentenced at the Quarter Sessions.

Some months later there was an inspection of the workhouse. The report
observed that 'there was not a healthy person in the house except the
Master and a portion of his family. . . . In three months there were eight
deaths, mostly from fever . . . the water supply was not pure and the supply
was short.'

1942 An inquest heard how, during a military exercise carried out on a
fast-flowing Sussex river – for security reasons, the river was not identified
– an assault boat was suddenly and unaccountably holed. Lieutenant
J. Smeltzer attempted to stop the flow by thrusting his fist into the hole but the
water poured in and within sixteen seconds the craft was submerged and went
below the surface with eight soldiers, all of them Canadians. When it almost
immediately came to the surface, now upside down, five men were clinging to

10 JANUARY

it, but so fast was the current that they were instantly swept away. Three of these men were rescued but in all six men were lost. Major F.B. Courtney who commanded the unit had stripped off his uniform and dived in the water to attempt a rescue. At the inquest he said, 'I kept up as long as I could against the current and was then picked up by a reconnaissance boat.'

The Coroner, returning a verdict of 'Misadventure', suggested that it might be advisable for lifesaving appliances to be available when such exercises were undertaken but conceded that 'they had to be carried out as realistically as possible and a certain risk was therefore inevitable'. All of the soldiers were wearing full equipment and carrying arms.

11 JANUARY **1936** The inquest on the body of Flying Officer Philip Agard-Butler, whose body was washed ashore in a dinghy the day after the aircraft he was flying was lost at sea, took place at Bognor Regis. Telegraphist John Hunter's body had not been recovered. The two men had ejected from the aircraft and had managed to inflate the dinghy which was large enough for three men and had enough fuel to last for several hours. The seas were extremely boisterous at the time. That the telegraphist had been in the dinghy was undeniable as his wireless headphones were found there. There was also a Verey pistol containing an empty cartridge and an undischarged marine distress signal. Agard-Butler had an extensive wound over his right eye but there was no damage to either skull or brain. The doctor thought that the cause of death was the accident to the eye and the shock following it which caused heart failure, but as there were no scorch marks on the face it was obvious that the airman had not been hit by the cartridge from the Verey pistol. The jury returned a verdict that 'death was due to the injury and shock as given in the medical evidence, there being no direct evidence to show how this was caused'.

12 JANUARY **1799** About 7 a.m. Mr Gregory of Heathfield found a dying black man, William Thompson, lying by the turnpike road near Cowfold. Thompson, a beggar, was well known in the neighbourhood. Unable to do anything to help, Gregory went to the Crabtree public house which was about a mile away. The landlord, 'with a degree of humanity that did credit to his feelings', immediately sent two men with a horse and cart to fetch him but he died shortly after he was put in the cart. He had 12d in his pockets but it was said that he had recently paid £50 into the bank at Horsham. Could it be true? At today's value £50 is worth £4,000. Was there that much money in begging? Or was it just a tale that got about?

13 JANUARY **1855** At about 11 o'clock, as he was passing the Ship public house, Inspector Battersby heard a dispute among females taking place in a house behind the pub. The language being used was not fit to be repeated, the policeman later told Hastings magistrates. Accompanied by a constable, Battersby entered the house where he found fourteen men and four prostitutes, two of whom were drunk. Two days later the Inspector went back to the house. This time he saw a man in the yard 'in a very indecent position with a drunken

prostitute'. The couple were persuaded to unravel themselves and return inside. Later the same evening Battersby returned yet again only to find the same couple resuming operations in the yard. 'I have frequently visited the room,' he was to tell the court, 'and have generally found several prostitutes there. I consider it to be a worse place than a common brothel.' The room was regularly hired out for 6s 2d a week. The defendant was fined 10s and 19s 6d in costs.

1805 'The soldier in custody for stealing meat in a butcher's shop, was on Monday tried by a Court Martial and found guilty. He was the next morning punished with 450 lashes.' Nothing perturbs the *Sussex Advertiser*. Typical of the time, it seems to accept 450 lashes as harsh but merited.

14 JANUARY
Contemporary cartoon attacking military floggings from the *Northern Star*, 1838. *(Author's collection)*

15 JANUARY

1925 For some weeks police had been investigating the disappearance of Elsie Cameron from Kensal Rise, and several times had questioned her fiancé, Norman Thorne, a chicken farmer at Crowborough. Confident that Thorne had done away with her, they arrested him on 14 January and began a closer search of the farm. Now, in the early hours, digging by oil lamp in the chicken run, police unearthed a biscuit box. Inside they found the missing girl's head. Lower down they found three more parcels – the torso with the upper limbs attached and the legs in separate bundles.

Thorne admitted dismembering the body but he insisted that he had not killed her. She had come to visit him unexpectedly and they had argued because he was losing interest in her. He claimed that in his absence she had hanged herself in the tiny shed in which he was living. In his statement he said: 'When I opened the hut door I saw Miss Cameron hanging from a beam by a piece of cord as used for the washing line. I cut the cord and laid her on the bed. She was dead. I then put out the lights. She had her frock off and her hair was down . . . I was about to go to Dr. Turle and knock up someone to go for the police and I

Norman Thorne
standing over Elsie
Cameron's grave.
(Daily Mirror)

realized the position I was in.' After burning Elsie's clothes, 'I got my hacksaw . . . I sawed off her legs, and the head, by the glow of the fire.' Then he had buried the parts.

At his trial at Lewes the medical evidence hinged on one question – did Elsie Cameron commit suicide or did Thorne murder her? The jury concluded the latter and he was hanged on 22 April.

16 JANUARY **1920** Nurse Florence Nightingale Shore – named after her godmother – died in hospital four days after being found unconscious on the London to Hastings train. She had been badly beaten about the head, possibly by a revolver butt. Her killer had propped up the body so that she appeared to be sleeping. Two platelayers who got into the carriage paid no attention to her until she began to slip off her seat. Then they noticed there was blood on her face, some of which was dripping down on to a magazine in her lap. Her smashed spectacles were later found on the floor. The case remains unsolved.

17 JANUARY **1851** The *Sussex Advertiser* records yet again one of the greatest offences, another crime against property. 'Eliza Bonniface (Colgate Forest), a woman about 40 years of age, and as rough and wild as a forest colt, appeared to a summons for having, on Monday 6th inst., unlawfully and maliciously injured a calf, the property of Thomas Gent, by cutting it with a heath hook. Fine 5s or one month's confinement.

'Jonah Bonniface, son of the defendant in the previous case, and about 16 years of age, was committed to Petworth for one month, for setting a wire for the purpose of catching game.'

1749 At two o'clock, with Guards and Dragoons in attendance, six smugglers who over several days had so savagely murdered Galley and Chater, both of them old men, were marched through Chichester to the Broyle. They climbed into a long wagon placed under the gallows. Tapner, Hammond, Cobby and Carter addressed the dense crowd, forgiving everyone, even the informants, but 'Major' Mills and his son were less forgiving, refusing even at this stage to accept that they were guilty.

A letter from a Chichester correspondent, dated 20 January 1749, describes the occasion: 'Young Mills talk't very narrowly and said we shall have a very

Chater and Galley, mounted on one horse, are whipped by the smugglers as they go to their protracted deaths. *(Author's collection)*

Smugglers toss stones down Harris's Well where they have thrown the dying Chater. *(Author's collection)*

Galley, still alive, is thrown into his grave at Harting Combe. (*Author's collection*)

jolly Hang of it and at the place of execution he said it was very hard to be refused a pint of beer which he had asked for. The father would have smok'd from the Gaol to the gallows but was prevented.' The writer complains that the executioner produced ropes that were too short, which meant an hour's delay as someone had to be sent for new ropes. 'Young Mills,' says the correspondent, 'amused himself most of the time in looking up at the executioner who sat across the gallows, and smiled several times as is supposed at the hangman's going so awkwardly about his work.'

'Major' Mills, defiant to the last, had to stand on tiptoe as the rope finally went round his neck. It was still too short. 'Don't hang me by inches,' he called out. Finally the horse was driven away and the six murderers were left to dance 'the hempen jig'.

Carter's body was gibbeted at Rake; Chapman's at Rook's Hill near Chichester; and Cobby's and Hammond's corpses were sited near Selsey Bill. The bodies of the two Mills men were flung into a hole near the gallows.

The Galley and Chater murders, so cruel and violent, involving long torture of the two men by the smugglers, led to increased government activity against the great smuggling gangs of the eighteenth century.

19 JANUARY **1786** Diarist John Burgess, a leather worker from Ditchling and a leading member of his local Baptist chapel, suggests in his 'Jernal' how the law was sometimes maintained in days before a police force was established: 'This forenoon went to Kymer with Several people in persuit of the person soposed to have Robd Mrs Browns Shop it was soposed he was concealed in old Mooryes House & by virtue of a warrant we serched his house but did not

find the man But found several things soposed to have been stolen a quantity of wheat in the Chafe and a large quantity of old Timber Concealed in a very secret place upon the cealing over the chamber &c a Great Number of people was there.'

1778 John Wesley records a visit to Sussex in his journal: 20 JANUARY

I went through most miserable roads to Robertsbridge, Mr Holman's widow being extremely desirous that I should lodge at Carborough, two miles from Rye. She sent a servant to show me the way, which was a dirty road and slippery enough, cast up between two impassible [sic] marshes. Many rough journeys I have had, but such a one I never had before. It was one of the darkest nights I ever saw, it blew a storm yet poured down with rain. The descent in the going out of town was near as steep as the ridge of a house. John Bradford whom I had taken into the chaise, perceiving how things were, immediately got out and walked at the head of the horses (who could not possibly keep their eyes open the rain was so violently beating in their faces) through rain, wind, mud and water, 'til in less than an hour he brought us safe to Crowborough.

1838 In Kirdford churchyard is the headstone, 'To the memory of George 21 JANUARY Norman, aged 17, Charles Newman, aged 13, Thomas Rapley, aged 14, George Puttick, aged 13 and William Boxall, aged 19 years, who died at Sladeland on 21st of January, 1838, from having placed green wood ashes in their bedroom. In the midst of life we are in death.'

All of the boys worked at Sladeland where they shared a bedroom. As there was no chimney they were in the habit of taking a bucket of ashes from the grate of the brick oven downstairs to warm up the room. Ventilation had been by a broken windowpane. Alas, this was repaired and the unsuspecting boys suffocated.

1824 Samuel Greenyer was working in a chalk pit at Denton near 22 JANUARY Newhaven when, 3ft below the surface, he came across the skeleton of a female. He had found the remains of a local woman who had disappeared thirty years earlier.

1879 Medical Officer of Health, Hastings: Summary of Annual Report, 1878: 23 JANUARY 'As usual, the mortality amongst children is very great. No less a number than 227 died under five years of age, being one third of the total deaths from all causes. I need scarcely repeat that a vast number of these lives might be annually saved if more discretion and knowledge in the feeding of children which are obliged to be brought up by hand were shown by those in charge of them. Surely a few philanthropic ladies, with some knowledge of how to support infant life, and a capacity for importing their knowledge to their poorer and uneducated neighbours, might well devote a few occasional hours to such laudable work.'

24 JANUARY **1838** The *Sussex Agricultural Express* relates the following alarming tale: 'DALLINGTON. On Wednesday night last, Cooper, the gate keeper at Wood's Corner, while in his bed, was surprised by the forcible entrance of two villains, who directly seized him and thrust a silk handkerchief into his mouth to prevent his giving alarm and afterwards bound him down to his bed. The ruffians then purloined his money, amounting to nearly £300 with which they got clear off. The poor fellow remained in his unpleasant situation nearly three hours before he was released.'

25 JANUARY **1802** 'The following robbery was committed on Thursday evening in the parish of Slaugham,' says the *Sussex Advertiser*. 'As Mr. Cremer, a master warrener, was without-side his house putting up his window shutters, he was accosted by two men who demanded of him whether any person was within his house. On his answering that could be no business of theirs, and asking whether they meant to rob him, one of them replied that they had come for that purpose, and instantly seizing him by the collar, dragged him into the house, and with presented pistols robbed him of forty pounds in cash.'

26 JANUARY **1786** The following return for the virulence of the smallpox in Brighton reveals how serious the outbreak was among a population of 3,620. The first column indicates those who had the smallpox and the second those who had escaped it.

West Street	351	322
Middle Street and Lanes	231	272
North St. and Lanes	234	295
Ship and Blk-Lyon Lanes	318	336
Knab, Cliff, Brighton Place and Little East Street	260	291
East Street and North Row, Steyne and Pool Lane	308	291
Poor in the house	31	50
Number supposed after taking numbers	0	30
Total	1,733	1,887

The 1,887 people who escaped the disease were inoculated and charged as follows: the poor and day-labourers *2s 6d* each; others *7s 6d*.

27 JANUARY **1860** A grim story from a headstone in St Peter's Church at Bexhill: 'In Memory of William Harris who was accidentally killed in the Parish of St Mary's Bulverhythe by his wagon passing over him on the 27th of January 1860. Aged 35 years.'

Oh! Let my sudden doom
A Warning be to all
E'en while thou bendest o'er my tomb
Thou may'st as quickly fall.'

1748 The murder of Richard Hawkins, a farm labourer from Walberton, took place only a fortnight before the even more horrifying murders of Galley and Chater. John 'Smoker' Mills was involved in all of these murders. Suspecting Hawkins of the theft of two bags of tea, Mills and Jeremiah 'Butler' Curtis took him to the Dog and Partridge on Slindon Common where he was murdered. The following account of Mills's trial was written by 'A Gentleman of Chichester' a few months after the event:

28 JANUARY

Thomas Winter, alias the Coachman, an accomplice, deposed that one day the latter end of January was twelvemonth, he, with Jerry Curtis, alias Pollard, were at the prisoner Reynolds's house, who kept The Dog and Partridge; that Curtis presently went away from him, and promised to come to him again very soon, for he was to pay this witness some money he owed him; that this deponent stayed at The Dog and Partridge the rest of the day; that towards evening Richard Rowland, alias Robb, came to the house, asked for his master Curtis and stayed with this deponent till night, when the prisoners Mills and Curtis came; that Curtis called for Robb and said, 'Robb, we have got a prisoner here'; then Hawkins got down from behind Mills, and all went in together, to a parlour in the prisoner Reynolds's house; that they all, viz., Hawkins (the deceased), Curtis, Mills, Rowland, otherwise Robb, and this deponent, sat down together; that then they began to examine Hawkins about the two bags of tea, which he denied, saying he knew nothing of the matter; that Curtis said, 'D——n you, you do know, and if you do not confess I shall whip you till you do, for, d——n you, I have whipped many a rogue, and washed my hands in his blood'; that the prisoner Reynolds came in when they were urging the deceased to confess, and said to the deceased,

Murder of Hawkins at the Dog and Partridge, Slindon. *(Author's collection)*

'Dick, you had better confess, it will be better for you'; his answer was, 'I know nothing of it.' After Reynolds was gone, Mills and Robb were angry with the deceased; that Robb struck him in the face and made his nose bleed, and threatened to whip him to death; that Mills showed he was pleased with what Robb had done, and again threatened the deceased who said, 'If you whip me to death, I know nothing of it'; that then Mills and Robb made the deceased strip to his shirt, then they began to whip him over the face, arms and body, till they were out of breath, he all the while crying out that he was innocent, and begged them, for God's sake, and Christ's sake, to spare his life for the sake of his wife and child; that when they were out of breath, they pulled off their clothes to the shirts, and whipped him again till he fell down; when he was down they whipped him over the legs and belly, and upon the deceased kicking up his legs to save his belly, they saw his private parts; then they took aim thereat, and whipped him so that he roared out most grievously; then they kicked him over the private parts and belly; they in the intervals asking after the tea; the deceased mentioned his father and brother; that upon this Curtis and Mills took their horses, and said they would go and fetch them, and rode away, leaving the deceased with Robb and this deponent. That after they were gone, he and Robb placed the deceased in a chair by the fire, where he died.

Two months later Hawkins's body was found weighted with stones in a pond in Parham Park. In consequence of this evidence by Thomas Winter, John Mills was hanged. Jeremiah Curtis escaped to France.

29 JANUARY **1763** Thomas Turner, the East Hoathly grocer, records in his diary: 'The frost began to thaw today, after having continued very severe for five weeks; the ice was seven inches thick.'

30 JANUARY **1789** Another extract from John Burgess's diary: 'We have had a remarkable Sharp Frost Great deal of Snow likewise the frost began Nov 24th 1788 & Lasted about 8 weeks many people say it more severe Cold then it was in the hard Winter Water was scarce and very bad many wells dry has been so very dry for so long time Great Numbers of fish was perished as Well as birds &c.'

31 JANUARY **1885** Medical Officer of Health, Hastings, Summary of Annual Report, 1884: 'Diarrhoea caused 31 deaths, so large a number having only occurred once before during the last ten years. . . . Twenty-two of the deaths were of children under five years of age. Eighteen of the 31 deaths occurred during the September quarter among children under two years of age.'

FEBRUARY

Dead Man's Hand – the women have pressed the hand of the newly executed felon to their throats hoping it will cure them of goitre. *(From a print by Isaac Cruikshank. Courtesy of the Neil Storey Archive)*

1866 The murder of Mrs Harton was celebrated, as were many murders, in a popular penny paper, typical of its time, printed by c. Phillips of Market Street, Brighton. The Victorians enjoyed lurid and dramatic expositions of tragic events but the story behind Leigh's murder of Mrs Harton is not touched on. The murderer, son of the American consul, and known locally as 'Mad' Leigh, was a deeply disturbed man, who regularly beat his wife. Finally her sister, the victim Harriet Harton, advised her not to have anything to do with him. The consequences are described in Phillips's lumbering verse.

On the first of February,
In Brighton we see,
There did appear a murderer,
By name John William Leigh.
He led a dissipated life,
To wickedness gave way,
That fatal night he left his wife,
And he did her sister slay.

For this cruel murder he must die,
And end his days on the gallows high.

With a six-barrelled revolver,
He went on Thursday night,
To The Jolly Fisherman, in Market Street,
To take away the life
Of the landlady, Mrs Harton,
He was by Satan led –
Where her husband, Mr Harton,
Had been ten months ill in bed.

He fired the fatal weapon,
Oh, twice he fired the shot,
His victim soon lay bleeding,
Upon that fatal spot;
Her husband, ill, ran trembling,
And there beheld his wife,
By the hand of a wicked murderer,
Deprived of her life.

John William Leigh, the murderer,
In Brighton town did dwell,
A very wicked troublesome man,
And many knew him well;
He, mad with desperation,
If he could but had his way,
The police, and all around him,
The murderer would slay.

In the American service,
A Confederate he had been,
Though aged only twenty-eight,
Much villainy had seen;
There is nothing now can save him,
For that atrocious deed.
Of such an audacious scoundrel
We scarcely ever read.

Leigh left his wife and entered
The Jolly Fisherman;
He looked just like a demon,
With the revolver in his hand,
He killed his own wife's sister.
Alas! She soon lay dead,
And her poor afflicted husband,
Lay consumptive in his bed.

He had no consideration,
No pity in his breast,
His wicked desperation
Caused horror and distress.
Confined in Lewes dungeon,
For a short time he must be,
Then for the Brighton murder,
They will hang the prisoner.

Leigh a native was of Brighton,
To the family a disgrace,
By everyone detested,
Who knew him in the place.
She was his own wife's sister,
Who received the fatal wound,
Which has caused such consternation,
Many miles round Brighton town.

1852 The inquest into William French's sudden death at Gun Hill was convened for the third time and Professor Taylor of Guy's Hospital, who had analysed the whole of his stomach and intestines, presented his findings to the Coroner and jury at the Six Bells, Chiddingly. He estimated French might have been given up to eleven grains of arsenic in several small doses but he was confident that one large dose had been administered on the day he died. So after a faltering start the investigation into the Onion Pie murder, one of the classic crimes of the county, was under way. Among the most powerful witness statements was that of Henry Hickman, father of James, the lover of Sarah French, the victim's wife. Henry Hickman told the court:

2 FEBRUARY

The Six Bells,
Chiddingly.
(Alan Skinner)

I had a conversation with the deceased on the Sunday week before he died.
I met him coming from Chapel; he was alone; it was towards one o'clock.
He overtook me and I said, 'Well, Mr. French, how be you?'

He replied, 'Not very well.'

I asked him who that was before us.

He said, 'It is my wife and your Jim' and he said, 'I don't very well like it.'

I said, 'No more do I.'

He said then, 'I wish you would tell him to keep away from my house.'

I asked if he ever saw any underhand dealings between my son and
his wife.

He said, 'No.'

I said, 'He tells me you asked him to come and read a book to the little
boy [French's son] who was ill.'

He said, 'I did.'

I asked him why he did not tell him to keep away if he did not like it.

He said the reason why he did not tell him to do so was, if he spoke to his
wife, she would say he was jealous of her and he thought she would make
away with herself.

The following Sunday I saw the deceased going to Chapel with his
wife arm-in-arm . . . I told my son what Mr. French had said, and he
replied, if Mr. French had told him he did not want him to come he
would not have gone. I have frequently told him not to go there. He said
French had asked him to go and read to his little boy who was ill.

After this James Hickman admitted that he and Mrs French sometimes kissed, that she sometimes sat on his knee, that they had talked of marriage, and that he had been at the house on the night that French ate the onion pie. He admitted that he heard the sick man upstairs, retching and vomiting violently on the night he died.

It did not take the inquest jury long to return a verdict of Wilful Murder against Sarah French and she was committed for trial at the Sussex Spring Assizes. She was hanged in April. Her 20-year-old lover, James Hickman, was acquitted.

1824 For ten nights, between Rottingdean and Littlehampton, there was a continual blaze of light as smugglers, frustrated by the strenuous activity of the Coast Blockade and, on land, by the coastguards and other revenue officers, kept signalling out to sea to warn incoming craft laden with contraband. One gang of smugglers was taken, trying to land 130 casks of spirits at Littlehampton Pier. Another gang tried a different tack and under cover of early morning darkness sneaked into Newhaven harbour with their craft. But the customs officers were on the lookout for unusual activity and spotted the smugglers' boat, following it 6 miles up the river to Glynde Reach. By the time the coastguards arrived the smugglers had unloaded the greater part of the cargo, but 54 casks of spirits were impounded. In the same week 140 casks of spirits were seized at Hastings.

3 February

1839 'WADHURST. The disgraceful riots which so frequently occur at beer shops and ale houses in our parish will now, it is hoped, soon be put a stop to,' says the *Sussex Agricultural Express*. 'Warrants are issued against James Sivyer, commonly called Turk, Richard Darnell, a sweep, and Frederick Lee, the principal ring leaders concerned in a riot at Wadhurst Fair on the 1st November last.'

4 February

1926 Perhaps Jack Delaney felt himself to be safe and secure, tucked away as he was in a very remote country cottage near Shipley. Sadly for Delaney, this was the day of his arrest for running what Mr Justice Horridge would later call 'a very extensive factory with very elaborate appliances for turning out both pound and ten shilling Treasury notes'. After manufacture was completed his girlfriend travelled all over the country distributing them. Suspicions were aroused in the Horsham area when several notes were passed in various shops.

5 February

Delaney, 29 years old and described as an engineer, had previously served three years' imprisonment for forgery and had two convictions for other offences. He had been released from Parkhurst only the previous year with part of his sentence remitted for good behaviour. He claimed in court that with his record he could not find work and therefore had been obliged to fall back on forgery as a means of earning a living. He received five years for this offence, added to which were 273 days from his previous sentence.

As for the unnamed girl, the judge was of the view that she had been influenced by Delaney. She had not been charged by the police who were apparently of the same opinion.

6 FEBRUARY **1795** The serious effect of the winter storms is recorded in the *Sussex Advertiser*:

> The turnpike road between Brighton and Stanmer is so much damaged that an expenditure of some hundreds of pounds will be needed to repair it. At Preston 22 sheep and several hogs were drowned in a close belonging to Mr Smithers, who also suffered a loss of upwards of twenty pounds in his brewery. At Patcham the turnpike was several feet under water. The rivulets about this town swelled to an amazing height; the mill pond stream overflowed its bridges, and the tan yard of Mr Fuller, where also considerable mischief was done. At Goodwood three fatting hogs were drowned; 13 others that were in the same sty were with difficulty saved. At Halnaker, 13 or 14 lean hogs were drowned; and at Lavant, near Chichester, a number of lambs shared the same fate. In short, the damages that have been sustained in this county are inconceivable; to enumerate a description of them all would more than fill our paper. But what is more alarming than all the rest, 'tis greatly to be feared that the injurious effects of this watery visitation have been extended to the wheatlands, not only partially, from the torrents that in many parts ran over them and laid the grain bare, but generally, from being exposed, in their very wet state to the perishing powers of the frost that immediately succeeded the thaw, which may indeed prove a very distressing circumstance, as in that case, no plentiful crops, so necessary to supply our wants, can be expected.

7 FEBRUARY **1881** In Hastings the Special Relief Committee announced that altogether £50 18s 6d [approximately £3,300 in 2007] had been handed out to relieve 'the necessitous poor'. The Committee added 'with commendable satisfaction, that so liberal were the donors that the Committee have still as much as £37 8s 6d [today worth approximately £2,500] in hand for future use'.

8 FEBRUARY **1798** Charles Scrase Dickens, the High Sheriff of Sussex, was returning to Brighton from London with his family, when a highwayman stopped his carriage, just 3 miles from home. When a pistol was pointed at his son's head, the High Sheriff handed over 9 guineas and a watch and the highwayman rode off. He was described as 'a young man of very genteel appearance, and received his booty with a trembling hand'.

9 FEBRUARY **1942** A Warship Week exhibition at Brighton Corn Exchange turned into a tragedy. There were the usual demonstrations of weapons and the public, not surprisingly in time of war, were curious to look at Bren guns and P17 rifles, at grenades and stick bombs, at intercoms and signalling systems and at charts illustrating aircraft, both allied and enemy. All sorts of items of which the public had only heard were there to be shown and explained by the soldiers, sailors and airmen on duty.

A knot of visitors was having the mechanism of a machine gun explained, its breech, its bolt, its trigger, when suddenly and quite accidentally there was a burst of fire. One soldier, a Canadian, was killed and a 14-year-old boy, Joseph Luper, was taken to hospital with wounds.

POLICE NOTICE

AIR RAID DANGER

Conceal your Lights

All windows, skylights, glass doors, etc., in private houses, shops, factories, and other premises must, as from to-day, be completely screened after dusk, so that no light is visible from the outside. Dark coverings must be used so that the presence of a light within the building cannot be detected from outside.

All illuminated advertisements, signs and external lights of all kinds must be extinguished, excepting any specially authorised traffic or railway signal lights or other specially exempted lights.

Lights on all vehicles on roads must be dimmed and screened. The Police will issue leaflets describing the restrictions to be observed.

THESE MEASURES ARE NECESSARY FOR YOUR PROTECTION IN CASE OF AIR ATTACK.

Police notice
about air raids.
(*Eastbourne Gazette*)

1943 Four high-explosive bombs dropped on Horsham in the late afternoon. Two houses were completely demolished, another was very seriously damaged and others received substantial damage. About eighty-five houses suffered minor damage. Fortunately there was no loss of life. Three people were seriously injured and three others received slight injuries.

10 FEBRUARY

11 FEBRUARY

1843 PC Beck writes in his notebook: '10 a.m. Stopped two females of the name of Puttick and Smith with two bags full of wood. Resides in the Parish of Bignor. Obtained leave from Mr Wales to have it.' So PC Thomas Beck recorded the first significant event of his day in the Duty Book. He was the constable for the parishes of Bignor, Westburton, Bury and Sutton. In the course of his day, indeed in the course of his two years in the district, he would constantly keep an eye out for vagrants, trespassers, poachers, pedlars, pub card players and a variety of other malefactors. But, to continue his day: '4 p.m. Stopt Mrs Carver, residing in the Parish of Watersfield, with a quantity of swede tops and a bundle of sticks. Brought them from Stroud. 4.30 p.m. Stopped one of Mr Newland's men coming out of a copse with a Bundle of wood. Allowed to have it. Patrolled the district 1 p.m. And found all correct.'

The struggle against vagrants was never ending. Thomas Geering, writing of this period, recalled the men and women who used to doss down in a huge barn at Hailsham, 'as motley a company of scoundrels and cheats, of knaves and liars, schemers, soft talkers and hard swearers as eye ever looked upon'. Among them were the 'one-legged turnpike sailor' and 'the soldier minus an arm in the street', who miraculously each night no longer suffered any physical handicaps.

12 FEBRUARY

1924 There was a mysterious wounding in Cambridge Street, Brighton, which involved George Anscombe, a 47-year-old naval pensioner, and his 15-year-old niece, Rose. They had been alone in the house and he allegedly attacked her with a chopper. Rose ran outside, blood pouring from her head, and fetched her mother from a local cinema. When the police arrived at the house they found Anscombe suffering from serious wounds to the throat. After some days Rose was released from hospital, but her uncle died from his injuries.

13 FEBRUARY

1933 The wording of the notice opposite is still reminiscent of the preceding century: 'At a Meeting of the Persons whose names and Places of Abode are hereunder written held at the Crown Inn, Arundel, on the twelfth Day of April One Thousand seven hundred and ninety-six the following Articles agreed upon and signed for the establishing of a Society and raising a Fund for prosecuting Persons who shall rob or defraud any Member of this Society or his Property and for offering and paying such Rewards as are hereinafter mentioned that such Offenders may be discovered and brought to justice.'

Each member paid an entrance fee of half a guinea and a yearly subscription of 5s. Payments into the fund stopped when the balance reached £100 and recommenced when it fell to £50. Rewards were offered for information leading to conviction of all categories of crime, including murder, against members. The first prosecution was in December 1798 when two men were convicted at Chichester of stealing three geese and four fowls. There were many such Prosecuting Societies throughout the county.

ARUNDEL SOCIETY
FOR
PROSECUTING
FELONS, THIEVES, &c.

The Society, consisting of the Persons whose names are hereunder printed, will give the undermentioned

REWARDS

To be paid by the Treasurer to the Person or Persons (other than the Constabulary) giving such information as shall lead to the conviction of the Offender, and if more than one, in such parts or shares and in such manner as the Members at their next Annual Meeting shall direct; but no Reward will be given unless the majority of the Members present at such Meeting shall think the case deserving of it:

A REWARD OF TWENTY POUNDS,
On the conviction of any person wilfully MURDERING any Member of the said Society.

A REWARD OF FIVE POUNDS,
On the Conviction of any Person or accomplice Breaking into or Robbing any House or Building belonging to any Member of the said Society; or Robbing any Member on the Highway; or maliciously setting fire to any House or Building, Stack of Corn, Hay or any other property belonging to any Member of the said Society.

A REWARD OF FIVE POUNDS,
On the Conviction of any Person Stealing any Horse, Mare, Gelding, Colt, Filly, Bull, Cow, Ox, Heifer, Calf, Ram, Ewe, Sheep, Lamb, Goat, or Pig belonging to any Member of the said Society.

A REWARD OF TWO POUNDS,
On the Conviction of any Person Stealing any Hay, Corn, Iron, Lead, Wood, Coals, Poultry, Fish, Rabbits, Wool, Sheep Skins, or such like Property belonging to any Member of the said Society.

A REWARD OF ONE POUND,
On the Conviction of any Person Stealing, Destroying, or Damaging with intent to Steal, any Plant, Root, Fruit, or Vegetable Production growing in any Garden, Orchard, Nursery Ground, Hot-House, or Conservatory belonging to any Member of the said Society.

A REWARD OF TEN SHILLINGS,
On the Conviction of any Person Stealing, Destroying, or Damaging with intent to Steal, any Cultivated Root or Plant used for the food of Man or Beast, or wilfully or maliciously Damaging, Injuring or Spoiling any real or personal Property belonging to any Member of the said Society.

A REWARD OF TEN SHILLINGS,
On the Conviction of any Person or Persons for Trespassing in search of Game upon land owned by or in the occupation of any Member of the said Society.

THE FOLLOWING IS A LIST OF THE MEMBERS OF THE SAID SOCIETY.

ARUNDEL, 13th February, 1933.

HERBERT A. E. HEY, Clerk.

Mitchell & Co. (Printers), Ltd., West Sussex Gazette Offices, Arundel.

Left: Notice of Arundel Prosecuting Society, 1933. (*Sussex Advertiser*)

Below: Wisborough Green Prosecuting Society notice, 1792. (*Sussex Advertiser*)

1837 Labourer George Head, 14, was charged with having stolen nine worsted cravats, valued at 4s, at Brighton.

A previous conviction for a felony dating back to 10 October 1836 was also taken into consideration by the judge, who decided to sentence him to seven years' transportation.

14 FEBRUARY

Wisborough Green
PROSECUTING SOCIETY,
Established March 8th, 1792,

FOR RAISING A FUND TO PROSECUTE
Felons, Thieves, Receivers of Stolen Goods, &c.
AND FOR PAYING
REWARDS ON CONVICTION.

1849 Edward Cresy, Superintending Inspector, began his investigations at Hastings into 'Sewerage, Drainage and Supply of Water and the Sanitary Condition of the Inhabitants'. His report was completed the following year. Under the section headed 'Present State of Drainage' he gave illuminating information on the condition of many homes. There follow some descriptions representative of the wretched conditions which obtained in so many houses in the town.

> Eastbourne Street: In the Tanhouse lived Wenham and his wife, both of whom were attacked with cholera, and a child with diarrhoea. The husband, wife and child died. Four other families resided in this house, and several were under the medical attendant's hands but recovered. Each of these families make use of a small bucket, which, as often as used, is covered with ashes from the grate, and placed in a closet or in one angle of the room. When entirely filled, it is carried out to be emptied in the street or the first convenient location. These families each occupy two rooms, about 12 feet by 10. . . . There is neither sink, water supply, nor privy, and the medical gentleman who attended observed that fever was never absent from the Tanhouse.

> Bosham Square: There are four houses, one of which is occupied by Grisbrook, a bricklayer, who recovered from an attack of cholera. Upon examination of his house, in which lived eight other persons, it was found to be without proper drains, and a tub, instead of a privy, without cover, retained in each room, and emptied only when positively full. There was a cesspool, but it was overflowing, and 'no-one's business to cleanse it'.

> William's Row houses consist of six tenements, which have neither water-supply, sinks, nor drainage; two of them have their ventilation intercepted by a high wall in front; four privies are constructed over one cesspool. The plan given is that occupied by Mrs Page, two men, two women, five children; Mrs Sutton, husband and four children; woman and her husband and two children; a man and woman lodger: making in all twenty-five persons.

> Henbery's Row of nine cottages are in a filthy condition: the drain at the back is open and ineffective. The six houses beyond are only one storey high, and two privies are constructed against the back wall of No. 4. Disease and fever are never, it is reported, absent from this place, and most of the inhabitants are receiving relief from the parish. Mrs Harmer and all her children, residing at No. 4, were then suffering from fever. These houses consist each of two rooms, with only one fireplace. There is no ceiling, the bare rafters being evident, and the floors are paved with brick.

1794 A DESERTER. Deserted, last night, from the PRINCE of WALES's Regiment of Light Dragoons, quartered at BRIGHTON, RICHARD BRISTOW, 26 years of age, fresh complexion, brown hair, hazle [sic] eyes, by trade a labourer, born in the parish of Ninfield Stocks, Sussex – Had on when he deserted a smock frock, a round hat, white regimental leather breeches, and brown worsted hose, with copper clasps in his shoes.

Whoever will apprehend the said RICHARD BRISTOW, and cause him to be lodged in any of His Majesty's Gaols, shall receive FIVE GUINEAS, over and above the allowance by Act of Parliament, on application to the Commanding Officer at Brighton; or to Messrs COX and GREENWOOD, Craig's Court, Charing-Cross, London.

FEBRUARY 16, 1794.
A DESERTER.
DESERTED, last night, from the PRINCE of WALES's Regiment of Light Dragoons, quartered at BRIGHTON, RICHARD BRISTOW, 26 years of age, fresh complexion, brown hair, hazle eyes, by trade a labourer, born in the parish of Ninfield Stocks, Sussex.—Had on when he deserted a smock frock, a round hat, white regimental leather breeches, and brown worsted hose, with copper clasps in his shoes.
Whoever will apprehend the said RICHARD BRISTOW, and cause him to be lodged in any of His Majesty's Gaols, shall receive FIVE GUINEAS, over and above the allowance by Act of Parliament, on application to the Commanding Officer a Brighton; or to Messrs. Cox and GREENWOOD, Craig's-Court, Charing-Cross, London.

The original notice regarding the deserter in 1794. (*Sussex Advertiser*)

The iron stocks at Ninfield are here set picturesquely on tended grass among spring flowers. (*Tony Spencer*)

1794 A lady named Goldsmith, living at Laughton, was safely delivered of her twenty-fifth child.

1893 A marble cross in the garden of the George and Dragon pub at Dragons Green reads: 'In loving memory of Walter the Albino son of Alfred and

The cross in front of the George and Dragon, Dragons Green. *(Alan Skinner)*

Charlotte Budd. Born February 12th 1867. Died February 18th 1893. May God forgive those who forgot their duty to him who was just and afflicted.'

Always an outsider on account of his being different, Walter was bullied throughout his life. A deeply unhappy man, he drowned himself shortly after being accused, probably falsely, of a minor theft. The memorial was erected in Shipley churchyard, but several people in the village, and particularly the vicar, the Revd H. Gorham, resented the last line of the epitaph and asked Walter's parents, local publicans, to remove it from the churchyard. As an act of defiance, they transferred the cross to its present position.

1842 Fifteen-year-old Frances Emary was brought before the Brighton magistrates, for the second time in weeks, charged under the Vagrancy Act. Hers was a sad history. She had been left an orphan when very young and for a considerable time had lived in the workhouse at Steyning, the village to which her parents had belonged. Later the Overseers of the Poor had sent her to live with her grandmother, paying a weekly sum for her support. When the union workhouses were opened in 1834 under the New Poor Law, this payment was discontinued. At this point Frances was sent to Shoreham workhouse where she stayed two years. After this, aged about 11 years, she began a variety of jobs as a house-servant.

Recently she had found herself out of work and returned to the Shoreham workhouse where she stayed for a fortnight. Then, without any prospect of employment, she was ejected. She returned to Brighton where a policeman found her in the street in the early hours, homeless and destitute. The Brighton magistrates referred the matter to the assistant overseer who sent her back to the Shoreham workhouse where she was again refused admission. Frances returned once more to Brighton and for several weeks lived by prostitution until she found herself before the magistrates for the second time. Again the magistrates consulted the assistant overseer who undertook to find a place for her somewhere, but driven from pillar to post, like many of the poor, Frances's outlook was bleak.

19 FEBRUARY

The building in the centre of the picture, drawn in 1844, was Steyning Workhouse between 1729 and 1835. (*Steyning Museum*)

20 FEBRUARY   **1794** Coarse Mary and Dick Cat, two well-known Lewes characters, died of smallpox. The *Sussex Advertiser* comments: 'The former had good reason to believe she had had distemper, having been nursed for it many years ago, and very often since been among it. The latter, who was deficient of intellect, fell a sacrifice to his own obstinacy as no-one could prevail upon him to be inoculated.'

21 FEBRUARY   **1861** The collapse of the spire of Chichester Cathedral was a dramatic event. 'It was twenty-five minutes to two when the spire fell,' said one witness. 'I had gone into my back room when I was called out, and I saw the spire and the tower sink softly down as a candle sinks down into the socket. As it went, it quivered a little, and appeared to part in two from the base of the spire upwards to within twenty feet of the top, and that piece fell entire . . . as it sank, there was a slight bearing of the spire to the south side; but it came down within its own area. The sound was only like that of stones or coals shot down into the street. I am told that the weight of the falling mass was about 1,600 tons.'

Chichester Cathedral before the collapse of the spire. *(Illustrated London News)*

It was perhaps no surprise to this witness or to others that the spire and tower of Chichester Cathedral collapsed. Renovation work had revealed its weaknesses. The old Norman piers which held up the central tower were in danger of falling. Their very core was rotten and the foundations were no longer capable of sustaining the loads which they had borne over the centuries. While the exterior of the tower and spire looked in good order, internal inspection proved otherwise.

The damage to the cathedral. *(Illustrated London News)*

'One topic engrosses all Chichester,' the local newspaper reported. 'Nobody seems to think, certainly nobody cares to talk of anything else. How it had been feared; how it had been declared incredible; how it had come to be regarded as possible; how the hour arrived and the cathedral was deserted, and the streets were filled with hundreds of sad spectators; how, at last, the crash came, and the spire was gone; how the city became desolate and unbearable without it.'

1799 A Brighton man, Staines, sold his wife to James Marten for 5s and eight pots of beer. There was a signed document apparently making the new arrangement acceptable to both parties. It may seem odd, but divorce was too costly for a working man.

22 February

23 FEBRUARY **1819** Either on Tuesday night or early on the following morning three prisoners escaped from Lewes House of Correction. There were sometimes queries about the frequency of escapes and questions asked about the collusion of keepers at such times.

24 FEBRUARY **1789** The *Sussex Advertiser* is rightly concerned that a child had been snatched, although something about this story seems dubious. How did the woman rescue the child so easily? Why were there no attempts made to catch the perpetrators? Or was it simply a familiar anti-gypsy tale? 'Some gypsies enticed away a child about 6 years old, belonging to Mr Reed, plumber of Chichester; they were proceeding with it out of the city with great expedition when a woman who saw them pass by and who happily knew the child, immediately followed them and brought it back. They had made the little innocent quite dirty, and enticed it away by the trifling reward of a cake; it is with great concern we inform the public that these vile wretches escaped unpunished.'

25 FEBRUARY **1890** 'HALFPENNY DINNERS: NEW SHOREHAM. There was another distribution of halfpenny dinners at the Town Hall, New Shoreham,' says the *Sussex Daily News* with some satisfaction. 'There were from 120 to 130 children, all of whom paid their halfpennies, but in the very poorest and deserving families three children received a dinner for a penny. The dinner consisted of two large pieces of bread with a basin of gravy and meat.'

26 FEBRUARY **1949** In the course of their investigations into the disappearance of the wealthy widow Mrs Durand-Deacon, the police became interested in one of

her fellow residents at Onslow Court Hotel in Kensington, John George Haigh, who was a dapper, articulate little man. They learned about a workshop in Crawley where, as an inventor and engineer, he carried out 'experimental work'. The police went round to Leopold Road where the workshop, a rackety two-storey brick building surrounded by a 6ft wooden fence, was situated.

Inside the whitewashed storeroom they found paint pots, pieces of wood and metal, old rags, tools and benches. Not really surprising perhaps. But there were also a rubber apron, rubber boots, a gas mask, a pair of rubber gloves and a riding mac. There were a stirrup pump, two large carboys and several large oil drums. There was a receipt, dated 19 February, from a cleaner in Reigate, for a Persian lamb coat. And in a hat box were a .38 Enfield revolver and eight live rounds.

Haigh later confessed that he had shot Mrs Durand-Deacon. 'I then donned the rest of my equipment for I had found it necessary to protect myself from the acid. I had a rubber mackintosh which I kept specially for this purpose, rubber gloves, a gas mask to protect myself from the acid fumes, a rubber apron and rubber boots.' Then using

John George Haigh.
(News of the World)

the stirrup pump he had filled the oil drum with sulphuric acid and placed the body inside. He was so sure of himself. After all, he had got away with at least five murders and possibly others, all for gain.

1804 William Souter of Cootham Common, Storrington, was already in bed at 8 p.m. when a gang of armed men burst into his cottage. He was tied up and bustled out of the house, his wife and young children terrified and powerless. Souter had been captured by the press gang from Littlehampton led by Lieutenant Spry and taken to Havant.

27 February

Souter's kidnapping was an act of revenge, initiated by James Searle, landlord of the Crown Inn at Cootham, who had brooded for years about what he regarded as a betrayal. In the past both men had been heavily involved in smuggling. But then Souter had given information to the customs men about smuggling activities. It seems likely that he had been threatened with court proceedings, possibly with a severe sentence, perhaps even transportation to New South Wales, if he did not tell what he knew. Many a gang – the ruthless raiders from Shipley, the greatly feared Hawkhurst gang, the less important groups at Firle and Barcombe, Stanton Collins's followers at Alfriston – was brought down by informers desperate to avoid being 'boated'.

Now, Searle had persuaded Lieutenant Spry to impress Souter into the Navy. Fortunately Souter had a friend in Thomas Broad, Comptroller of Customs for the port of Arundel. Broad had not forgotten the help that Souter had given him. It was Broad's intervention on his behalf that led to his release. Had he not done so Souter might have served years in His Majesty's Navy with little chance of being freed. In this case Broad pleaded quite justifiably that the Littlehampton men were operating outside their legitimate area.

> By the Commissioners for Executing the Office of Lord High Admiral of the United Kingdom of *Great Britain* and *Ireland*, &c. and of all His Majesty's Plantations, &c.
>
> IN Pursuance of His Majesty's Order in Council, dated the Sixteenth Day of *November*, 1804, We do hereby Impower and Direct you to impress, or cause to be impressed, so many Seamen, Seafaring Men and Persons whose Occupations and Callings are to work in Vessels and Boats upon Rivers, as shall be neccesary either to Man His Majesty's Ship under your Command or any other of His Majesty's Ships, giving unto each Man so impressed One Shilling for Prest Money. And in the execution hereof, you are to take care that neither yourself nor any Officer authorised by you do demand or receive any Money, Gratuity, Reward or other Consideration whatsoever, for the sparing, Exchanging, or Discharging, any Person or Persons impressed or to be impressed as you will answer to it at your Peril. You are not to intrust any Person with the execution of this Warrant, but a Commission Officer and to insert his Name and Office in the Deputation on the other side hereof, and set your Hand and Seal thereto. ---This Warrant to continue in Force till the Thirty First Day of December 1809, and in the due execution thereof, all Mayors, Sheriffs, Justices of the Peace, Bailiffs, Constables Headboroughs, and all other His Majesty's Officers and Subjects whom it may concern, are hereby required to be aiding and assisting unto you, and those employed by you, as they tender His Majesty's Service, and will answer the contrary at their Perils.
>
> Given under our Hands and the Seal of the Office of Admiralty, the   1809.
>
> *Captain*
> *Commander of His Majesty's*
> *the*
>
> *By Command of their Lordships,*

But Souter was left to make his own way home from Havant. He walked 18 miles to Broad's house, arriving there in a state of collapse. He had been beaten unmercifully and he did not recover. Within six days he was dead. Spry and three members of his press gang were found guilty at the Assizes and all served gaol sentences.

Press gang warrant, 1809, authorising a ship's captain to seize men aged between 18 and 55 for naval service. *(East Sussex Record Office)*

28 FEBRUARY   **1851** This matter-of-fact report comes from the *Sussex Agricultural Express*:

> Alfred Witten, a little urchin, aged eleven years, was charged with stealing ducks eggs belonging to Mr. Breach. Poiney deposed that Mr. Breach, complaining that he had lost several eggs, he offered to watch, and he saw the prisoner crawl through the hedge and take two from a nest: he laid them down and was just pulling his shoes off to go into the pond after another when Poiney pounced on him.
>
> The boy was ordered to be taken to the lock-up and once there privately whipped by the police officer. The boy's father was in court and told he might be present when the punishment was inflicted.

29 FEBRUARY   **1884** John Coker Egerton, rector of Burwash, records in his journal: 'Carried up a wreath to Charles Coppard's. Saw Mrs Coppard, poor thing, to be left in a fort[night] w. no children at all is indeed sad.' All three of Charles Coppard's children had died of diphtheria within days of each other, victims of primitive sanitation. The family pig-sties were close to the house; the lavatory, a recent addition, was badly fitted and the effluent, going straight into an unventilated cesspool, polluted the water in the well.

MARCH

Itinerant bear keeper with dancing bear at Arundel, *c.* 1900.
His trumpet was used to announce his arrival. Dancing bears were
commonly seen until about 1914. *(Arundel Museum and Heritage Centre)*

1 MARCH **1869** John Coker Egerton, the rector of Burwash, called on Mr Isted, one of his wretchedly poor parishioners. 'Wife confined 11 times, besides mishaps; has had 13 children, once 3 at a birth; 6 now living, eldest 14; none of them earn anything except the eldest who is a girl & does a little hop-tying & a little hop-picking, tho' the biggest part of this last she lost having to attend her mother, who is permanent invalid.'

2 MARCH **1801** The *Sussex Advertiser* offers a warning: 'A CAUTION – A man of low stature, swarthy complexion, with hair a little grey and queued to the fashion, wearing dark-colour'd clothes and short spatterdashes bound with red, and who travels with a portfolio or parcel at his back, on his way from Battle to Horsebridge, on Thursday last, imposed on several persons by selling them watches for two guineas and a half and three guineas, though in reality not worth one guinea. He facilitates the imposition by pretending to be a Hungarian man-cook, out of place, and in great distress, which compels him to part with his watch as the only means left of procuring subsistence.'

3 MARCH **1892** Short of funds, the long-established Brighton and Hove Kitchen for the Aged, Sick and Hungry Children appealed to the public for financial support. The Kitchen in Cavendish Street, a very efficient charity, was run by distinctly middle-class volunteers who sought to ensure that the recipients looked upon themselves as 'partakers' rather than receivers of handouts. Many of the volunteers spent hours each week offering practical help as there was no paid staff. Dinners of beef, mutton and potatoes were served on Wednesdays and Fridays. The greatest care was taken that vouchers for these meals were given only to those in genuine need. Those not regarded as so were turned away. There were 181 people known to be 'deserving' on the books. In addition to the dinners, suppers were provided to 400 poor children every Tuesday and Friday. The *Sussex Daily News* comments: 'Owing to the large amount of sickness this winter and the pitiful weakness to which, through lack of proper nourishing food, so many of the poor, and especially mothers of large families, have been reduced, it would be most deplorable if the distribution of these dinners had to be stopped.'

4 MARCH **1863** Kate Richardson, 18, was charged with attempting to poison William Halsted and his mother, Martha, by police at New Fishbourne near Chichester. In the privy a bottle labelled, 'Woods: Chichester Lotion – Poison' had been found.

　　In December 1861 Richardson had taken up her post as the Halsteds' only servant. She was said to be 'a quiet and good girl about the house'. But on 18 February she was given notice by Mrs Halsted. There had been soldiers calling at the house for the girl and this would not do. The order was strictly 'No followers'. The girl was given the chance to leave at once or to stay on until April. At dinner that day the usual beer was on the table but when it was poured out its colour and taste were peculiar. Halsted went into the kitchen and asked Richardson if she had put anything into the beer. 'Why should I poison you?' she had asked. 'We have no quarrel.' Later that day

Richardson left. Halsted sent the beer for analysis and it was found to contain either mercury or lead but he took no further action, having no proof that it had been deliberately tampered with. And then, by chance, weeks later he found the bottle in the privy and sent for the police.

At the Assizes the following year Richardson was found not guilty of attempted murder. There was no evidence against her. The prosecution could not find any motive. There had been no quarrel. And the poison bottle was not found until after Richardson had left. The question lingers. Did she put poison in a bottle? Because if not . . .

1924 The worst blackmail case that the Lord Chief Justice claimed to have heard was tried at Lewes Assizes. John Halsey, a 28-year-old stoker, and his brother William, a barman aged 30, were each charged with demanding £20 with menaces from Walter Heaver, a Bosham nurseryman. The cases against the two men were heard separately. **5 MARCH**

The court heard of systematic blackmail carried out since 1915 when the first demands were made. John Halsey had gone to work for Heaver in 1912 when he was 17 years old. After several months he had left to join the Navy but he and his former employer had kept up a correspondence. When he was on leave the two men met on a number of occasions during which indecent acts took place. Over the years demands for money were made. By 1915 Halsey had received £75 and by 1923 he had received about £2,000 (in today's terms, £75,000). But now the demands for money were accompanied by threats. Sometimes Halsey threatened to inform the police; once he had hinted that he might shoot Heaver. There was strong evidence that both brothers drank heavily and that John took cocaine.

William Halsey, who also claimed to have been seduced by Heaver, was making heavy demands on him. By 1924 Heaver decided to stop the whole matter. He informed the police of what was happening. The brothers were each sentenced to twelve years' imprisonment.

1906 Two boys from Rusper, 11-year-old John Farley and his friend Edwin Jenkins, were on their way to do some stone-picking to earn a few coppers. On the way they slid on a pond where the ice was thick enough to bear their weight. Later they stopped at the pond at Cobb's Pit. Farley took a run, sliding towards the middle when the ice cracked and he fell through. Jenkins ran 200yd for help, returning with a length of cord, but there was now no sign of his friend. When the local blacksmith came on the scene he located the body, but only after a twenty minute search. **6 MARCH**

1935 A 21-year-old motor mechanic, Percy Charles Anderson, pleaded not guilty at Sussex Assizes to the murder of Edith Constance Drew-Bear, also aged 21. Her body had been found in a water tank on East Brighton golf course. **7 MARCH**

For the prosecution Sir Henry Curtis Bennett, a giant of the legal world, alleged that after firing three shots into the girl's body Anderson

Percy Charles
Anderson and Edith
Drew-Bear. *(Both
Sunday Graphic)*

strangled her by tying his scarf round her neck. Later, Anderson boarded a bus, dripping wet, without boots, jacket or waistcoat. He had told the police, 'I got a pain in my head. I started swimming for my life. I cannot remember any more from the time I sat down with my young lady until I found myself in the sea.' He had further admitted that he had had a quarrel with the girl who had accused him of smiling at another girl.

Throughout his trial Anderson claimed that he had no memory of harming his girlfriend. A defence plea of insanity was rejected and Anderson was found guilty and hanged at Wandsworth on 16 April.

8 MARCH 1890 The *Sussex Daily News* says that 'The Soup Kitchen, having been kept open for four months, was closed for the season, having been served to the schoolchildren during the whole of this time. Soup had also been provided at the same rate for home consumption. The total cost to the subscribers has been £6 7s 6d.'

9 MARCH 1842 Late in the evening the storm began with torrential rain and violent winds. Buildings were shaken to their foundations in weather conditions that had not been experienced for many years. In several houses chimneys collapsed and fell through the roofs, in at least two cases narrowly missing the occupants. In the Channel a number of craft foundered. In one, the brig *Economy*, returning to Littlehampton from Sunderland with a cargo of coal, the crew of six along with two pilots lost their lives. Half a dozen other coal vessels in the Littlehampton roads succeeded in making the harbour. The Shoreham lifeboat put out to sea in appalling weather to aid a schooner. The schooner was lost but some of her crew were rescued.

10 MARCH 1800

WHEREAS JOHN BAKER (otherwise Green), effected his escape in the night of the 2nd of this instant March, from the Common Gaol in the town and port of Hastings, in the county of Sussex, to which Gaol he was committed for Felony.

The said John Baker, alias Green, was born in the parish of Hollington, in the said county, is about twenty-two years of age, about 5 feet 8 inches high; sallow complexion; short brown hair; speaks slowly and with a little impediment in his speech; rather blear eyed; a small cut on the right side of his face, and has a hurt on his left hip.

Whoever will apprehend the said John Baker, otherwise Green, and secure him in any of his Majesty's Gaols, or give such information as may be the means of his being secured, to JOHN WEATHERMAN, the Keeper of the said Gaol at Hastings, shall receive from him a reward of TWENTY POUNDS.

1837 'About half past eight o'clock, as Mr. James Whitfield's carter was on return to his master's farm at Falmer, he was stopped on the highway by three men and two women. He was pinioned by the shoulders and arms while one of the female depredators robbed him of a yellow canvas bag containing in gold, silver and copper, £3 17s 6d, the remaining change of a £5 note, with which he had been entrusted to pay his master's workmen. The miscreants got clear off.' The *Sussex Agricultural Express* is undeniably outraged. 'When will this disgraceful state of things be put an end to by the authorities?' the editor demands. 'Depredations are now so frequent on this road that it is now palpably unsafe to travel alone and unarmed.'

1930 The nine-day trial of Sidney Harry Fox, one of the most riveting of the decade, opened at Lewes. Despite the fact that Mrs Fox, the accused man's mother, died at the Hotel Metropole in Margate, in the interests of justice he was tried away from the area, where the feelings of jurymen might have been clouded. After all, matricide is rare. Fox, a 28-year-old homosexual, sometimes claiming to be an Old Etonian, at others to be an officer in the RAF, was simply a deep-rootedly dishonest and plausible former convict. In 1928, after release from prison, he was moving from town to town, from hotel to hotel, most often in the company of his mother Rosaline, herself not an especially reliable woman. Behind them they left a trail of debts. At a time when his finances were low, Fox was due to inherit Rosaline's few possessions. When they settled in the Margate hotel, Sidney increased his mother's life insurance to £3,000 (at today's value £120,000).

On the evening of 23 October he raised the fire alarm. There was a fire in his mother's room. Although Rosaline was dragged out she died shortly afterwards. 'Misadventure' was the verdict of the Coroner's court.

Sidney Harry Fox
and Rosaline Fox.
(*Both Daily Mirror*)

But Sidney was too keen for the money, too callous, and suspicions were roused. There was an investigation and he was charged with murder. At his trial the prosecution advanced the theory that Sidney plied his mother with port and then, when she was drowsy, strangled her and then set fire to the carpet under the chair she was sitting on. He was found guilty and removed to Maidstone for execution.

13 MARCH   **1821** A headstone at All Saints' Church, Hastings, reads:

> This Stone Sacred to the Memory of Joseph Swain Fisherman was erected at the expense of the members of the Friendly Society of Hastings in commiseration of his cruel and untimely death, and as a record of the public indignation at the needless and sanguinary violence of which he was the unoffending victim. . . . He was shot by Geo England one of the sailors employ'd in the Coast blockade Service in open day on the 13th March 1821 and almost instantly expired in the twenty-ninth year of Age leaving a widow and five small children to lament his loss.

Swain, described as 'an industrious, sober Fisherman', had just returned from sea when he was approached by George England, a coastguard, who insisted on searching his boat. There was an argument and then Swain apparently agreed to England's demand. But after this there were further words, a struggle and then a shot which passed through the seaman's body. England was tried at Horsham Assizes and was given a free pardon.

As ever, Austin the Hastings printer was at work to immortalise the event and express the popular feeling in the following broadsheet. His ten-verse 'Lines on the Death of Joseph Swain who was maliciously shot on 13th March 1821, Aged 29 years' begins:

> The wicked tyrant did surround
> The boat it was on shore
> To kill a youth it was well known
> And left him in his grave.

And ends:

> For blockade in the coast along
> His life must freely pay
> His blood will cry for vengeance
> On the great judgment day.

14 MARCH   **1927** Arthur Cheshire and Joseph Lucas, both of them Metropolitan Police constables, were each sentenced to six months' imprisonment with hard labour at Sussex Assizes. Sentenced with them was Edwin Bottom, 61, who was charged with making a corrupt gift of silver coins to the constables, both of whom were charged with receiving the coins. This was the second trial of this case, as the first jury had been unable to agree.

It was alleged that at Goodwood racecourse the previous July Bottom gave each of the policemen *2s 6d* (£5 today). Sergeant Albert Jones of the West Sussex Constabulary said that he had been keeping Bottom, a known bad character, under observation at the course. The sergeant said that he saw him hand coins to the two constables and saw them put the coins in their pockets. The sergeant and a PC went to arrest Bottom, who resisted violently. A number of men then swept down upon the two arresting officers calling 'Let him go! He belongs to us!' After this, four plain-clothes officers came on the scene and helped the arresting officers. Bottom then asked them to call a sergeant. 'He will tell you I'm all right,' he claimed. When arrested Bottom, described as a labourer, had on him a sum of £58 (today £2,100). He claimed to be financing two bookmakers on the course. The corruption of some police officers enabled the protection rackets to flourish on racecourses.

1853 Twelve-year-old James Haffenden, described frankly in the newspapers as 'a stupid looking boy', pleaded guilty to a charge of setting fire to a stack of straw. He had been playing with 'lucifer' matches near the stack and this

15 MARCH

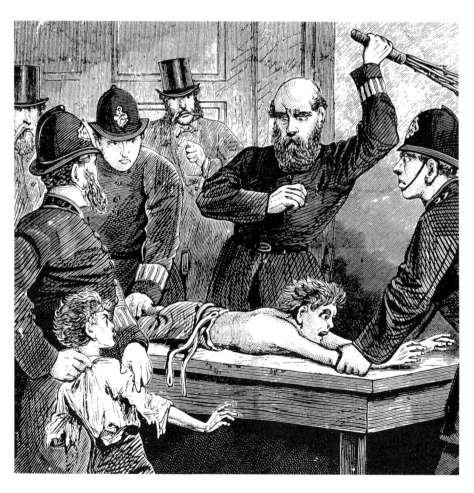

Illustration of a flogging. *(Courtesy of the Neil Storey Archive)*

was how it came to catch fire. Passing sentence, the judge, Baron Alderson, explained to the boy that he had committed a very mischievous act and he was very glad that there was an Act of Parliament which gave him what he considered to be the very best punishment under the circumstances. He ordered the prisoner to receive a sound flogging at once in the gaol, privately, and then to be delivered to his friends.

16 MARCH   **1807** Henry Christian, a 42-year-old labourer, was found guilty at the Assizes of stealing 'one wether sheep valued twenty shillings, the property of Mr John Fry of Mayfield'. His death sentence was commuted and he was sentenced to transportation 'beyond the Seas to the Coast of New South Wales for the term of his natural life'. As it was, Christian never went further than the prison hulks at Portland – an appalling enough fate – from where he was discharged a free man in February 1815.

17 MARCH   **1853** Early in the morning Brighton was roused by an enormous explosion. A train due shortly to leave the station for Shoreham, Worthing and Littlehampton was left in a heap of fragments after its boiler burst. Pieces of machinery were driven through the iron roof of the shed, which flew a distance of 35ft in the blast. The station flagstones were torn up and the eastern wall seemed ready to topple. But there was worse. Three men had been caught in the explosion and fragments of their flesh were everywhere. The body of a fireman, John Elliot, was hurled through the shed on the London side and the other two bodies, of John Young, the driver, and Richard Baker, a fitter, were blown over Terminus Road in the opposite direction. Baker's head was found halfway up the road. The driver's head and limbs were torn from the trunk, one leg breaking the window of a house over 100yd distant. Elliot's body landed on top of a roof. Dreadful . . . too dreadful to go into the further fine detail offered by the daily newspapers. But the Victorians, those sometimes sentimental, often hardheaded, folk, always wanted the detail of drama and the awfulness of the human condition which even *The Times* provided in the fullest lurid detail.

18 MARCH   **1845** George Curd, 26, described as a labourer but nevertheless exceedingly well dressed, was charged at Lewes Assizes with passing a forged £10 note in 1840. There was a separate charge of passing a forged £5 note in the same year.

    Curd had been connected with a gang who, in those earlier years, were very active, passing off their forgeries throughout the county. For the past four years and up to December 1844 Curd had evaded the police and, judging by his clothing, he was still involved in some or other lucrative criminal enterprise. When he was arrested in London he offered the arresting officer £10 – one wonders how genuine the note might have been – if he would let him go but the offer was rejected. Witnesses were called to swear positively to his having passed the two forged notes five years earlier. Curd, not unnaturally, claimed that it was a case of mistaken identity but the jury had no hesitation in finding him guilty.

1818 Maria Walton, who appeared at Horsham Assizes charged with bigamy, created something of a stir. But then she always had done. When her first husband, Ensign Cox, an officer in the East India Company army, took her to Bombay in 1801 she was known for 'the celebrity of her character'. Some years after Cox's death, still in India, she married another 'Gentleman in the Company's services'. On their return to England they separated, Maria living both in Brighton and Lewes where she still had many admirers. She had resumed her original married name, Cox, and more recently had married Mr Walton, 'a young gentleman', but they separated and he soon ended up in gaol, unable to settle the debts with which she had left him. So now, here was Maria Walton in the dock with a crowd in the public seats anxious to see her. The press speak of her 'exceedingly prepossessing countenance' and describe her outfit with some wonder, the striking white dress with its white light-coloured pelisse, her round black hat with feathers and black veil. Walton's mother, seemingly wealthy, was determined to pay back the woman who had so embarrassed her son. It was she who had brought this prosecution.

Mr Wilkins, husband number two, was apparently still alive and living in Horsham, and he and Maria had never divorced. It looked to be an open and shut case. Not so. Maria told the court that she thought Wilkins had remarried and therefore that she was free to marry; that she did not believe her marriage in India to Wilkins was really legal in the absence of witnesses; that she had not deceived Walton about her status but had been frank with him.

After the jury had returned a verdict of guilty with a recommendation to mercy, Mr Baron Graham, the judge, remarked on the 'frank and open manner' in which she had told Walton of her marital situation and as a result of this 'she would be visited with the least punishment the law in such cases has provided'. Sentencing her to six months in Lewes House of Correction, he expressed the wish 'that it should be attended with as gentle treatment as was suitable to her situation'.

1871 Harvey, a professional criminal with more than one alias, was convicted of attempted burglary at Kingston by Sea, near Shoreham. He had been arrested on the spot, in his possession the tools of his trade: a

The distinctive dress of various classes of convict. *(Lloyd's News, courtesy of the NCCL Galleries of Justice)*

jemmy, a pair of pliers to turn keys in locks, a centre-bit used to cut holes in shutters, a pair of slippers and a cosh. The tools were beautifully made, appropriate for their purpose. At the house where he had been caught he had used the centre-bit to cut a hole in one of the shutters, just large enough to allow his hand entry to remove the security bar. The judge observed that the prisoner was clearly a man to make an example of. Not only was he a regular burglar but with the cosh he was obviously prepared to put up a murderous resistance to anyone attempting to stop him. Harvey was given twelve years' penal servitude.

21 MARCH **1782** '21 March. Sat a few minutes with a neighbour, Mrs King,' Mary Capper, staying at Wilmington, writes in her diary. 'She has been afflicted with the ague [malaria] for several months, and her children are in the same pitiable condition. Agues are frequent here, and very difficult to remove.'

22 MARCH **1849** At the Assizes John Pearson, a 23-year-old groom, was charged with the murder of Mary Ann Newman on 12 November 1848.

When Mr Moore and his sister returned from church to Cattarina Villa, the house they shared in St Leonards, they had found the doors locked on the inside and they had to enter through a window. They found the cook, Mary Newman, unconscious, lying in the passage off the kitchen. She had received dreadful head injuries and by her side was a bloodied spade. A good deal of valuable property had been stolen and it was obvious that the theft had been perpetrated by someone who knew the household habits. Every Sunday, both the Moores and their coachman and housemaid went to church. Only the cook was left in the house. Pearson was quickly arrested and charged with robbery and assault. The charge changed to murder two days later when Mary Newman died. In the meantime a gamekeeper had seen someone lurking in his woodland and had been suspicious. When he searched, he found under a pile of leaves all of the stolen property, wrapped up in a large handkerchief.

John Pearson was a former groom at the Moore household, dismissed only days earlier. He had gone to live in London but on the day before the murder he had returned to Hastings.

It was estimated the murder had taken place at midday and it was shortly after this that Pearson was seen in a public house close to the Moores' house. Another witness claimed to have seen him near Cattarina Villa on the Sunday morning. After this he went to his mother's nearby house, asking for a clean shirt and handkerchief. Footmarks found in the woodland and outside the Moores' garden matched Pearson's boots. And so the evidence piled up.

For much of the time the result of this case, heard from 9 o'clock in the morning until midnight, must have seemed cut and dried. But a brilliant defence saved the day for Pearson. So successfully was doubt sown about the footmarks and the handkerchief that what in the middle of the evening must have seemed an inescapable guilty verdict had, by the end of the day, been overturned and Pearson was found not guilty on charges of both theft and murder.

1913 On the wet and stormy evening of Easter Monday, only a handful of people, thirty or so, turned up to hear the McWhirter Quintet on Worthing pier. Part of the way through the programme they were forced to flee to the promenade for safety, for the storm had reached hurricane force. It continued through the night and by morning the whole centre structure had been washed away, leaving the South Pavilion stranded out at sea.

23 MARCH

Worthing Pier
wreckage.
*(West Sussex
Library Service)*

24 MARCH **1795**

COCKING

Two mains [fights] of cocks will be fought between the Gentlemen of Henfield and Steyning, against the Gentlemen of Horsham for five guineas a battle, and 20 the odd. Also two shake bags for 20 guineas. The first main will be fought on Monday, the 30th March, at the Chequers Inn, Steyning, the second main will be fought on Monday, the 20th April at the Lamb Inn, Horsham. To fight in silver, and to go to the Pit at 1 o'clock. Hammond and Holding, Feeders.

The Chequer Inn at Steyning. *(Alan Skinner)*

N.B. – A good ordinary at one o'clock.

25 MARCH **1794** The head of a Brighton prostitute named Hadely was found in a well near the Sussex Tavern in East Street. Nothing more is known of this murder, although the story that she had serviced the Prince Regent is still quoted.

26 MARCH **1811** At Sussex Assizes, held at Horsham, Robert Bingham was 'charged, on suspicion, of having feloniously and unlawfully sent a threatening Letter, without a Name subscribed thereto, to Mr Richard Jenner, of Maresfield: And also, on suspicion of having feloniously set Fire to a Dwelling House, then in his possession, at Maresfield'. Both of these charges carried the death sentence.

Rev. Mr. BINGHAM's TRIAL,

At the SUSSEX ASSIZES, before the LORD CHIEF BARON.

On Saturday next, will be published,
BY W. AND A. LEE,
Price 2s. 6d.

THE TRIAL, AT LARGE,

OF THE

Rev. ROBERT BINGHAM,

Charged, on suspicion, of having feloniously and unlawfully sent a threatening Letter, without a Name subscribed thereto, to Mr. RICHARD JENNER, of Maresfield:

And also, on suspicion of having feloniously and maliciously set Fire to a Dwelling House, then in his possession, at Maresfield, &c. &c.

As taken at Horsham, on Tuesday, the 26th of March, 1811,

BY J. V. BUTTON, B. A.

☞ Orders for the above, very interesting Trial, will be received at the OFFICES of the PUBLISHERS, at LEWES; or by their several NEWSCARRIERS, throughout the County.

The letter, received by Jenner, a farmer, in December of the previous year, was ill spelt, unpunctuated and ungrammatical:

MURDER FIRE and REVENGE
Fifty of us are detarmd to keep our land or have revenge therefore pason churchwards and farmers your barns and houses shall burn if you take our land your lives two shall pay your sheep we will eat your oxen we can mame your stacks shall blaze Dick you shall be shuted as you comes from markt or fares we are United an are sworn to stand biy one another.
FIFTY GOOD FELLOWS

At first it was supposed that the letter had been sent by squatters living in the Ashdown Forest and who were consistently at loggerheads with the farmers and others in authority in the Maresfield area.

Accounts of major trials were of great public interest, as this advertisement shows. (East Sussex Record Office)

Cottage in the
Ashdown Forest.
(Boys Firmin)

The dwelling house which was set alight was in fact the vicarage where the Revd Mr Bingham lived as curate-in-charge with his wife and nine of his twelve children. And it was he who was ultimately charged with both offences. But he was found not guilty on both charges. Why would he have concocted the bogus letter to a man whom he considered to be a friend? Could he really have endangered the ten other members of his family as part of an insurance fraud? Guilty or not, Robert Bingham never returned to Maresfield, moving instead to a living in the north.

27 MARCH 1805

At the Assizes there were 29 prisoners for trial, 15 of whom were capitally convicted, and received sentence of death, viz. George Williams, aged 28, for stealing divers bridles and saddles, the property of different persons – Edward Byrne, aged 22, James Birmingham, 25, John Cole and John Stone, 19 years each, soldiers in the 88th Regiment, for sheep-stealing – William King, 64, also for sheep-stealing – William Harris, 49 years old, for a burglary in the dwelling house of John Tooth of East Grinstead – Ann Davis alias Gordon, aged 27, for the wilful murder of her newborn female infant – Samuel Harman, aged 14, for stealing in the dwelling house of Alexander Walker, three notes, value one pound each – John Bedwell, aged 39, for sheep-stealing – James Maidlow, aged 17, for a burglary in the house of James Wood – John Sacre, 55, for sheep-stealing – Sophia Turner, aged 18, for stealing a silver watch and seal, the property of Messrs. Levy and Yates – Thomas Piper, aged 25, for a burglary in the house of John Richardson of Withyham – and Mary Ann Bartholomew, aged 15, for feloniously stealing a £20 Lewes Bank Note, the property of her master, Mr. New of Ringmer.

The first named eight of the capital convicts are left for execution; the remaining seven were reprieved before the Judges left the town.

It is the final paragraph which tells us something of our forefathers' attitudes, for they are not thirsting for revenge. Rather they are anxious that the girl should make her peace with God before her execution. It is her state of mind and not her execution which most concerns the writer of this passage:

The unhappy young woman, for the murder of her bastard child, was to have suffered on Tuesday last, but it being represented to the Judge that her mind was in a state of distraction from the effects of her sentence, he humanely granted her a respite, until her mind should become more quiet, and she was better reconciled to her melancholy fate; but of this she betrays no symptoms, as her excessive perturbation continues, and shuts out all hope of consolation, and her death is, we hear, in consequence daily expected.

1807 The *Sussex Advertiser* reports: 28 MARCH

William Ball, the unfortunate young man who at our last Summer Assizes was found guilty of forgery on the Bank of England, and whose judgment was respited, in consequence of an exception which in point of law had been taken, was brought to the bar, and informed that his case had been submitted to the opinion of the Judges, whose decision was that his conviction was right. The dreadful sentence of the law was then pronounced against him, which he heard with firmness, and in a manner highly becoming one in his unhappy situation. The debt due to the offended laws of his country will be cancelled with his life on next Saturday se'nnight, at the fatal tree, and we may venture to assert amid the commiserations of all present.

Again, something of public attitudes to crime and punishment is evident. The *Sussex Advertiser* accepts that the man must hang but expresses its sympathy towards him.

1822 The case against Mary Mathews, 'a young woman of about 20', was   29 MARCH
heard at the Assizes at Horsham. She was accused of keeping a disorderly house, 'of the very worst description', in Brighton. Working for her were 'several young creatures under the age of 14, and one not more than 11'. She was found guilty, fined £10 (£700 today) and imprisoned in the House of Correction for a year.

30 MARCH **1820** 'At our House of Correction, Flagellation was the Order of the Day. The Governor had to superintend six private and two public whippings, which latter punishment attracted the curiosity of several women who, without shame, pressed forward to view the bloody backs of the offenders, Edward Ridley for corn stealing and Thomas Blaber for a misdemeanour.' Note the *Sussex Advertiser*'s acceptance of public flogging and its disapproval of the women who 'pressed forward'.

31 MARCH **1817** Lydia Astell, a dazzlingly beautiful young woman, came before the Assize court for having in her possession a forged £5 note, and knowing it to be forged. The Bank of England had first intended that Lydia would be charged with trying to pass a forged £5 note in a Horsham draper's shop, but as this would have meant a hanging had she been found guilty, she was charged with the less serious offence of having the note in her possession without lawful excuse. Tried in Horsham, her home town, this was a case which grabbed the attention of the locals.

Not that Lydia ever failed to grab attention. On both days of the trial she turned up in the most elegant and fashionable outfit, with feathers in her bonnet and a crimson velvet fur-lined cloak. The second day her hair, covered with a black veil, was in the latest fashion, though some observed that the rest of her outfit seemed better suited to the ballroom than to the court room. She pleaded guilty to the charge and to her horror was sentenced to fourteen years' transportation.

Young though she was, Lydia had had a remarkable career. She was of a respectable family but had taken up with soldiers – several of them by all accounts – with one of whom she went to live in London. After he abandoned her she found an engagement as a singer at the fashionable Astley's Amphitheatre where she was very popular, but she seems to have pursued a rackety lifestyle and in recent months had ended up living with a jockey who was described as 'profligate'.

APRIL

Sussex County Gaol, Horsham, drawn by Henry Burstow, who was present at the execution of John Lawrence in 1844. The cross indicates the position of the gallows. *(SCM)*

1 APRIL **1799** At the Assizes 13-year-old Thomas Lucas was sentenced to death for stealing a letter containing a £10 cheque from Arundel Post Office where he worked. He had fallen under the influence of a notorious woman, owner of a fruit shop in the town; 'Through the artful seduction of an infamous prostitute, mistress, who fitted him to her purpose by occasional drink' is how the *Sussex Advertiser* puts it. She had said to him that even if he were caught, because he was so young he would not be severely punished. And now here he was in court, taking all of the blame because 'the abandoned woman' had agreed to act as a prosecution witness against young Lucas and 'thereby saved her own neck from the halter'. The judge observed that the woman ought to have been indicted as the principal offender, and the jury was clearly in agreement. Even prosecution counsel was affected and 'he could not refrain from shedding tears'.

Within days the boy received a free pardon but, says the Advertiser with some satisfaction, 'the woman has been very properly abandoned to the poor house, where, it is hoped, she will find repentance in the bitter cup of reflection'.

2 APRIL **1904** Frank Burt was charged with neglecting to maintain his wife at Worthing. The relieving officer stated that Mrs Burt and her child had become chargeable to the East Preston Union, and that Burt had made no attempt to contribute in any way to their support. The Burts were married in March 1903, at East Preston, but he disappeared in November of the same year. He was then earning £1 per week. He was sent to gaol for one calendar month's imprisonment.

3 APRIL **1797** The *Sussex Advertiser* reports with some relish that a man from Isfield got drunk and beat his wife savagely. Local women were incensed. Seventeen of them 'seized upon the masculine offender, and tossed him in a blanket 'till they were heartily tired of the discipline; after which they threw him into an adjacent horse-pond amidst the shouts of a little multitude who had become spectators of this summary mode of punishing a bad husband'.

Excessive drinking was a serious problem in rural areas during this period. On the same date, ten years earlier, John Boxall, a labourer from Storrington, had already drunk a huge amount of gin when he was offered a challenge. Friends offered him two more half-pints of gin, provided he drank the whole amount in two draughts. He did so and 'immediately sank into a state of stupefaction and died about a half an hour afterwards'.

The same fate, more or less on the same date in 1791, befell William Edwards of Midhurst. He had been drunk for two days and wagered that, if his drinking companion paid the bill, he would drink eighteen glasses of gin. He managed seventeen glasses and had begun the eighteenth when he fell over, and was carried to a cottage 'where he soon gave up the ghost'.

On a wall at Kirdford is the warning headed 'Degradation of Drinking'. It reads:

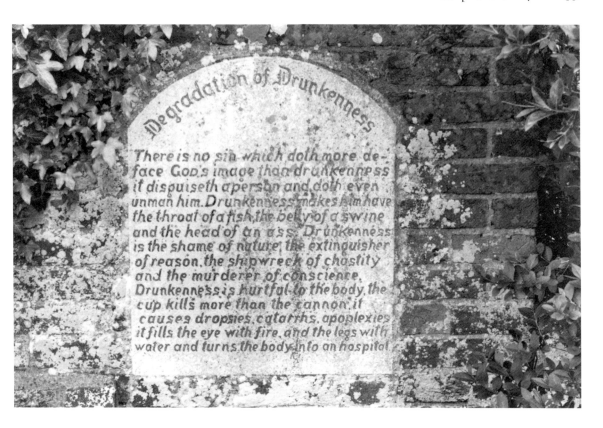

There is no sin which doth more deface God's image than drunkenness it disguiseth a person and doth even unman him. Drunkenness makes him have the throat of a fish, the belly of a swine and the head of an ass. Drunkenness is the shame of nature, the extinguisher of reason, the shipwreck of chastity and the murderer of conscience. Drunkenness is hurtful to the body, the cup kills more than the cannon, it causes dropsies, catarrhs, apoplexies, it fills the eye with fire, and the legs with water and turns the body into an hospital.

Degradation of Drunkenness warning at Kirdford. *(Alan Skinner)*

4 APRIL

1807 Bob Bignall of Clayton quit this life in style. Like others called to Horsham 'Hang Fair', he arrived in a horse-drawn cart, sitting on his coffin, and wearing a handsome greatcoat and fine boots. A well-known criminal – footpad, horse-thief, burglar, poacher, gaol-escaper – a distinct glamour attached to him.

Bignall accompanied the clergyman in prayer. Then, standing on the flat bed of the cart, he made the kind of farewell speech that hanging mobs felt themselves entitled to hear, warning his listeners against idleness, whoredom, dishonesty and drunkenness. The *Sussex Advertiser*'s account of the execution ends, 'Before the body was cut down, which was after hanging the usual time, two young women with enlarged necks, appeared under the gallows, and had the affected parts stroked for some minutes with the dead man's hand.'

Bob Bignall's failed attempt to escape from Lewes Gaol and his subsequent execution at Horsham was the subject of this print, published in 1807. *(SCM)*

In March 1803 Bignall had been tried for the murder of Jack Webber, a Hurstpierpoint farmer and noted smuggler. On this occasion Bignall was on the side of the law, assisting (for a fee) Joseph Howe, an Excise man. They had met Webber and six of his smuggling gang, all of them on horseback, on the Patcham to Hurstpierpoint road, and an argument had ensued. The shouting, the swearing, the threats and the accusations continued all the way to Stone Cross where all parties dismounted. What then followed is garbled. Some swore that Bignall had shouted out, 'Stop or I shall shoot you.' Howe told the court that Webber had encouraged his followers with shouts of 'Let us murder them both.'

'Damn your eyes,' Webber had dared Bignall, 'why don't you shoot me through the body, you damned excising bugger, for I would rather die than live.' And at some point Bignall shot him. Webber died of his wounds some days later. At the Assizes Bignall and Howe were found not guilty of murder.

Bignall's life of crime continued. In September 1806 he escaped from Rochester gaol. Months later, after a housebreaking at Albourne, he was arrested and taken to Lewes House of Correction. But his ingenuity did not fail him even then. Waiting in the prison yard for the coach to take him to Horsham gaol, he found a rope-ladder. It sounds incredible but there it was, lying there by chance, or possibly deliberately. Climbing down the ladder to freedom on the other side of the prison wall, he was seized with cramp and fell to the ground. Before he could recover he was recaptured. And there was to be no further escape.

1828 The *Exeter Weekly News* of 5 April carries the story of the fracas at   5 APRIL
Sidley on 3 January when upwards of 200 heavily armed smugglers fought a pitched battle with preventative men. The stakes were high: 300 gallons of brandy and 300 gallons of gin. In the course of the fight Quartermaster Charles Collins of HMS *Hyperion* was killed, as was Timothy Smithurst, one of the smugglers.

A Coroner's inquest on Collins had returned a verdict of 'wilful murder against some person or persons unknown' but information then led to the arrest of Charles Hills of Bexhill, and several others. At length Hills volunteered to become an 'approver' – that is, a prosecution witness – and he named sixty others involved in the affair. Searches in the area in and around Bexhill led to further arrests but, says the *Exeter Weekly News*, 'a great number of men, besides those in custody, have absconded, no other resource for their families, but the workhouse; and in one parish alone, Bexhill, no less than twenty-five families have been thrown upon the parochial funds, which were before very heavily burdened. Consequences of a still more melancholy nature have been produced in some of the families resulting from this unhappy conflict. In one instance a young woman, who had lain-in but a few hours, experienced so dreadful a shock on seeing her husband, one of the accused, dragged from the house, that she died in a state of madness the following day.'

Eight men appeared at the Old Bailey on 10 April, all pleading guilty to 'aiding and assisting in the illegal landing, running and carrying away certain unaccustomed goods'. The death of Quartermaster Collins was not mentioned. All were sentenced to death, later commuted to transportation.

6 APRIL **1844** John Lawrence was arrested for stealing a carpet in Brighton and taken to the police station. In the tiny office of Henry Solomon, the Chief Officer of Police, he suddenly seized a poker and beat in the policeman's skull. Found guilty of murder, he was the last man to be hanged at Horsham. Lawrence's 'Last Dying Confession', a cheap pamphlet typical of the period, was sold to the crowds who attended his execution:

> Good people all, I pray draw near,
> A dreadful story you shall hear.
> Overcome with grief and fear,
> I am condemned to die.
> I do lament and sore repent
> The evil deed which I have done;
> My time is come, my glass is run,
> I now behold the setting sun,
> All in the prime of life.
>
> *Chorus*
> John Lawrence is my name,
> To grief and shame
> I brought myself this world may see;
> Young men a warning take by me,
> At Horsham on a fatal tree,
> Alas, I am doomed to die.

John Lawrence and
Henry Solomon.
(SCM)

1904 In the Magistrates' Court Michael Cooper was charged with begging   7 APRIL
at Worthing on 4 March. Cooper said that he had walked from Brighton
because work was slack there and that he hoped to find a job in Worthing.
He was sentenced to seven days' imprisonment.

1793 Edward Howell and James Rooke were hanged at noon before a crowd   8 APRIL
of 14,000. After an hour their bodies were taken down and hung in chains at
Goldstone Bottom, the scene of their crime, on a 25ft-high gibbet, Howell on the
eastern arm, Rooke on the westward.

The two men had robbed the 12-year-old Steyning post-boy the previous
November, stopping him in Goldstone Bottom and taking his mailbags from
him. They had ridden off on the boy's horse but were captured later. Howell, a
well-known criminal, was one of a gang which had earlier robbed a Chiddingly
miller of £800 and then thrown him, gagged and bound, into a ditch. On
another occasion he had set fire to the public house belonging to the notorious
Jevington Jigg, whose sister had spurned his advances. Rooke, the younger
man, was immortalised in the Tennyson poem 'Rizpah', which tells how
Rooke's mother paid nightly visits to the gibbet to collect the bones that had
fallen from her son's skeleton. She took them home, placed them in a chest and
finally buried them outside the walls of Old Shoreham church.

Do you think I was scared by the bones? I kiss'd 'em, I buried 'em all –
I can't dig deep, I am old – in the night by the churchyard wall.
My Willy 'ill rise up whole when the trumpet of judgment 'ill sound,
But I charge you never to say that I laid him in holy ground.

1919 At last Miss Barham of Crowborough learnt of her fiancé's fate. Since   9 APRIL
Private Jack Gilbert, fighting on the Western Front, had been reported
'missing' on 26 April 1918, neither she nor any of his family had had
news of him. All efforts to trace him had proved futile. Then letters arrived
from some of his former comrades. One man wrote to say that 'he saw
Private Gilbert killed instantaneously by a machine gun bullet and knows
he did not suffer'. In another letter Miss Barham was told that her fiancé
was killed in the early morning, just at dawn. The writer could not say for
certain what became of the body because the 'Germans delivered a strong
counter-attack and took all the ground back, so no doubt he was buried
by them'. Private Cecil Herbert wrote to Miss Barham, telling her that 'the
last time I saw him was on the morning of 26 April. We went over the top
at 5.30 a.m. at Hangard Wood. It was a proper hell and I wonder anyone
came out alive.'

1823 Coastguards at Seaford had had warning of a landing of tubs of spirits   10 APRIL
in the early hours and when the suspect craft came in sight they carefully
tracked it until they were able to make certain that there could be no escape.
They boarded the boat and found twenty tubs under tarpaulins. After
unloading the tubs and ensuring that the crew was under guard, they tapped
the barrels to find that each of them contained nothing more than sea water.

While they had been attending to the decoy boat 300 tubs of spirits had been unloaded not half a mile away at Newhaven Tidemills and made off with up-country.

11 APRIL 1795 The *Sussex Advertiser* reports that 'the eastern part of the county is again infested by a very dangerous gang of horse stealers, who prosecute their plans so systematically that it is extremely difficult to detect them. On the same night the two horses advertised in our last were stolen at Ardingly, three others were stolen from Bromley in Kent, two of which were a valuable pair of coach horses.'

12 APRIL 1796 A mob at Petworth burnt the effigy of a miller after carrying it about the town and whipping it at the public post. The charge against the miller was that he had prevented a reduction in the price of flour. 'To such a pitch did the populace carry their resentment,' the *Sussex Advertiser* tells its readers, 'that 'twas judged expedient to call forth Lord Egremont's troop of Yeomanry Cavalry by whom tranquillity was very speedily restored.' In the same week farmers and corn merchants were stoned and jostled by angry townsfolk.

13 APRIL 1799 Robert and William Drewett, charged with robbing the mail at North Heath near Midhurst, were sentenced to death at East Grinstead Assizes. When they returned to Horsham gaol to await their fate there were suggestions that there would be a rescue attempt and guards were placed outside the gaol for several nights before the execution. The brothers were escorted by a strong military guard to the execution ground on Horsham Heath, where the crowds were enormous. The bodies were gibbeted at North Heath, the scene of their crime, where they hung for three years.

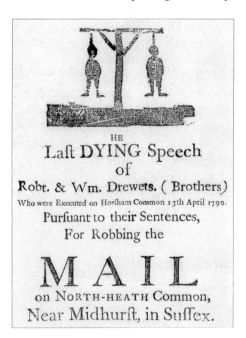

HE
Laſt DYING Speech
of
Robt. & Wm. Drewets. (Brothers)
Who were Executed on Horſham Common 13th April 1799.
Purſuant to their Sentences,
For Robbing the

MAIL

on NORTH-HEATH Common,
Near Midhurſt, in Suſſex.

Notice of execution of the Drewett brothers. *(SCM)*

1820 An endless litany of crimes is recorded in the *Sussex Advertiser*, yet never is there any observation on the inconsistency of sentencing. The gallows, transportation, whipping, gaol for a year or for a week; the sentences suggest how punishment was a lottery: 'Peter Thomas, for stealing one hempen sack, the property of James Foard, of Petworth – One month's solitary confinement. . . . John Berryman and John Goble, convicted of stealing three fowls and one turkey in the parish of Sutton and William Chantler, convicted of stealing 14 live fowls, the property of Ann Kempshall, of Horsham, were severally sentenced to Seven Years Transportation.'

14 APRIL

1853 James Wellerd, keeper of Hastings Gaol, records in his diary: 'At 5 p.m. Edward Goodsell received seven lashes on the britch with a birch rod in pursuance of sentence at Petty Sessions on 14th April under the Juvenile Offender Act. The mayor and Mr Duke, Surgeon, present.' Goodsell was given a further twelve strokes in September for another offence. He was 12 years old.

15 APRIL

1924 Ladies' man Patrick Mahon, handsome, intelligent and deeply dishonest, was carrying on an affair with a girlfriend, Emily Kaye. They were staying at an old coastguard cottage, Officer's House, near Eastbourne. Mahon's statement to the police gives his version of how Emily came by her death:

16 APRIL

Patrick Mahon.
(*Daily Mirror*)

During that night, 16 April, we quarrelled over certain things and in a violent temper she threw an axe at me. It was a coal axe. It hit me a glancing blow. Then I saw red. We fought and struggled. She was a very big strong girl. She appeared to be quite mad with anger and rage. During our struggle we overturned a chair and her head fell on an iron coal scuttle and it appeared to stun her. This happened about 12 o'clock, midnight. I attempted to revive her but I could not. I put the body in the spare bedroom and covered it up with her fur coat.

I came up to London on the morning of 17 April and returned to the bungalow fairly late, taking with me a knife which I had bought in a shop in Victoria Street. I also bought at the same shop a small saw.

When I got back to the bungalow I was still so upset and worried that I could not then carry out my intention to decapitate the body. I did so on Good Friday. I severed the legs from the hips, the head, and left the arms on. I then put the various parts in a trunk in the bedroom and locked the door.

I again went to the bungalow on Tuesday and on that day I burnt the head in the sitting room grate and also the feet and legs.

The dismemberment was so unpleasant that for several days he was unable to look at the body, but then he resumed the task at about 10 a.m. on Saturday, 26 April.

I had to cut up the trunk. I also cut off the arms. I burned portions of them. The smell was appalling and I had to think of some method of disposing of the portions. I then boiled some portions in a large pot in the bungalow, cut the portions up small, put them in the brown bag, and I threw them out of the train while travelling between Waterloo and Richmond.

Mahon deposited the trunk in a Gladstone bag at Waterloo station. His wife, suspicious, found the left luggage ticket in his jacket pocket and from that point his days of philandering were over.

At the trial Sir Bernard Spilsbury, who had conducted the post-mortem in the garden at Officer's House as the stench of death had been so overpowering, dismissed the idea of Emily's death being accidental. The coal scuttle against which Mahon said she had hit her head was too flimsy an item to cause anyone's death.

Mahon hanged at Wandsworth Prison on 3 September 1924.

17 APRIL **1802** John Beatson, nearly 70 years of age, and his stepson William, the Great Mail Robbers, hanged side by side at the scene of their crime at Wall Hill, Forest Row. They had left Horsham gaol earlier in the day and made the slow 20-mile journey by horse-drawn cart, sitting on their coffins. Awaiting them was a crowd of 3,000, some of them perched in trees. The *Sussex Advertiser* reports the final moments: 'The old man who appeared as it were to spring from the cart as it was drawn from under him, died without a struggle; but the young one exhibited strong symptoms of life for near a quarter of an hour after he was suspended, owing to the shifting of the rope, which was not skilfully placed by the executioner.'

The Beatsons were respectable, hard-working men who had fallen on hard times and were desperate not to have to spend their days in the poor house. At midnight on 20 July 1801 they had held up the mail cart at Wall Hill outside Forest Row, escaping with £4,000 in bank notes, the equivalent today to approximately £500,000. They abandoned drafts and bills. They made their way on foot to Westerham from where they took a coach to London. They were finally captured at Liverpool attempting to escape to Ireland.

GENERAL POST-OFFICE,

Monday Morning, 20th July, 1801.

THE Poſt Boy conveying the Mail from Lewes to Eaſt Grinſtead, was ſtopt this Morning within about two Miles and a Quarter of Eaſt Grinſtead, by two Men on Foot, who robbed him of the following Bags of Letters, namely

Brighton,
Shoreḥam,
Steyning,   } for London.
Lewes,
AND
Uckfield,

and Five Bye-Bags, viz. Brighton for Croydon, ditto for Eaſt Grinſtead, ditto for Lewes, Lewes for Croydon, ditto for Eaſt Grinſtead.

Whoever ſhall apprehend and conviĉt, or cauſe to be apprehended and conviĉted, the Perſons who committed this Robbery, will be entitled to a Reward of TWO HUNDRED POUNDS, over and above the Reward given by Aĉt of Parliament for apprehending Highwaymen :/ Or if either of the Perſons concerned therein will ſurrender himſelf, and make Diſcovery, whereby the other Perſon who committed the Robbery may be apprehended and brought to Juſtice, ſuch Diſcoverer will be entitled to the ſaid Reward, and will alſo receive His Majeſty's moſt gracious Pardon.

By Commⁱˢ of His Majeſty's Poſtmaſter-General,

FRANCIS FREELING,
SECRETARY.

Wanted notice issued by the GPO, 1802. (West Sussex Record Office)

18 APRIL **1852** 'This Board still entertain the opinion that the Children in the Seaford School [Work]house should not be taught to write as they would otherwise be in a better situation than the children of a considerable number of the independent Agricultural labourers in this Union who do not have the opportunity in the National Schools.'

1920 After months of litigation and years of scandal, the rector of Rusper, the Revd Edward Synnott, was finally cleared by the Consistory Court of Chichester of all charges against him. It had been alleged that on 21 May 1917 he had raped Mrs Alice Harris, the charwoman, as she was tidying his bedroom. Inevitably there was an enormous furore which went far beyond the boundaries of the village. There was a conspiracy against him, Synnott claimed, and there were those who were perhaps too ready to believe the worst of the somewhat aggressive Irishman who was 'too Protestant' in his services. Synnott was to describe his experiences in *Five Years' Hell in a Country Parish*: there had been malicious gossip, allegations of lewd conversation and intemperance, anonymous letters and threats of blackmail; the parish had been divided; his daughter had been scorned; his wife had had a nervous breakdown; and he had been bankrupted. The livestock on the farm he had worked for three years as his contribution to the war effort had been reduced from a fine herd of cattle to a couple of chickens. Months after being cleared by the court he was bound over by the Horsham magistrates for hitting a parishioner in the kitchen of the rectory before insisting that he sign a document, promising not to defame his character in future.

19 APRIL

The Revd Edward Synnott. (*Daily Sketch*)

1816 'John Ayling, for stealing a faggot of wood, of the value of twopence, the property of John Sargent, Esq., of Woolavington and Edward Legatt for stealing at Eastergate, one faggot of wood, the property of Francis Bine. Each, one month's solitary confinement on bread and water.' And not an expression of surprise from the *Sussex Advertiser* about the charge.

20 APRIL

1865 Edward Evans, who ran the Bargeman's Arms in Cliffe, Lewes, was committed to trial for keeping a disorderly house. Magistrates learnt that his beer shop, known familiarly as 'Harriet's', was frequented by men and women of loose reputation.

21 APRIL

1811 'Last Wednesday,' the *Sussex Advertiser* informs its readers, 'Mary Dennis and Mary Richardson, her daughter, were committed to the House of Correction at Lewes, charged with stealing in the shop of Mr Bodle in Alfriston, about 80 yards of ribbon of different sorts, in rolls, the greatest part of which, in searching them, was found concealed under the peak of their stays.'

22 APRIL

1810 'On Monday, the Easter Holiday folks, in all the brilliance of Sunday finery, assembled in great numbers at the Bear public house, about a mile north of the town, on the grounds contiguous to which they were

23 APRIL

subsequently entertained with the polished diversions of cock fighting, and the baiting of a badger.' Unsurprisingly the *Sussex Advertiser* finds nothing unsporting or cruel in these events.

24 APRIL, **1863** William White, also known as George Warren, a prisoner at Lewes gaol, committed suicide by hanging himself from the ventilator grating inside his cell. A ropemaker by trade, he had twisted together two handkerchiefs and a prison towel to make a ligature. He had been convicted of a petty theft at East Grinstead, for which he was sentenced to nine months' imprisonment.

This was the second suicide at the prison within three months. A 15-year-old boy, Thomas Jones, two weeks before release from a two-month sentence, had tied a handkerchief to the gas pipe in his cell.

The prison regime, designed in part to reform and in part to punish and deter, was unremittingly harsh. It was an existence of hard labour, poor food, gaol fever, verminous clothing, airless cells. Small wonder it had its victims.

25 APRIL, **1817** When Martha Young of Lewes eloped with Henry Bourn, 'an Agent for granting Licences to Hawkers, Pedlars, &c' and taking with her 'divers articles, my property', her husband declared in an announcement in the *Sussex Advertiser* that it was his intention 'to caution all persons against trusting her, on my account, as I will not pay any Debts she may contract'.

26 APRIL, **1858** John Coker Egerton records in a mixture of sadness and optimism in his usual note form 'the disheartening news that 6 or 7 girls, if not more, close at hand in the vill. Were in the family way. It indeed is sad beyond expression. . . . Such a fact makes one almost a sceptic as to schools or anything else. . . . Still it is not right to doubt. . . . Bad as things are, they surely cd. be worse if the voice of warning & exhortation to turn to Christianity were altogether dumb.'

27 APRIL, **1798** Another grim event, not the first nor the last dreadful explosion to appear in the pages of the *Sussex Advertiser*. 'About noon on 27 April, one of the Battle Powder Mills with a Drying House and Store-room nearly adjoining

An early nineteenth-century lithograph of a powder mill. *(East Sussex Record Office)*

were blown up with two tremendous explosions and totally destroyed. Three men employed at the Mill were blown into the air and killed. Seven separate buildings were completely destroyed, though only two reports were distinguishable; the quantity of powder exploded exceeded fifteen tons in weight and the damage was estimated at upwards of £5,000.'

1941 At Chichester police court William Flack, a 21-year-old driver in the Royal Corps of Signals, was committed for trial at the next Sussex Assizes. He was charged with the murder of Mrs Lillian Welch, a member of the ATS, whose body was found some weeks earlier near Sennicotts Church on the verge of the carriageway, in Funtington Road. Her head was crushed and evidence showed that she had been hit from behind by a heavy vehicle.   28 APRIL

Flack eventually admitted that he had accidentally collided with the cyclist. He had stopped his lorry and had dragged the body to the roadside. Realising he could not help her, he had, in a panic, disarranged the dead woman's clothing, to make it appear an assault had been committed.

The prosecution's case was that Flack had deliberately run the woman down, intending to rape her, but that when he found she was dead he had fled the scene. There was no evidence of sexual interference.

At the Assizes in July a witness from Carmarthen, Miss Eiluned Bridgeman, said that in January she had been knocked off her cycle by a lorry driver whom she identified as Flack. He had stopped and carried her to his lorry and indecently assaulted her. When she shouted he had driven off. Flack admitted hitting Miss Bridgeman accidentally and claimed that when he picked her up he was only trying to help her, but when she screamed he had left her.

There was strong evidence that Flack's eyesight was so bad that he ought not to be driving any kind of vehicle. Mr Justice Humphreys told the jury that unless they were satisfied beyond all reasonable doubt that Flack had deliberately driven into Mrs Welch he must be acquitted. The jury returned a verdict of guilty of manslaughter. The court then heard that although he had been before the court for other offences, including indecency and an assault on a female, Flack had never been in prison. Sentencing him to seven years for manslaughter, the judge said he was satisfied that Flack had twice knocked women off their cycles 'in order to gratify some feeling'.

1839 According to the *Sussex Advertiser*, 'The Royal Commission on Police was informed that Brighton contained numerous lodging houses, the keepers of which furnish matches, songs, laces, and many other petty articles which are hawked about as an excuse of vagrancy and it gives them opportunities of greater consequence, observing the fastenings and other circumstances that may lead to robbery. The principal robberies have been concocted in vagrant lodging houses and rendered effectual through the agencies of the Keepers. Intelligence is given and received by clients.'   29 APRIL

30 APRIL   **1814** 'There has been', according to a Horsham witness, 'hot work between the soldiers and the townspeople. About 250 of the former attacked the town with clubs, stones, etc., but were repulsed.' Sadly this was no isolated incident. Such events were repeated wherever the military were billeted: Brighton, Hastings, Worthing, Newhaven, Seaford and several other locations. The soldiers, usually from some far-off county, not infrequently drank too much, their presence encouraging prostitution and general rowdiness. On the other hand, soldiers were good for trade. In Alfriston the town's leather industry, its brewery, its public houses and beer shops prospered from the presence of the military.

MAY

Lewes Law Courts, 2005. *(Andy Gammon)*

1 MAY **1797** Soldiers from Horsham barracks are reported to have behaved badly at Slinfold Fair. They had torn down the stalls, chased off many local people, had taken over the only pub where they had ordered great quantities of beer, and then not only had they refused to pay but had smashed all the beer mugs and crockery. On their way back to barracks they had broken down the doors of a pub at Broadbridge Heath and had finally made off with a flitch of bacon.

2 MAY **1764** Thomas Turner of East Hoathly writes in his diary: 'This day was fought a main of cocks at our public house between the gentlemen of East Grinstead and the gentlemen of East Hoathly for half a guinea a battle and 2 guineas the odd battle, which was won by the gentlemen of East Grinstead, they winning 5 battles out of the six fought in the main. I saw three battles fought, but as I laid no bets, I could neither win nor lose, though I believe there was a great deal of money sported on both sides.'

3 MAY **1829** At Lewes Quarter Sessions the court heard the extraordinary case of 12-year-old Mary Anne Soffe, 'an intelligent looking girl', who had been in the workhouse in St John's parish until she was sent the previous November to work for Mr and Mrs Philp, shopkeepers in North Street, Brighton. When one day Mary was accused of having burnt the hearthrug, her mistress would not accept her denials. Mrs Philp, 'a young, rather good-looking woman', told the girl that if she confessed to it, she would not be punished but if she refused to admit to what she had done she would suffer. Afraid of what might happen to her, Mary confessed that she was responsible for the damage. At dinner Mrs Philp, despite her husband's attempts to persuade her otherwise, threatened to strip the girl. After Mr Philp had gone out Mrs Philp made Mary take off her frock, her pinafore and her underclothes. She was then ordered to take the dinner plates and cutlery down to the kitchen. After that Mrs Philp told the girl to go upstairs to dust the drawing room, make the bed and empty the slops. Mary was naked for the whole afternoon. In that time she was beaten with a birch rod, hit with a broom and violently kicked.

When Mr Philp returned he remonstrated mildly with his wife but it had little effect. When she went out that evening Mrs Philp left some stockings for Mary to mend. Returning home very late, she was angry that the work had not been completed. She pushed the girl and pulled a handful of hair out of her head. Mary suffered a black eye when she was thrust violently against a doorpost. Finally, because her mistress said that she had been slacking that evening, she was made to stand by her bed all night.

The court heard a catalogue of gross ill-treatment over the weeks. Finally Mrs Philp was sentenced to three months in Horsham gaol and fined £20. Her ineffectual husband received no punishment.

4 MAY **1838** A formal letter from the Eastbourne Union Workhouse Guardians firmly states its view of one of the 'undeserving poor'. 'The Board of Guardians of this Union have requested me to inform the Poor Law Commissioners for England and Wales that the worthless character of John Chapman was the reason that induced the Board to refuse him outdoor relief.'

1835 John Mance, the Keeper of the Petworth House of Correction, and a martinet, was the inventor of the Ergometer, a machine used at Lewes and Petworth to measure the amount of 'work' done on the treadmill. When the prescribed amount of work was completed the Ergometer rang an alarm bell. Mance was asked by a Government Select Committee enquiring into the effectiveness of the prison regime:

5 MAY

> Q. Are you of the opinion that the system of enacting silence in the prisons is one which is likely to be beneficial?
> A. I am decidedly of that opinion.
> Q. Do you not think that, wherever practicable, separate cells for every prisoner before and after trial should be provided?
> A. I have no doubt of it; and if prisoners were separately employed I think it would be still more beneficial.

For years reformers such as John Howard had pleaded for more humane conditions in prisons but even so, many reformers advocated systems of

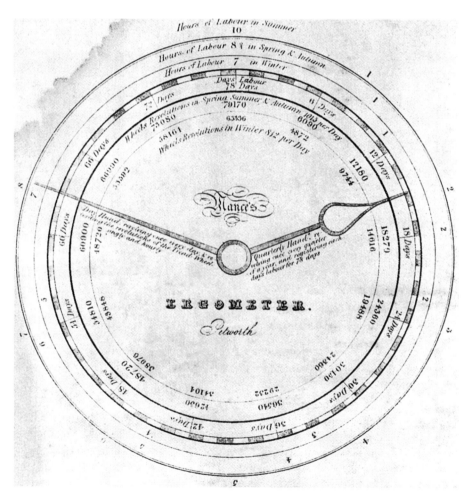

Mance's Ergometer.
(SCM)

Pentonville prisoners wearing masks exercising in the prison yard. *(Illustrated London News)*

total isolation and complete silence for prisoners, as at Petworth and Lewes. Here they sometimes operated looms in their cells, worked the treadmill each in his own separate partition, and every day went to the chapel in which each had his own private cubicle. The earnest reformers were anxious that in their mute solitude the prisoners would have time to reflect upon their various wickednesses – poaching, robbing barns of bags of corn, taking flour from mills – and eventually be released from prison as better human beings. Mance expressed the view that a prisoner's mask, such as was worn at Pentonville, would be desirable, but it was not introduced at Petworth or Lewes. Total silence, total separation and total anonymity was his ideal.

6 MAY **1796** The body of William Upton, a servant, was found hanging from a tree on Selsfield Common, West Hoathly. He had suddenly left his workplace 'and 'tis supposed went immediately and committed the horrid act of suicide. The Coroner's jury brought in their verdict, Felo-de-se; and the body was in consequence by order of the Coroner buried at the crossroads.'

1830 A young surgeon named Griffith travelled up to London on business, intending to stay for a week. The day after his arrival a friend who called on him found him incoherent and so uncontrolled that he was forcibly placed under restraint. At the sight of any liquid offered him he broke out into the most awful paroxysms. A doctor called in said that Dr Griffith was suffering from hydrophobia. At one point, during a lucid interval, he said that about a couple of months earlier a dog had bitten him on the lower part of the leg. He was sent immediately to the Middlesex Hospital whose wards he had walked at the beginning of his career, but 'notwithstanding the very best care and advice, the effects of the fatal disorder became hourly more strong, and on the night of Saturday terminated in the death of the unfortunate patient, whose sufferings were most dreadful to the last'. The newspapers of the period frequently refer to rabid dogs on the loose.

7 MAY

1791 'Mr Payne, Surgeon, of East Hoathly delivered a poor woman of Waldron, of three children, two girls and a boy, who with their mother are doing well. Perhaps a greater scene of poverty does not often appear than presented itself at the lying-in of this miserable woman who has not a scrap of clothes provided for her new-born infants, which was witnessed by the Minister of the Parish that attended to baptise them, and who made them Christians, but half covered with the ragged remnants of some old aprons. We are told that she is the mother of nine children, and that her fourth, fifth and sixth born are, from poverty and neglect, yet unable to stand alone, but crawl about the house like frogs.' Is the *Sussex Advertiser* simply struck by the novelty of the scene, the children crawling about the house like frogs, or is it just amazed at the survival of so many children in such squalor?

8 MAY

1840 Thomas Vidler was charged with stealing at Burwash twenty pieces of hop pole, valued at 3*d*, belonging to Edward Maynard. He pleaded guilty and said that he picked up the wood to burn. He was given one week's imprisonment in solitary confinement.

9 MAY

1934 At some time during the evening Violette Kaye, one-time stage dancer but now a faded prostitute, died in a flat in 44 Park Crescent, Brighton. She had suffered a violent blow to the head. At his trial her boyfriend-cum-pimp,

10 MAY

Toni Mancini – his real name was Cecil England – told the court that she was dead on his arrival home from his work at a seaside café. As he had a police record – relatively minor, despite his dubious claims to have worked with the Sabini racecourse gang – he had not reported her death, fearing that he would be charged with murder.

Apparently he did nothing immediately, sitting for hours until rigor mortis had almost set in. Then he squeezed Violette's body into the wardrobe. The next day he purchased a black trunk and transferred her body to it. He moved

Toni Mancini.
(News of the World)

to new rooms in 52 Kemp Street, now using the trunk, covered with a pretty cloth, as a table. He also resumed his old life, visiting pubs and billiard halls, dancing at Sherry's and the Regent and squiring girls.

It was a warm summer and some of his visitors commented on the smell. Disinfectant, he told one. Somebody had died in the room recently. Another visitor was told that his sweaty football boots were responsible. And when the trunk leaked a brown fluid he told his landlady that it was a unique French floor polish which would enhance the floorboards. Convinced, she asked him for a quote: how much would it cost to do the whole floor?

In mid-July Toni Mancini was arrested and charged with murder. His counsel, Norman Birkett KC, convinced the trial jury of his innocence.

11 MAY

Below and opposite:
Jet crash at Southwick.
(Daily Sketch)

1956 A Valiant jet bomber piloted by Squadron Leader Kenneth Orman crashed on to the railway track at Southwick. The plane, with a four-man crew, had left Farnborough and because the main runway was temporarily unserviceable it had taken off from a shorter runway. In consequence of this it could not take on sufficient fuel for the tests it was to undergo. It had therefore landed at Wisley in Surrey for more fuel. Once more in the air, it was at this point that a serious electrical fault developed. The problem facing the pilot was that the plane could not return immediately to Farnborough as it was now too heavily laden with fuel. It was decided to make for the coast to burn off the excess weight over the sea. But then matters worsened and finally it became impossible to control the aircraft: Squadron Leader Orman gave the order to bale out.

At the inquest Flight Lieutenant Colin Preece, the co-pilot and only survivor, explained that although two of his colleagues, Flight Lieutenant Evans and a Ministry of Supply technician called Knight, had no ejector seats, they did have parachutes and a door through which to bale out. 'I am sure', Preece told the court, 'that Squadron Leader Orman stayed in the plane to make sure that we all got out.' Shortly afterwards the Valiant, a ball of fire, crashed on to the railway tracks. Had it done so a minute or two later it would most certainly have hit a passenger train. The power lines it had cut through writhed on the ground, spitting blue sparks.

Others too had fortunate escapes that day. Despite the enormous explosion on impact and the wreckage, scattered for a mile around, only six people on the ground received slight injuries and thirteen houses were damaged. Most fortunate were the children at two local schools, all of them out enjoying playtime. Part of the landing gear along with a storm of broken glass fell in the playground of Southwick Junior Boys' School. Many years later Mick Bird, a pupil at Manor Hall Road School, still vividly recalled the events of that day. 'There were flames and clouds of smoke. You have to remember that we were still very much aware of the atom bomb, and for us children it was terrifying. Once the shock was over, though, we began to collect souvenirs. There were cartridges still warm to the touch. However, we were mustered in the school hall and told that it was a crime to keep any bits and pieces, so we had to hand everything over.'

1886 A young cow boy who worked on a farm at Wiston near Steyning, was milking the cows in the byre. An 8-year-old boy came in for a pail of milk and while waiting he succeeded in annoying the cow boy. Perhaps he was baiting the adolescent as he sat at his stool, possibly name-calling, insulting him in some childish way. When the milking was finished the cow boy, aiming to teach the youngster a lesson, took a length of rope and tied him to the hind leg of a cow, and then he set the animal loose. But the cow took fright and ran off, dragging the child with him out of the yard. Realising what he had done the cow boy frantically tried to stop the animal but failed. The little boy's head was dashed against a post and within a few hours he died. At the Assizes the cow boy's counsel said that his client, a normally well-behaved youngster, had not deliberately intended to harm the child. The animal, he said, was normally very gentle and the yard gate had been opened by accident. The jury found the prisoner guilty but recommended him to mercy. The judge accepted that no serious injury had been intended. He would normally have passed a three-month sentence but the cow boy had already been in prison for three months and so he was sentenced to two days' imprisonment, with the consequence that he was immediately freed.

1837 'EAST HOATHLY – a few nights since some thieves carried off from the farm of Mr. Marten, the leaden pump and piping. This they accomplished without creating alarm there being no residence at hand. Lead stealing has of late increased and several felons are now in the Lewes Gaol, awaiting their trials for offences of this kind.' Even so, and despite the *Sussex Advertiser*'s evident satisfaction that felons were awaiting trial, thefts of lead remained common.

1913 In the evening there was a riotous disturbance in Hastings. Two suffragettes had refused to pay their taxes and in consequence their property had been seized and its sale by auction was to be held in the town. A suffragette procession set

12 MAY

13 MAY

14 MAY

A suffragette arrested at Hastings. *(Hastings Reference Library)*

A suffragette note. *(Hastings and St Leonards Pictorial Advertiser)*

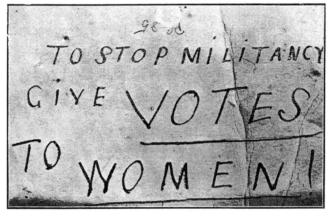

off along the seafront, the two heroines in carriages, a band in front and a banner-carrying procession behind. On each side of the road a hostile crowd was prevented from attacking the women by an escort of policemen. But the opponents of the suffragettes managed to get into the sale room, throwing eggs and flour, tearing off the women's hats and destroying their banners. Outside, one of the carriages was overturned. While the women escaped from the building without serious harm, not a single article was sold.

15 MAY **1826** 'Last Monday', says the *Sussex Weekly Advertiser*, 'a labouring man named Russell was found lying dead in a wood, nigh to Burwash. He had left his home the same morning, apparently in good health. An inquisition has been since held on view of the body, which we understand, for the satisfaction of the jury, was opened; some circumstances having appeared which led to the suspicion that the deceased had swallowed arsenic.'

The Wheel, Burwash
Weald, *c.* 1890.
*(Courtesy of the
present landlords)*

Benjamin Russell and his wife Hannah ran The Wheel, a public house
at Burwash Weald. As soon as his body was found, even before the post-
mortem, there were rumours that Russell was the victim of his wife and their
19-year-old lodger Daniel Leany, with whom she had conducted a very open
affair. The newspapers were to write of the 31-year-old Hannah speaking
of Daniel 'in terms of gross affection'. The couple were arrested and tried at
the Summer Assizes in Lewes. Leany was hanged, but there was a stay of
execution for Hannah as there was doubt about her part in the murder. Dr
Gideon Mantell, the famed natural historian living in Lewes, took up the case,
querying the medical evidence. It was through his intervention that she was
eventually pardoned and released.

1851   16 MAY

Mr. Holman deposed before the magistrates: I was returning home about a
quarter before five o'clock, along the Eastbourne road, in my pony chaise,
accompanied by my son Thomas who is aged 11 years. At a spot about
three quarters of a mile before East Hoathly village, between two woods, I
saw the prisoner come upon the road about 20 yards in front of me, from
behind some bushes on the right hand side of the road. He came across a
swampy piece of ground in the direction of my chaise with his right hand
in his jacket pocket. I whipped the pony and drove faster. When I came
on a level with him, he pulled a pistol from his pocket and presented it.

He said, 'Stop, stop, your money or —.' I was riding rather fast and my pony being a spirited animal, I got out of hearing. I got the constable and several persons to go immediately in pursuit. I accompanied them and came up with the man in about an hour afterwards at Laughton Pound. Mr. Starnes [the constable] took the man into custody. He struggled with Starnes and got away and threw away a bundle. We then discovered that it contained a jacket, a pistol and some other articles.

It does seem that pistols were cheap and easily come by.

17 MAY **1944** At the inquest at Shoreham on the bodies of two victims, killed on the previous Sunday's shelling of Steyning, Lieutenant W.H. Marshall, senior gunnery officer of an Army unit, said that the 75mm guns of the Sherman tanks were firing at a clump of trees. When they were told by a dispatch rider that mortar bombs were falling on Steyning he reduced the range as a precaution, although his ammunition bore no relation to mortar bombs. When officers then came to tell him that shells were falling in the wrong place he stopped the firing. Rather than offer an explanation as to why the shells, if they were his, fell in and around Steyning, the lieutenant said that he wished to await the findings of a military investigation. A verdict of 'Accidental Death' was recorded.

18 MAY **1928** Ernest Smith, a 67-year-old retired druggist, died in a nursing home as a result of injuries received on 14 April when he was attacked and savagely beaten on Brighton seafront. Three men had taken him in a car up to Race Hill where they stole his money and a gold watch. They had left him there with 2s to get home.

Smith had left home at 7.30 p.m. ostensibly to take a walk. When he returned after 10 p.m. his wife had scarcely been able to recognise him. Despite the fact that he was unwilling to tell the police much about what happened to him, three men were ultimately arrested and charged with murder. Percy Taylor, a painter, James Weaver, a hawker, and Thomas Donovan, a motor mechanic, were said to have attacked Smith on the sea front. It is likely that they used a woman as a decoy and this may be the reason for Smith's reluctance to talk about the matter.

Several incriminating remarks were offered in evidence against the three men. Mrs Rhoda Spraggs, with whom Donovan went to stay in Hastings, said he had told her: 'The splits are after me. We hit an old man on the jaw and he never lived to tell the tale.' Taylor when arrested asked, 'Can the old man identify me? I mean, the fellers who were there.' Weaver said to the police, 'You don't want to look for us on this job. It's Donovan you want.'

All three were sentenced to death but were reprieved. The judge himself had thought that a manslaughter charge might have been more appropriate, and this might have led to the reprieve.

19 MAY **1794** 'Elizabeth Lavender was executed at Horsham, pursuant to her sentence at our late Assizes, for the murder of her male bastard child. Her behaviour at

the gallows was such as became one in her unhappy situation. She trembled and wept much, but nevertheless seemed to listen to the clergyman who attended her, and having expressed the hope that all other females take warning by her untimely fate, she was turned off about half past twelve, and expired without any apparent agony.'

The *Sussex Advertiser* seems to say that all went off well. Elizabeth was upset, had listened to the clergyman, expressed regrets and had apparently not suffered much pain. But is the newspaper callous or simply being matter-of-fact? Elizabeth Lavender was 17 years old.

1850 Tough times in the county: the *Sussex Agricultural Express* reports a pub disturbance. 'Stephen Doust, P.C. – I recollect the Rodmill Club night on the 20th May. The club is held at the Abergavenny Arms. About ten at night I was sent for to quell a disturbance between parties who had previously been quarrelling. I was thrown down on the floor, and one of the party, William Robinson, thrust his fingers in my throat. I had about ten men on top of me. The prisoner at the bar, when I was released, followed me out of the door, and I heard him say, "A ring, a ring" and he pulled his clothes off. A party closed round, amongst whom was the prisoner. I was knocked down and I am quite sure the prisoner was one of the men who struck at me. My staff was taken from me but I am not aware whether or not I was struck with it. I was under the care of a surgeon for more than a week.' 20 MAY

1794 There was a riot in the centre of Lewes when the Hereford Militia came to town on their way to their camp in Eastbourne. In the evening they paraded in the High Street where their band attracted a huge crowd. There was some pushing, shoving and jostling between locals and the military. A scuffle involving a young baker started in Keere Street and the sergeant major, fearing that matters would worsen, reported to the colonel who confronted the baker and tried to arrest him. The town constable now turned up, saying that the colonel had no authority to arrest a civilian. They seem to have reached some compromise but scuffles continued. Then the soldiers broke ranks and waded in. The constable was knocked down and forced to find shelter in a nearby house. A man who was helping him was struck in the eye by an officer's cane. Others were severely beaten by the soldiers and sought refuge in nearby houses and shops. Finally order was restored. 21 MAY

There was always disorder in towns with the arrival of soldiers from distant parts of the country. They were resented by the locals, especially the young; in turn, the incomers disdained the stay-at-home bumpkins.

1783 Thomas Noakes, a 24-year-old Hastings smuggler, was shot at sea by a customs officer. He was buried in St Clement's churchyard. His headstone reads: 22 MAY

> May it be known, tho' I am clay
> A base man took my life away;
> But freely him I do forgive
> And hope in Heaven we shall live.

23 MAY   **1839** At a meeting of the Board of Hastings Guardians, reported in the *Cinque Ports Chronicle*, one of the members proposed the establishment of a library for the use of inmates of the workhouse. 'The Chairman thought it very absurd to provide paupers in a union house with a library of books; they could have copy books and slates when wanted. Mr Luck thought that a man was much better without education than with it.'

24 MAY   **1817** 'A man between 70 and 80 years of age, named Holloway, fell down in the Cliffe and fractured one of his legs in a shocking manner: the bone protruded through the integuments at least five inches, the end of which the surgeon was under the necessity of taking it off.' Like any newspaper of its time, the *Sussex Advertiser* does not flinch from recording the grim facts.

25 MAY   **1841** Throughout the century there were scandals about workhouses and this at Petworth was one of the earliest. John Penfold, Master of Petworth workhouse, eventually resigned after complaints about his behaviour had been investigated by Mr Tufnell, the Assistant Poor Law Commissioner for East Sussex, and Mr Daintrey, the Secretary of the Petworth Poor Law Guardians. The statements of several inmates of the workhouse were included in the report presented to the Poor Law Commission.

Emma Lucas had come from London six years previously and had been in the workhouse ever since. She delivered a male child on 16 February. She had left the workhouse in June when she was in the family way again and had another child in Wisborough Green workhouse. She claimed that Penfold was the father of both children. He had asked her to leave soon after he got her into trouble and gave her 17s two or three times. She told Daintrey that no one else had given her money and that she had resisted his advances in the larder: 'He persisted and wanted "to have connection with me". I refused but he laid hold of me and took liberty with me.'

Mary Ann Dummer claimed that Penfold 'put his hands up my clothes and also made me put my hands in his breeches. Other nights when mistress was in bed he used to put his hands up our clothes. He told us not to tell or else he would be cross with us. Once I caught Master and Emma Lucas in the storeroom and another time with her clothes rumpled.'

Priscilla Lucas, aged 17, confirmed the pattern. 'Penfold used to put his hands up our clothes and put our hands in his trousers. Master first took liberties with me about four months ago and gave me two sixpences and four pence. He told us if we told we would have no holidays. The rumpling of Lucas's clothes was talked of downstairs.'

Hannah Henley went into the workhouse the previous October and Penfold put his hands up her petticoat in the winter. She said she did not resist him or complain much. 'When I objected, he gave me one shilling twice not to say anything about it.' Hannah boasted to the others that she had the power of turning her Master on at half an hour's notice.

Sarah Grant said, 'I never asked how, only said "Ooh, is that right Hannah?"'

1875 John Coker Egerton, the humane and deeply concerned rector of Burwash, was aware that some ratepayers were concerned about the way in which some people were content to live on benefits. 'It seems there is not the slightest desire to be hard upon the poor people, but there is a strong feeling, that all widows & all who can work ought to do so, & that there is a tendency on the part of many who can at any rate help to maintain themselves, to get by [to avoid] work altogether. I don't know how this is, but the labour test falls very heavily on some of them I am sure.'

26 MAY

Under the provisions of the Labour Test, if the local workhouse was full, outdoor relief could be awarded to the able-bodied provided that they could prove that they had made energetic efforts to find work. Among the able-bodied were included widows and the partly physically handicapped.

1837 'BRIGHTON – About two o'clock, a baker named Gregory, was aroused from his slumbers by his wife who heard a noise downstairs. Gregory immediately went downstairs with a pistol in his hand, where he found two men who had effected an entrance through the bakehouse, and had collected together considerable booty. The pistol was not loaded and the baker in his hurry presented the butt end of it and courageously exclaimed, "If you stir, I'll shoot you." Fortunately the cover of night befriended the baker and the burglars, inasmuch as they did not discover his mistake, being alarmed at his sudden appearance, begged for mercy. His wife in the meantime had alarmed the neighbourhood and two policemen coming up, they were given into their custody and safely placed in durance vile.'

27 MAY

The *Brighton Gazette* seems less perturbed about the use of firearms than perhaps we might be today.

1818 Mr Arthur Thistlewood was imprisoned at Horsham for twelve months and asked to provide sureties of £300 and two others for £150 each. He had challenged the Home Secretary, Lord Sidmouth, to a duel. In 1820 Thistlewood was hanged for High Treason after plotting to murder the members of the Cabinet.

28 MAY

1891 The Salvation Army's arrival in Eastbourne quite outraged the citizens of the sedate town.

29 MAY

Handbill from Eastbourne Council about the Salvation Army. (*Eastbourne Citadel Centenary Brochure*)

30 MAY **1928** Grace Marjorie Cooper, a 32-year-old clerk, was charged at Hove Police Court with bigamy, forgery and theft. In November 1914 she had married a man called Cole. The marriage was not dissolved when in 1917 she had met a flying officer, 'Mr X' as he was termed in court, and had gone through a form of marriage with him, calling herself Grace Marjorie Kathleen Lloyd. They had two children but in July 1926 she had left him.

Cooper was further charged with stealing a diamond and emerald brooch valued at £200 (today worth about £8,000) from her employer, Mrs Holman, living in Hove. In December 1927 Mrs Holman's jewellery was returned from the valuers and was placed on a table. Later Cooper handed Mrs Holman a small bag saying she had sewn all her jewellery in the bag and that she would sew the bag inside her fur coat for security. It was several days before Mrs Holman missed the brooch and by then Cooper had apparently gone on holiday.

Mrs Holman sent a telegram to Cooper who replied in a letter that she was not returning to work. She had, she explained, inherited 'a decent sum of money from my Uncle Bill'. In reality, she had sold the brooch in London for £100. She admitted that she had altered her marriage certificate, saying, 'I did it, and I would have done anything at the time to keep him.' Now, she said, when the bigamy was discovered, she was 'cast off like an old shoe'.

31 MAY **1882** Benjamin Birch, a casual at Westhampnett workhouse, argued with the Master after refusing to do his oakum picking. When the Master insisted that he finish the task, Birch picked up a broomstick and broke sixty-four panes of glass. When he appeared before the magistrates he said that he had been too ill to work but was sentenced to two months' imprisonment with hard labour.

JUNE

Treadmill at Brighton House of Correction. *(SCM)*

1 JUNE **1931** Mrs Caroline Tornoe, wife of a former Norwegian consul, booked into Mrs Emily Tuffin's nursing home in Powis Road, Brighton, intending to stay for a week. But, she said, from the moment of her arrival she was subjected to the most bizarre treatment. She was taken to a basement room where two women came in and spoke nonsense to her. Then after three hours left on her own a man and six women entered the room and without a word the women took her by the legs, stripped her, dragged her to a chair and injected her with a syringe. Before she passed out Mrs Tuffin told her: 'There is the bell but if you dare use it I'll have it removed.' She woke up the following morning and tried to make her escape but was stopped. After a further struggle and a visit from a doctor she was told that she might go home. On the way out Mrs Tuffin told her, 'You are very lucky to escape.'

At the Assizes the following year, Mrs Tornoe claimed that it was Mrs Tuffin's intention to detain her as a long-term patient. But the court found for the defendant and Mrs Tornoe's claim for damages for false imprisonment and assault was dismissed. Witnesses attested to Mrs Tornoe's alcohol problem.

2 JUNE **1800** The *Sussex Weekly Advertiser* sounds the alarm:

BROKE OUT of the HOUSE OF CORRECTION, at Lewes, in the County of Sussex, on Tuesday, the 27th day of May, instant:

RICHARD TEELING, the younger, late of STOCK-FERRY, in the parish of Piddinghoe, near Lewes, aforesaid, who at the last General Quarter Sessions for the Eastern Division of Sussex, was sentenced to be confined until he could find sureties of the peace towards THOMAS CARR, of Beddingham, Esq., the High Sheriff of the County of Sussex, for the space of two years.

The said Richard Teeling is a tall thin man, of the age of 30 years or thereabouts, light complexion, light brown hair, which he wears loose and long, slender made, dull heavy countenance; by trade, a shoemaker; formerly in the Sussex Militia, and has lately followed his trade of a Huckster, in buying fish at the seaside and retailing them in the country. Is well known to the smugglers on the coast.

Whomsoever will apprehend the said Richard Teeling and lodge him in any of His Majesty's Gaols, and give information thereof at the House of Correction at Lewes, shall receive a reward of TWENTY POUNDS, from me.

William Cramp, keeper.

The original notice reporting the escape from the House of Correction. (*Sussex Advertiser*)

3 JUNE **1879** Report of the Medical Officer of Health, Hastings, Quarter ended 31 March, 1878: 'The Deaths registered were 185; viz. 84 males and 101 females. This is a death-rate of 19.20 against 18.51 in the corresponding quarter of 1877 and 17.7 in that of 1876. This unfavourable contrast is

accounted for by a greater number of deaths occurring from Bronchitis and Pneumonia among children under five years of age and also more deaths for all causes among the aged. There were but two Accidental Deaths in the quarter, one of which was a visitor who was washed off the Pier steps and drowned.'

1955 The Royal Air Force Association's biggest conference was held at Eastbourne. To mark the occasion an RAF Coastal Command Sunderland flying boat appeared at 9 o'clock and for half an hour circled slowly over the town, watched by excited crowds. Then, as arranged, it made its descent, landing a mile out to sea.   **4 June**

The Sunderland made an apparently perfect landing, but suddenly and inexplicably the tail shot up in the air and then the whole aircraft was quickly submerged, settling below the surface of the water. RAF launches and the Eastbourne lifeboat *Beryl Tollemache*, and the pleasure boat *William Allchorn* went to the rescue. Ten men out of the fourteen on board were saved. Later four bodies were discovered inside the aircraft. The cause of the dramatic end of the flying boat was never discovered. There was no suggestion of pilot error and the aircraft had been well maintained.

The Sunderland flying boat: the smoke float attached to the fuselage ignited and there was a danger of the fuel tanks exploding. (*Brian Allchorn*)

1820 Nine-year-old John Archdeacon's gravestone at All Saints' Church in Hastings briefly tells the story of the boy's death: **5 June**

> Here lies an only darling boy
> Who was his widow'd mother's joy,
> Her grief and sad affliction prove
> How tenderly she did him love.
>
> In childish play he teased a mule
> Which rag'd its owner's angry soul,
> And thro' whose cruel blows and spleen
> This child so soon a corpse was seen.

This Mother now is left to mourn
The loss of her beloved Son,
Tho' sighs and tears will prove in vain
She hopes in Heaven to meet again.

At the Sussex Assizes at the beginning of August William Picknell, aged 45, was charged with manslaughter, 'feloniously killing and slaying John Archdeacon in the parish of the Holy Trinity within the Liberty of the Town and Port of Hastings'. Picknell was acquitted.

6 JUNE **1811** A bare-fist fight between Silverthorne and Tom Belcher at Crawley Heath for a £150 purse lasted seven rounds. The ferocious first round was described by Pierce Egan who was present: 'Belcher, upon the alert, stopped a tremendous blow aimed at his stomach by Silverthorne and returned two sharp hits left and right in Silverthorne's face which immediately produced a sharp discharge of blood. . . . It is supposed that such a first round was never before witnessed, wherein so much punishment was dealt out to one combatant. Silverthorne fell from the severe effects of Belcher's blows.'

The bloody contest continued and in the fourth round 'Belcher put in a terrible blow, then closed, and threw his opponent a cross-buttock enough to knock all the breath out of his body.' In the final round, 'Belcher did as he liked with his opponent and finished the contest by a desperate hit to the throat which knocked him down. When Belcher was proclaimed the conqueror he instantly, to show how little he was the worse for the contest, threw a somerset.'

Title page of Pierce Egan's Boxiana, printed in 1812. *(Author's collection)*

7 JUNE **1841** William Mundy was fined £3 and costs at Petworth Petty Sessions for an assault on Henry Johnson, landlord of the White Horse Inn at Sutton, on club night. He had become very noisy and was told to stop dancing on the table. When Johnson tried to pull him down, after first telling him to get down, he refused. Mundy then emptied a pot of beer over him, after which he threw the pot, striking him on the head.

1743 John Breads, a butcher, was executed at Rye for the murder of Alan Grebell, a local magistrate. Driven, so he claimed, by 'a parcel of devils', Breads had stabbed Grebell in the churchyard but he had mistaken his prey in the dark. His intended victim was Grebell's brother-in-law, James Lamb, Mayor of the town. Breads was hanged and his body exhibited in a gibbet 'suit' on Gibbet Marsh, where it stayed for twenty years.

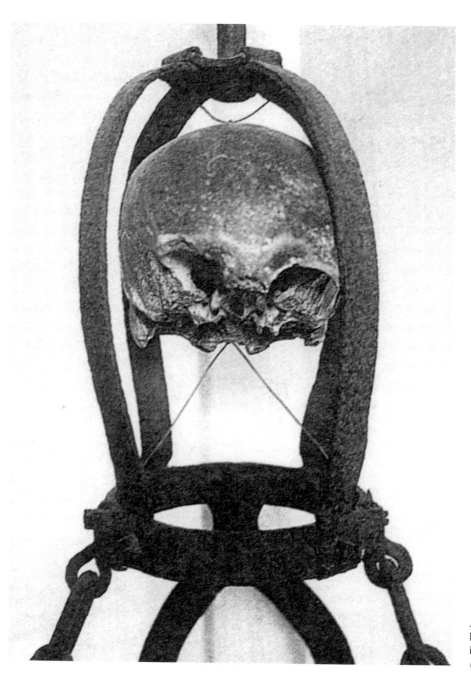

A fragment of John Breads' skull, now in Rye Town Hall. (*SCM*)

9 JUNE **1941** In a case brought by the rationing authority, Worthing Rural Food Control Committee, a fine was imposed on Alexander Low, formerly of Dorlo House, Ferring, for permitting food to be wasted in wartime. In March it was reported that the house, now empty, had been broken into and the police, in their searching of the premises, found that a considerable quantity of foodstuffs had been left there by the former occupier. There were over 300 tins of different kinds of food, 'comprising things which made their mouths water'. There were 29 tins of golden syrup, 27 tins of tinned milk, 28 jars of jam, 118lb of sugar, 11lb of butter, 10lb of mincemeat, 44 jars of marmalade, 100lb of honey, 11lb of butter and 7lb of tea. There were also tins of salmon and fruit. Most of these foodstuffs were now either rationed or not available. Much of the food found by the police had now gone off.

Low explained that he had been quartermaster of the Norfolk Broads Cruise for Boys and also honorary treasurer of a mission in London. In consequence he purchased food in considerable quantities for the various camps and the mission. When war broke out he had transferred the foodstuffs from Norfolk to Ferring, believing it to be a less vulnerable area. Then the camps had been discontinued and the mission taken over by another authority. In June 1940, after the collapse of France, fearing invasion, he and his family evacuated themselves from Ferring and went to live at Minehead. He had left the food behind.

10 JUNE **1919** A public meeting to air the grievances of service and ex-servicemen, especially with regard to housing, unemployment gratuities and war pensions, was held in Gildredge Park. The first resolution read: 'that this mass meeting of service, ex-service men and women and burgesses of Eastbourne enters its emphatic protest against the large number of aliens engaged in occupations and filling situations which could and should be filled by those who have fought for their country, and that government should be called upon to immediately take action to remedy this evil'. It was argued that the aliens question was of great importance as hotels and boarding houses had for many years been 'infested' with 'pseudo' French-Swiss and other foreigners, many of them of German extraction, who had deprived Englishmen of employment. Various trades had also been overwhelmed by alien employees. 'After Englishmen had fought and endured hardships for their country it was up to the country to see that they did not stand to lose by their patriotism.'

11 JUNE **1895** A doctor was called in to the East Preston home of Frederick and Emily Hughes, described as herbalists, to attend 1-year-old Ethel Mabel May who was dying. She weighed only 5lb rather than the expected 30lb. The Hughes were charged with murder and causing unnecessary suffering; they appeared at the Assizes in December. They had placed advertisements in the local newspapers offering to adopt a healthy little child for a premium of £12. On 6 March a mother had taken her baby to the Hughes' house and paid the premium. In the next few weeks neighbours heard a child crying and it appeared that she was being slapped, although no one ever saw it happening.

No evidence was offered in support of the murder charge and the judge was of the view that it would be unsafe to convict on the charge of 'unnecessary suffering'. He did say, however, that it was right that the case should have been investigated because £12 was a very small sum of money to provide for the future of the child. A verdict of 'not guilty' was returned on both charges.

1871 Sidney Barker, 4 years old, died of strychnine poisoning after eating chocolate creams. But this was not the only poisoning case in Brighton. Sweets had been left at random in other places about the town where any child might pick one up. Some had actually been found in Maynard's sweet shop, presumably purchased there, then poisoned and replaced on the shelves. Some people were sent parcels of poisoned cakes and sweets through the post.

12 June

It was small consolation for Sidney Barker's father to receive three anonymous letters expressing sympathy and suggesting that the fault lay with the sweet shop. The trail ultimately led to 42-year-old spinster Christiana Edmunds, a comfortably off, well-educated woman living in the town. She had visited Mrs Emily Beard, the wife of her doctor, and had given her some chocolate drops which had made her ill. As a consequence there was an unsurprising cooling-off in the friendly relations which had existed between the Beards and Miss Edmunds, who followed up this episode with rambling letters to Dr Beard, couched in the most affectionate terms. One of them begins, 'Caro Mio, I have been so miserable since my last letter to you. I can't go on without ever speaking to you.'

Christiana Edmunds was obsessively in love with Beard and when he insisted that she cease writing to him the doctor's wife received a box of cakes; remarkably she seems not to have suspected who had sent them. Out of kindness she gave them to her servants, two of whom were violently ill. And so the source of the poison was traced back to Christiana Edmunds, who was arrested shortly afterwards and charged with Sidney Barker's murder. She was found guilty at the Central Criminal Court, sentenced to death but later reprieved.

1840 Lucy Sturt, 20 years old, was in her cottage at West Hoathly when at about midday two men, James Clarke, a railway navvy, and Robert Tandy, called on her. They asked if she would give them some cabbages but she refused. Her father would be angry with her, she said; she did not dare give them anything from the garden. Clarke then seized her and dragged her into the washhouse where he raped her. Tandy also assaulted her.

13 June

At Lewes Assizes both men were found guilty of rape, as was James McDonald, a tramp who eked out a living selling printed ballads around the country. He had entered the cottage of an 85-year-old woman. She had been feeling poorly and had gone to bed, which was where McDonald found her.

The judge ordered all three men to be placed at the bar, instructing that the sentence of death should be recorded against them. Even so, he spared their lives, sentencing them to life transportation instead.

14 JUNE

1795 On this Sunday morning hundreds of spectators crowded Goldstone Bottom, the traditional place of execution. Thirteen regiments of reluctant soldiers were drawn up to witness the scene. To ensure that neither they nor the many sympathetic civilians created any disturbance, artillery men from outside the district had their cannon trained on them. In addition 2,000 cavalrymen were in attendance, ready to restore order with their sabres.

The men due to be punished – volunteers from the Royal Oxfordshire Militia stationed at East Blatchington – had been charged with mutiny. Hungry and irregularly paid, they had taken matters into their own hands and with others had looted a grain ship at Seaford Tidemills. At the court martial two of the militiamen found guilty were sent to Horsham for execution and another was transported to Botany Bay. At Goldstone Bottom six men were to receive 1,000 lashes and Sergeant Edward Cooke and Private Henry Parrish were sentenced to public execution by firing squad.

The execution of Sergeant Cooke and Private Parrish. The chaplain was so distressed by the barbarity of the punishment that he is seen turning away. (Courtesy of Seaford Museum)

Three of those to be flogged were tied to whipping frames and given 300 lashes, after which the surgeon, anxious that the men might die, called a halt. The other three men awaiting the lash were then pardoned. Cooke and Parish then knelt in front of their open coffins and were shot. It is said that Sergeant Cooke gave the order to fire.

15 JUNE

1843 'A most daring and audacious burglary was committed at the house of Mr. Renville, a farmer at Bolney,' the *Sussex Agricultural Express* says in appropriately breathless tones. 'It seems that Mr. and Mrs. Renville were alone in the house, having given the man and maidservant they keep in the house liberty to go to Cowfold club and as they were sitting at supper a person knocked at the door and requested lodging. Mrs. Renville answered the man that they did not receive lodgers when she perceived another standing near, and as soon as Mr. Renville came to the door, they stepped in, followed by four men, the whole six being disguised by wearing crape over their faces. Two of them produced pistols and demanded money and at the same time Mr. Renville, who is an elderly man, was forced into the pantry and locked in, two of the men keeping watch over him. Two of the men stationed themselves at the outside of the house, and the remaining two obliged Mrs. Renville to accompany them upstairs and deliver the money.'

16 June

1797

LANCING SOCIETY

For Prosecuting Thieves etc.

In the night of Sunday, the 11th instant, A Hen Turkey, with eleven young ones, seven Ducks, and a Hen with thirteen chickens, were stolen from the premises of Mr Wm. Groom at Edburton.

A reward of Seven Guineas will be given to any person that will discover the offender or offenders, to be paid on his or their conviction by Mr Brooker of Brighthelmston, Treasurer of the Lancing Society.

June 16, 1797

The original notice offering a reward to catch a thief.
(*Sussex Advertiser*)

17 June

1934 'New brown canvas plywood battened suitcase with four hoops, measuring 27 in. by 17½ in. and 11 in., of a cheap type such as is sold by almost any dealer, usually for about 12s 6d.'

So ran the official description issued by the Chief Constable of Brighton after the discovery of a trunk in the left-luggage office at Brighton railway station. It had been deposited on 6 June and in the hot weather its smell had begun to disturb the men on duty. When the trunk was opened, police found the body of a woman aged between 20 and 30 years. The head, arms and legs were missing. The legs turned up two days later in another trunk deposited on 7 June at Kings Cross left-luggage office.

It was purely coincidental that this investigation should overlap the so-called 'Second Brighton Trunk Murder', the better-known case in which Toni Mancini was charged with the murder of Violette Kaye. The first trunk murder was never solved but there were suggestions that a high-class abortionist in Hove had bungled an operation and had used this crude method of getting rid of the evidence.

18 June

1918 One of the fiercest fires ever to have occurred in Sussex, its glare so bright that it was seen at Newhaven, broke out at Lewes in the early hours. It spread with such rapidity that one of the oldest hotels in the county and several granaries, each of them of several storeys, were practically gutted. The

Bear Hotel, where the fire had started in the garage, was left a charred ruin, nothing remaining but the outer walls and three chimney stacks.

The Lewes Town Fire Brigade was soon at the scene but the men were obliged to send for help from the Brighton Borough Fire Brigade, the Brighton Railway Fire Brigade and the Newhaven fire-float belonging to the Brighton and South Coast Railway.

Once it was clear that the hotel and the nearest granary were doomed the firemen concentrated on preventing the spread of the fire to the Cliffe. This was a task of no little difficulty as there was only a thoroughfare about 15ft wide separating the blazing hotel and granary from the mass of timbered properties. Fortunately there was little wind and the firemen successfully halted the conflagration. By 8.30 a.m. the huge outbreak was under control, although it was not completely extinguished until midday. Although there was no loss of life the damage was extensive.

19 JUNE **1799**
TO COOPERS
Eloped from his Apprenticeship
Richard Dumbrell, by trade a cooper
He left his master's service on Tuesday morning, the 4th inst, and is supposed to have gone to London. The said Richard Dumbrell is aged about 18 years, and is a fine grown healthy-looking youth, nearly 5 feet 10 inches high, and rather of light complexion. Any person giving particulars of the said apprentice to his Master John Wapham, Cooper at Lewes, shall be rewarded for their trouble; and anyone who shall hereafter harbour or employ him will be rigorously prosecuted.

20 JUNE **1872** Because he had heard, or said that he had heard, that his buildings were to be burnt down, William Geatrell increased his insurance on Napper's Farm to £300 (£18,000 at today's value). He had moved into the 20-acre farm earlier in the year and in May had had it valued and insured with the Royal Exchange Society. But, he said, the rumours worried him. Justifiably so. The barn at Napper's Farm was burnt down on 20 August. But in December at the Assizes he was charged with arson and sentenced to five years' imprisonment.

21 JUNE **1919** The *Sussex Daily News* reported the inquest on Major Harold Hughes-Hallett whose home was in Arundel. He was found dead in a bedroom of an Eastbourne hotel, the muzzle of his service revolver still in his mouth. He had been on sick leave with a serious heart condition and was deeply depressed because he feared that he might never be able to return to the Army. A verdict of 'suicide whilst temporarily insane' was returned.

22 JUNE **1777** Prison reformer John Howard published *The State of Prisons* in England and Wales, the product of many years of investigation of prison conditions both in this country and on the continent. In the course of his journeys he covered 42,000 miles in all weathers, encountering hostile prison keepers,

Petworth House of Correction, *c.* 1815. *(Weald and Downland Open Air Museum)*

dangerous prisoners, squalid living conditions, outbreaks of gaol fever, smallpox and cholera. In a summary Howard wrote:

Food: Many criminals are half starved: some come out almost famished, scarce able to move, and for weeks incapable of any labour.

Bedding: In many jails, and in most bridewells, there is no allowance of bedding or straw for prisoners to sleep on. Some lie on rags, others upon the bare floor.

Use of irons: Loading prisoners in the heavy irons which make their walking, and even lying down to sleep, difficult and painful, is another custom which I cannot but condemn. Even the women do not escape this severity.

The insane: In some few jails are confined idiots and lunatics. Where these are not kept separate, they distract and terrify other prisoners.

In the course of his many visits to Sussex he found prisoners awaiting trial at East Grinstead locked up in a butcher's cellar. At Petworth prisoners had only a 7½oz loaf of bread each day and were 'upon discharge, much weakened by the close confinement and small allowance'. His intervention led to an increased bread allowance of 2lb a day. Even so, in the extreme cold of the winter of 1779 three prisoners died there.

At Horsham prisoners were allowed only 18oz of bread each day, and worse, the debtors were allowed nothing. 'The wards are dark, dirty and small,' Howard writes. 'There is not the least outlet for felons or debtors, but the poor unhappy creatures are ever confined without the least breath of fresh air.' While Howard was visiting, a group of prisoners, perhaps unsurprisingly, was planning to escape. 'The felons had been for two or three days undermining the foundation of their room; and a general escape was intended that night. We were just in time to prevent it; for it was almost night when we went in. Our lives were at their mercy: but (thank God) they did not attempt to murder us, and rush out.'

23 June **1941** 'All persons over 65 not engaged in essential work should be shipped to Canada and the United States.' This was one of the suggestions for improving the country's food situation made at a meeting of experts by Dr Duncan Forbes, the former Medical Officer of Health for Brighton. The country was now a fortress, he said, and the deportation of 3 million people over 65 would save food. All useless animals – dogs in particular – should be destroyed. Those who fed pigeons in public gardens with grain and bread should be prosecuted. Condemned meat, if sterilised, could safely be sold for human food.

24 June **1882** Elementary education was compulsory for all but fees were paid, often reluctantly, by all classes. At Alfriston the Master recorded in the school logbook, 'Resolved that Thomas Marchant, Hy Baker, David Taylor, Chas Reed and G. Streekly have notice served them, that if arrears are not paid and School attendances amended they will be summoned.'

25 June **1928** Two brothers, both employed as valets, Alfred Nelson, 24, and Frederick Nelson, 19, were committed by Hove magistrates for trial at the Assizes. They were charged with breaking into two houses, one of which was the home of Frederick's former employer, Sir Herbert Dering. A policeman who found the brothers in a hut on the Western Esplanade said that Alfred was carrying two coshes and a jemmy. He also had a cloakroom ticket referring to a suitcase deposited in a London railway station which was found to contain stolen property.

26 June **1871** At Lower Beeding the engine house, barn, and other buildings, the property of Thomas Wright, were set on fire. Later in the year Charles Brown pleaded guilty to charges of arson and was sentenced to seven years' penal servitude.

27 June **1881** When the London Bridge train arrived at Preston Park, a passenger covered in blood staggered out of a first-class compartment. 'I have been murderously attacked and fired at,' he told railway employees. His name was

Arthur Lefroy. He had been fired at three times, he said, and knocked insensible from a blow on the head with a pistol. But his carriage had no other occupant. And what about a watch chain hanging out of the injured man's shoe? How did that get there? It was his, Lefroy told his questioners, put there for safety. He was plainly insane, his listeners thought. They decided to send him to Brighton to make a statement to the police and receive medical treatment.

At the police station at Brighton Town Hall the 22-year-old Lefroy explained that in the carriage from London Bridge there had been a 'countryman' aged about 50. Some time after leaving Croydon he had heard a loud report and knew nothing more until reviving just outside Preston Park. He suggested that his assailant must have jumped out of the train. The constable was also of the view that Lefroy was unbalanced.

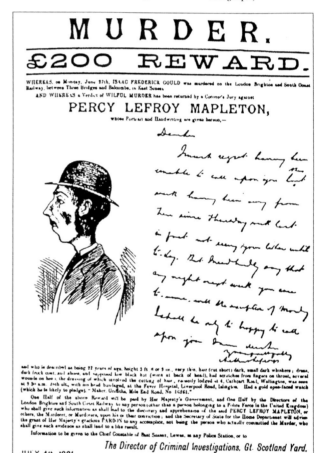

Wanted notice for Percy Lefroy Mapleton in the *Daily Telegraph*, the first such notice to appear in a newspaper. (*Daily Telegraph*)

After his wounds were dressed Lefroy returned to his home in Wallington. But, when the body of Isaac Frederick Gold, a 64-year-old coin dealer, was found in Balcombe tunnel and police went to Wallington to question him, Lefroy was missing. Days later he was arrested in Stepney.

At Maidstone Assizes the story came out. Lefroy – his real name was Percy Lefroy Mapleton – had travelled in the carriage with Gold. In Merstham tunnel Lefroy had shot but failed to kill the coin dealer who put up a struggle. Lefroy had then drawn a knife. There was a deep stab wound in Gold's eye. His face, cut to the bone, was gashed from the right ear to the lower jaw. His throat was cut and a thumb almost severed. When Gold was dead Lefroy threw the pistol out of the window. Gold was thrown out at Balcombe, his hat at Burgess Hill, his purse at Hassocks Gate and his umbrella in Clayton tunnel.

Some friends thought Lefroy a 'shy, gentle, timid, good-natured boy'. Others saw him as 'a wretched, friendless lad' and a fantasist. Penniless, puny and certainly insane, Lefroy was the first British-born railway murderer. He was hanged at Lewes on 29 November 1881.

1882 Walter Clifford, 29, alias Herbert Bramah, alias Ernest Siddons, described as a dramatic tutor, appeared at the East Sussex Quarter Sessions on charges of obtaining money by false pretences. Although there were only two charges before the court, evidence of Clifford's fraudulent operations proved that since the beginning of 1881 he had been deceiving people all over the country.

28 JUNE

Clifford's modus operandi was to advertise in theatrical papers, claiming to be on the lookout for promising amateur actors of both sexes for vacancies in provincial companies. Ernest Lovely of Eastbourne saw the advertisement and wrote to Clifford at Seaford. In reply Clifford promised to train Lovely as an actor but there was the matter of a premium. Lovely sent a 5s postal order to Clifford and later the two men met at Eastbourne where, after another payment, a formal agreement was drawn up. Clifford engaged to take Lovely into his acting company with a salary of 10s a week, travelling expenses and board and lodgings, commencing with a tour a few days later. But Lovely heard no more from Clifford. His unsuccessful entry into the theatre had cost him £1 11s, valued today at about £100.

Sidney Vincent had no aspirations to go on the stage but he applied for employment with Clifford when he saw an advertisement that seemed to promise interesting and well-paid work. As the promoter of high-class concerts Clifford drove from town to town and, so he said, he required a groom. Again the meeting took place in Eastbourne where Clifford was frank with the applicant. He had had some bad luck recently with his previous groom who had absconded with cash. He did not wish to be caught out again, and if Vincent were to become his employee he would have to pay a premium of £3, which Clifford would return at 10s a week. It all seemed satisfactory. They shook hands on the deal and while Clifford dashed off on urgent theatrical business in Pevensey, Vincent went to the lodgings which had been booked for him.

It was the landlady who first raised suspicions. The young man thought that his digs had been paid for, but she had received nothing from the man who had called to arrange the room.

Walter Clifford was finally picked up by Brighton police and at the Quarter Sessions was sentenced to twelve months' imprisonment with hard labour.

29 JUNE **1846** The *Brighton Gazette* relates this horrific tale: 'A lady, whose name is Burtonshaw, was crossing the line for the station-house at Balcombe, when the train was in sight, and on hearing the whistle she suddenly fell down on the rails and seemed quite motionless. The railway station clerk named Shaw, seeing her situation, immediately went to her assistance but before he could remove her the train came up, Shaw was knocked down by the buffer, and his head was completely cut off, while the unfortunate lady was dreadfully mutilated and died almost instantly.' The dead woman, whose name was later corrected to Louisa Murphy, was 32 years old. Patrick Shaw was 64.

30 JUNE **1764** Thomas Turner takes time out from his grocery business to record the following: 'Just at that instant of time as they was before my door, came by Mr Sam Beckett's postchaise and 4 horses in their road from Uckfield to Eastbourne (their home); and in driving a great pace and together with a sufficient degree of carelessness and audacity, they, in their passing the fore-horse in the team, in order to get into the road again before the other horses, drove against him and (I presume by accident) drove the shaft of the chaise into the rectum of the horse about 9 inches, and then it pierced through the gut into the body, of which wound the horse died in about 7 hours.'

JULY

Male ward at Petworth Workhouse, 1930.
(Weald and Downland Open Air Museum)

1 JULY **1870** Charles Septimus Ravenscroft, petitioning for a divorce from his wife Emilia on the grounds of her adultery with 'a person named Smith and another', was awarded a decree nisi. The court heard how the 'person named Smith', the son of a sheriff's officer, had gone to the Ravenscrofts' house in Hastings to execute a writ. He might well have discharged his legal function but on the same occasion, in company with 'another', he had bedded Mrs Ravenscroft. At the time Smith was not quite 16 years of age. The jury found for the petitioner, ordering costs of £100 against Smith, although these were never paid.

Two years later the Queen's Proctor intervened on the grounds that there had been collusion, suppression of material facts and wilful neglect and misconduct on the part of the petitioner, Charles Ravenscroft. He had turned out to be a serial fornicator, a man who had committed adultery with at least seven known women and countless others unknown. 'There was not one single case against the petitioner but a series of cases,' the prosecution announced. Now in court was revealed a saga of 'whoredom, adultery and profligacy'. Ravenscroft had committed adultery with a variety of women at different times and different places, including his business premises. He was 'the most sinister influence on every woman he came across', enjoying his women, customers and assistants alike, on the premises of 33 White Rock Place, even on occasions when his wife was present. Certainly one of his assistants had seen him during working hours busily occupied with one of his conquests in the kitchen of the salon.

Ravenscroft is known to have fathered three children and to have handed on to at least one of his sexual partners 'a certain illness arising from illicit intercourse'. His career was described as 'a course of as disgusting profligacy carried on at the establishment of the petitioner as ever had been exposed, even in the annals of this court'.

Ravenscroft was an upmarket hairdresser, the inventor of hair gel and a hair-brushing machine. The prosecution marvelled at the 'strange influence of this man upon the mind of females'. One of his ladies, Miss Cox, said to be 'suffering from a terrible disease which medical men call nymphomania', had even left him money in her will, which greatly eased his financial difficulties.

In February 1872 the decree nisi was rescinded.

2 JULY **1848** To the relief of many, so it seems, Ann Sergison, mistress of Cuckfield Park, finally died at the age of 85. Constantly at odds with her tenants and others who crossed her path, this wealthy woman was noted for her vicious temper. Known as 'Wicked Dame Sergison', it was said after her death that she was too wicked to rest. Apparently she continued to be a nuisance, now haunting the parkland, and the corridors and main stairway of the house. Carters passing along the road between Ansty and Cuckfield said that her apparition caused their horses to shy. There were some who spoke of her swinging on the oak entrance gates to the park and that as a result these were replaced by iron-spiked gates. As it was, there was an increasing fear of using the road at night. A midnight service to exorcise her wicked spirit, conducted by the vicar and curate of Cuckfield and the vicar of Balcombe,

is said to have been successful, the ghost itself apparently drowning in the font. But there is also the story that, years later, she put in an appearance at her daughter's wedding.

1840 A report on Lewes House of Correction stated that:

Hannah McDowell, under sentence of transportation, had petitioned for her discharge on the ground of ill-health; that the petition had been forwarded to the Secretary of State with a recommendation that the prayer of the petitioner should be granted; that Samuel Byfield, who was sentenced to be transported for life, had been committed to five years' imprisonment upon his petition and had been removed to the Penitentiary; that Richard Thompson, who was sentenced to fourteen years' transportation, prayed for his discharge from custody in consequence of ill-health, the Surgeon's certificate stating that his malady would increase with his imprisonment and advising his petition be forwarded to the Secretary of State, who had since given him his discharge; that a prisoner named George Primmer, committed on a charge of larceny and who had previously been committed nine times, was found dead in his cell on the 18th of June last, suspended by his neckerchief; and that another prisoner, David Cook, refused to behave properly in the House of Correction chapel and had been punished for a breach of the rules, in consequence of which he had been deprived of the privilege of attending chapel.

1798 More grim news from the *Sussex Advertiser*: 'As Mr Crow, of Ashurst, was
travelling in a chaise-cart from the place of his residence to Steyning, the horse took to kicking in so violent a manner that the carriage was almost literally broken to pieces, and before Mr Crow could clear himself from the fragments, he received so severe a blow from the heels of the furious animal, that he died in consequence a short time after.'

1925 Frederick Williams, 23, a gypsy, was charged with the murder of Sarah
Barton, 17, on the Downs at Falmer. They had been living together. The facts of the case seemed quite simple. The only question which might possibly arise, said Mr Cohen, the prosecutor at the police court, concerned the state of Williams's mind at the time the offence was committed. There were thirty-four stab wounds on the woman's head, face and neck, and seven on her hands. The prisoner was said to be dull and apathetic and apparently of low intelligence. He was committed for trial at the December Assizes. The verdict was that he was insane and unfit to plead. His manner made that all too evident. He 'appeared to be fixing his eyes on one of his barristers. He continually screwed up his eyes and seemed not to realise where he was.' The medical officer at Brixton prison where he had been awaiting trial said that Williams was in an advanced state of dementia and really did not understand the situation he was in. Williams was detained at His Majesty's Pleasure.

6 JULY **1841** Visiting magistrates were conducting an inquiry into the diet of prisoners at Lewes Gaol. The surgeon of the prison had concluded that the monotonous diet led to depression, which might stay with prisoners for the rest of their lives. This, he claimed, was a contributory factor in the high mortality rate in the Woolwich hulks. His view was that prisoners suffered most in the first two or three weeks of their imprisonment. The prison governor stated that he had seen prisoners break down in the first two weeks and never recover.

7 JULY **1944** In the late morning a flying bomb severely damaged houses at Westfield near Battle, and five hours later 250 houses at Polegate were seriously damaged. Minutes later a house was destroyed at Arlington and the owner killed. Other bombs landed at Dallington where a farm and fifty other properties received damage. Eighteen houses and shops were hit at Isfield. This day serves as a typical example of the random and terrifying nature of the sustained flying-bomb campaign, which had begun at the beginning of June and was to continue until the following spring. Towns and villages in East Sussex and Kent were bombed. Some 775 of these bombs fell in East Sussex, the more easterly area suffering particularly.

8 JULY **1918** George Sinden, a builder's foreman, was killed by a falling sandbag from an aeroplane looping the loop over the town. The pilot, unaware of the accident, flew on to France and learnt what had occurred only after his return to England some days later. He told the inquest that he had been giving the aircraft a thorough testing before it went into action. The inquest jury thought that the aircraft mechanics had been at fault for not properly securing the sandbag to the machine.

9 JULY **1760** Thomas Turner expresses his scepticism about cheapjack patent-medicine salesmen: 'In the afternoon my wife walked to Whitesmith to see a mountybank [sic] and his toad-eaters perform wonders, who has a stage built there and comes once a week to cuzen [sic] a parcel of poor deluded creatures out of their money by selling his packets, which are to cure people of more distempers than they had in their lives for 1 shilling each, by which means he takes sometimes £8 or £9 of a day.' The toad-eaters ate the toads in front of incredulous folk. They then collapsed, supposedly poisoned. At this point the mountebank stepped in with his cure-all.

10 JULY **1954** The Home Office announced that at Lewes Gaol a 19-year-old prisoner, serving twenty-one months for robbery with violence, had been given six strokes of the birch for 'gross personal violence on a prison officer'.

11 JULY **1787** Another horrific drama from the *Sussex Advertiser*:

> Between 10 and 11 o'clock in the forenoon, Brede Powdermill belonging to Messrs Brooke, Jenkins and Company, blew up, by which accident two men that were in it at the time were most miserably burnt, one

of whom named James Gutsel languished until the next day and then died in great agony, and the other lives with little hope of recovery. The deceased, though he had the presence of mind to strip himself of his clothes immediately after the accident, was scorched from head to foot, and in that miserable condition ran home to his family who lived about a quarter of a mile off. The other in some degree lessened his sufferings by jumping into a pond and extinguishing the fire about him. Had they been at the other side of the Mill, where the powder was running, they must have been blown to atoms. The explosion was felt at Westfield a few miles distant, like the shock of an earthquake. The accident was occasioned by driving a large iron bolt from the troughs. A powdermill at the same place blew up a few years ago, when one man was blown to pieces, whose limbs were afterwards found scattered a great distance from each other. Another man named Henley was seriously injured at the same time.

The report goes on to say that, on this occasion, bricks and stone from the buildings were thrown hundreds of yards. Years later a brick from this explosion was discovered, embedded in the trunk of a distant oak tree.

1906 What began as a jolly day out for an all-male party ended in tragedy. The *Sussex Daily News* described it as 'the most dreadful catastrophe which has occurred in the county of Sussex for some time . . . the most dreadful disaster which has occurred in this country to a motor bus since this means of locomotion was brought into everyday practical use.'

12 JULY

The bus accident at Handcross. *(Author's collection)*

Thirty-four members and friends of the St Mary Cray and Orpington Fire Brigade set off in an open-topped double-decker at 8 o'clock aiming to arrive in Brighton at midday. This was the first time they had hired a motor bus. After passing through Handcross they came to the top of a steep hill with a difficult bend. Witnesses reported seeing the bus lurching down the hill at estimated speeds of between 15 and 40mph, the driver wrestling with the steering wheel. Men on the top deck were shrieking with fear. Then the bus hit an oak tree and the top deck was scythed off. Upstairs passengers were hurled out, and downstairs bodies flew through the plate-glass windows. Machinery, glass, spars of wood, metal seats and personal belongings were scattered randomly along the road, over the hedges and into the wood beyond.

On the blood-spattered highway lay the dead and severely injured; in the hedge a corpse; in the trees hung two bodies, one suspended upside down. Four victims died instantly. Two men, both with broken backs, died shortly afterwards. 'One man who was dying called to me,' said the Revd Mr Boyd. 'Another man had his legs torn away and was pinned against the tree by the bus. A leg was left hanging in the tree, clean cut as if with a knife.' The next day two more men died and a ninth some days later. The inquest jury announced that the accident was caused by the breakage of machinery 'brought on by the efforts of the driver to check the speed of the motor omnibus when he found it was beginning to go too fast, the machinery not being of sufficient strength to stand up to the strain. We consider the driver, Blake, committed an error of judgment in allowing the bus to attain so high a speed before taking means to check it. We do not hold anyone criminally responsible. We are strongly of the opinion that this type of vehicle is unsuitable for use on country roads.'

13 JULY **1832** From Alfriston Burial Register, a stark marginal comment: '13 July 1832 Samuel Bussey aged 22. Buried in the night without service having died of the smallpox being in a dreadful state.'

14 JULY **1831** John Holloway – thief, wife-beater, all-round dissolute character – had deserted his wife, Celia, the mother of his child, and had gone to live at 7 Margaret Street, Brighton, with Ann Kennett. But the magistrates insisted that Holloway make provision for his wife and child. Running two homes is expensive. The matter had to be resolved. Holloway visited Celia, proposing that they live together again as man and wife. He had found an ideal cottage in North Steine Row, he told her. Happy now, she went to the cottage ready to start life anew. She was pregnant again, probably by Holloway.

Months later, awaiting trial in Horsham Gaol and already sure of its outcome, Holloway wrote *An Authentic and Faithful History of the Atrocious Murder of Celia Holloway*, telling what occurred when Celia arrived that day, unaware that Ann Kennett was already hiding in the house. Of Celia he says: 'I asked her to sit down on the stairs and then on the pretence of kissing her I passed a line around her neck and strangled her.'

But then, Holloway thought, just suppose that at some future time he and Ann were no longer lovers. Suppose that for some or other reason she

decided to tell what had happened to Celia. Holloway was now determined to involve Ann yet more deeply in the crime. 'As soon as I passed the line around her neck, I found it was rather more than I could manage,' he says. But Holloway was a strong man. How could he not finish off tiny, pregnant Celia? 'I called Ann and God knows she assisted me by taking hold of each end of the rope with me and she held the rope with me till the poor girl dropped.' And these words implicate Ann Kennett, as do those he claims she said: 'Do not let your heart fail you.'

'When I thought she was dead, or nearly dead,' Holloway goes on, 'I dragged her into a cupboard under the stairs and under the stairs there is some nails. I did not remove the cord but took an over-handed knot and I made the ends fast to the nails so that she was hanging by the neck.'

But the body had to be disposed of. 'I proposed then cutting her. Ann Kennett told me to wait until the blood settled.' They left the house, returning the following day to finish their work. 'I cut off the head first and I think the arms I carried with the head.' The head and limbs were taken back to Margaret Street and dropped in the common privy. And at night, with the remains in a trunk, they took their cargo in a wheelbarrow to Lovers Walk, a copse in Preston, and buried it there.

But crime will out, at least sometimes. The body was discovered, Holloway and Ann were arrested, and on 21 December 1831 he hanged at Horsham. Strangely enough, at a separate trial months later Ann Kennett was acquitted.

Left: John Holloway awaiting trial, painted in Horsham Gaol, drawn by J. Perez.

Above: Ann Kennett as she appeared at Holloway's trial, also drawn by J. Perez. *(Both SCM)*

15 JULY **1937** At Lewes Assizes four London men were charged with criminally assaulting a 16-year-old chambermaid in a Brighton hotel. Because of her age and the nature of the offence her name was not revealed.

On the evening of 22 May the girl, very mature for her age, was sitting alone at Sherry's dance hall, drinking port. She was joined by four men in their twenties. The men drank Scotch and she had two more glasses of port with them. After this they went to Hennekey's in Ship Street where they all continued drinking. The five then went outside and found a stall where they bought jellied eels. More drinks followed, after which they all went off in a car with the girl sitting in the back. Near Roedean the car was stopped. The girl claimed that she resisted the advances of one of the men and then she was struck several times on the face and body. Finally she lost consciousness and only came to, lying on the grass verge, wearing nothing but her stockings and with a coat draped over her. She was several miles from home on a wild night, the rain pouring down. Although she did not find it, most of her clothing had been thrown out of the car. Ultimately she hailed a bus to take her back to Brighton.

There seems little doubt that the girl had told the men she was 19 years old. It seems likely too that in the course of the evening and during the short car journey sexual matters were freely discussed and that she had kissed at least one of the men.

The jury had to decide whether the girl had encouraged the men. Did she consent to what had occurred? Did the men mistakenly think that she was willing to go along with what happened? Did she not, by her knowing behaviour, her drinking and smoking, give them a false impression? As far as the judge was concerned it did not matter if she had been raped by one or all of the men, and these facts were unclear. In his view all of the men were responsible for what occurred. Sad, he remarked, that they were men of 'perfectly good character'. All were sentenced to eighteen months' imprisonment.

16 JULY **1799** At the Quarter Sessions James Ripley was sentenced to three months for stealing hens. At the expiration of his sentence he was to be publicly whipped in the market place at Horsham. William Scrase who stole hay was sentenced to a public whipping at Lindfield, and Henry Blackman, for the theft of three pieces of linen, received six months' imprisonment, at the expiration of which he was to be 'publicly whipped up and down the said town of Uckfield'.

17 JULY **1873** Henry Coleman appeared at the Summer Assizes at Lewes charged with wounding with intent to do grievous bodily harm. Coleman was unpopular with his neighbours, who showed their disapproval of him in the old-fashioned way. They gave him 'rough music', assembling outside his house with kettles and bin lids and saucepans and beating them loudly. One evening, incensed at the treatment, Coleman met one of his tormentors, who had a kettle hidden under his smock, and cut him on the neck with a knife. The prosecution seems to have had some sympathy with Coleman and accepted the defence request for a reduced charge of 'unlawful wounding'. In view of this Coleman was given only three months' hard labour.

1795 Nine prostitutes, held to be largely responsible for the excessive sick list at Brighton Barracks, were recommitted until the next Quarter Sessions. But one of the girls, Sarah Mitchell, was immediately ordered to be privately whipped. She was given 450 lashes. Sarah appears in later years, still following the same line of work.

18 JULY

1789 'In the morning,' the *Sussex Advertiser* laments, 'a coat and hat known to be those belonging to a young man of Lewes named Brand, was found lying on the bank of our river, near the bridge, which furnished reason to believe he had drowned himself in consequence of which the river was dragged several hours for his body, but in vain, for it could not be found. On Thursday morning, however, the water being fallen, his feet appeared above the surface, when his body was taken out, being found erect, with his head sticking in the mud. The deceased was to have been married on the morning he drowned himself, but upon waiting on the object of his affections, to lead her to the altar of Hymen, she denied herself to him, which is supposed to have been the cause of his committing the above rash action.'

19 JULY

1932 At Lewes Assizes a 25-year-old commercial traveller, Edward Elvidge, pleaded guilty to making and uttering counterfeit half-crowns. He had told the police that he had learnt how to make the coins from a magazine article published in 1894. The judge, Mr Justice Goddard, commented that he had read the same article when he was at school. Elvidge's counsel said that a book describing quite simply how an amateur could make counterfeit coins and medals was available in public libraries. The judge was of the view that Elvidge was foolish rather than criminal and he was bound over, with a warning that if he offended again he would receive a gaol sentence.

At the same Assizes justice was less lenient with a wireless engineer who was sentenced to twenty-one months of imprisonment with hard labour on five charges of coining. As a 17-year-old he had been sentenced to three months for stealing a bicycle and it was while he was in Wandsworth Prison that he had learnt from fellow prisoners how to make counterfeit coins.

20 JULY

1800 'A melancholy accident happened on Wednesday last in the parish of Burwash.' The *Sussex Advertiser* never spares the detail. 'A wagon loaded with unslaked lime, on which a young man, an under-carter to Mr Jarvis of that parish, was riding, overturned in passing through a small stream on the road to Etchingham, when the lime, which had nearly buried the lad by its fall, on coming into contact with the water, heated so immediately and so excessively, that notwithstanding every exertion of his companion to extricate him, the unfortunate youth was literally flayed, from head to foot, and otherwise so miserably scalded that he died a few hours afterwards in excruciating torture.'

21 JULY

1938 Mrs Beatrice Clow, a wealthy widow living in Eaton Gardens, Hove, went to the cinema in the afternoon, leaving her long-serving housekeeper,

22 JULY

Dorcas Mace, and her husband George in the house. On Mrs Clow's return she found her bedroom in total disorder. The Maces had left the house with jewellery worth £7,691 (£320,000 in today's money), and £40 in cash.

The Maces were soon picked up because, although the faked burglary might have convinced investigators, the fact that they had forgotten to stage a faked entry to the house gave the game away. The Maces were questioned about a man who had visited them. He was named as George Husband and police were told that it was he who had stolen the jewellery. Within a couple of days Husband, a man with a prison record, was traced to a club in Putney where he put up no resistance. 'I will help you all I can,' he said. 'I did it when I was drunk. The stuff is in my pocket now.' Most of the money and jewellery was recovered. The three of them, Husband told the police, had planned the theft.

All three were committed for trial at the Quarter Sessions, where it was stated that the Maces, previously of good character, had fallen under the influence of Husband and that they were afraid of him.

Remarkably, Husband was sentenced to eighteen months in prison, reduced by the judge to twelve months on the grounds that he had made an effort to go straight. George Mace also received a twelve-month sentence and his 'wife' – for it turned out that theirs was a bigamous marriage – was bound over for twelve months.

23 JULY **1798** The following notice appeared in the *Sussex Weekly Advertiser*:

On Saturday, the 23rd of June last under a pretence of visiting a relative at Burpham, near Chichester, and who has not since been heard of, William Martin of Plumpton, near Lewes, Farmer.

Description of his person and dress

Aged about 50 years, 5 feet 6 inches high, thin or spare habit of body, light complexion, light hazel eyes, light brown hair, hanging rather lank, long, and loose on his shoulders, his speech rather low and mild, a scar on his forehead rather inclining over one eye, also a small knob or bunch on the upper part of his nose, occasioned by a blow he sometime since received; cloathed in a mixed slate-coloured second cloth coat, black velveteen waistcoat, ornamented with small gold impressed spots, with a fine white round frock [smock] over the same, plain dark coloured velvet breeches, blue cotton stockings, shoes with plain silver plated buckles.

N.B. – If the said William Martin left his home on account of his circumstances being deranged, and will return to his disconsolate wife and family, he will be cordially received and assisted.

Should any accident have happened to him or any person will give intimation of the same to Mr Homewood of Plumpton aforesaid, miller, every reasonable expense will be paid. Plumpton, July 1798.

24 JULY **1752** 'Anne Whale and Sarah Pledge were indicted at the Assizes at Horsham on 20 July 1752 for the murder of James Whale, husband of the said Anne, and being convicted upon the clearest evidence were sentenced to death.'

In the case of Sarah Pledge, the judge pronounced, 'Let her be hanged by the neck till she be dead, on Friday 24th July, and let her body be dissected and anatomised.' For Anne was reserved the old punishment for petty treason, the murder of a husband. 'Let her be taken from the jail and thence to be drawn upon a hurdle to the place of execution and there to be burned with fire till she be dead on Friday 24th July.'

The executions took place on Broadbridge Heath Common. Sarah was taken by cart from gaol. At half-past three she was hanged.

Two hours later Anne was chained to the stake. An account written at the time tells the rest:

The parson prayed for and with her for upwards of half an hour before she was strangled. This was about five minutes before the fire was kindled, which was one of the greatest ever known upon such a melancholy occasion. There were upwards of three hundred and one half of faggots and three loads of cordwood so that it must have continued burning till Saturday night or Sunday morning. The faggots eclipsed the sight of her for some time but, in about five minutes the violence of the flames consumed a part thereof which falling gave the spectators an opportunity of seeing her – a very affecting and disagreeable object, for she was all consumed to a skeleton. She said nothing at the place of execution – the whole ceremony was carried on with the strictest decorum and decency and there was the biggest concourse of people ever known on a like occasion. The body of Sarah Pledge was put into a tallow chandler's hamper and carried to Dr Dennet, junior, of Storrington, to be dissected agreeable to the late Act of Parliament.

A

GENUINE ACCOUNT

OF

ANNE WHALE and *SARAH PLEDGE,*

Who were tried and condemned at the Affizes held at *Hor-fham* in the County of *Suffex,*

Before the Right Honble Sir JOHN WILLES, Lord Chief Juftice of his Majefty's Court of *Common Pleas,*

AND

Sir THOMAS DENISON, K^nt, one of his Majefty's Juftices, the 20th of *July,* 1752.

For the barbarous and inhuman Murder of JAMES WHALE, Husband of the faid ANNE WHALE, by Poifon, when ANNE WHALE was fentenced to be burnt, in being guilty of Petty Treafon.

And SARAH PLEDGE to be hanged, as being an Acceffary, Aider and Abettor in the faid Crime, which Sentence was accordingly executed on them on *Friday* the 7th of *Auguft* 1752, at *Horfham* aforefaid.

Together with their Authentick Examinations and Confeffions, taken before JOHN WICKER, and SAMUEL BLUNT, Efqrs, two of his Majefty's Juftices of the Peace for the County of *Suffex.*

This Pamphlet is worthy the Perufal of Perfons of all Ranks and Denominations, as it contains a Series of uncommon Events, and more particularly the remarkable Contrivance of *Sarah Pledge,* in endeavouring to poifon the faid *James Whale,* by putting Spiders in his Beer.

L O N D O N:

Printed for M. COOPER, at the *Globe* in *Pater-nofter Row,* and Meffrs. VERRAL and LEE, at *Lewes.*

[Price Six-Pence.]

Front cover of a pamphlet of 1752 purporting to tell the true story of Anne Whale and Sarah Pledge. *(SCM)*

1820 The *Sussex Advertiser* reports:

25 JULY

At our Assizes seventeen prisoners were tried, seven of whom were capitally convicted, and received sentence of death, viz – Thomas Wren, for a felony, in the dwelling house of Mr W. Homewood of Frant – Thomas Summers, for a burglary in the dwelling house of the Revd W. Keating of Oving – George Miller, for robbing a mill, in the parish of Maresfield, of a quantity of peas – Wm Elliott, for sheep-stealing at Eastbourne – Edmund Martin, for stealing a lamb, in the parish of Aldingbourne – William Drewitt, for horse-stealing, in the parish of East Grinstead – and Thomas Jaques, for a rape on the body of Sarah Kingshatt, in the parish of Fernhurst. The Judge pronounced the awful sentence of the law, on this prisoner, in a very solemn and impressive manner; it pierced the very soul of the unhappy culprit, who went from the bar in great agony; but it moved not the haggard, squalid, and forbidding countenance of the persecutrix. – They were all reprieved by Lord Ellenborough [the judge] before he left the town.

26 JULY   **1788** Horse thief William Still, hanged at Horsham, did not appear to be concerned about his fate when he was taken to the place of execution. He more or less ignored the clergyman who prayed by him and 'he had nothing to say under the gallows'. This offhandedness was bad enough but the hangman's behaviour was even worse. 'Had not the malefactor himself been so insensible of shame, his sufferings must have been much augmented by the indecency of the executioner, who, to his infamy be it spoken, appeared at the gallows, so beastly drunk that to maintain his feet he was frequently obliged to lay hold of the poor wretch he was preparing to execute and whose dying moments were prolonged by the bungling manner in which he performed the fatal office.'

27 JULY   **1809** At Wellingham near Lewes a clergyman who had been chaplain and tutor to a well-connected family for nearly twenty years was in his bedroom with two of the children. There was a loaded pistol lying on a chest of drawers and it was thought that one of the children, a 9-year-old, took up the weapon to have a look at it. The pistol went off, the bullet hitting the clergyman in the forehead; 'his brains', according to the report, 'scattered on the floor'. The boy, questioned by the Coroner, insisted that he had not touched the gun and that it had gone off of its own accord.

28 JULY   **1874** There was considerable alarm in Lewes when it was learnt that there were seven cases of cholera in the town. Within two weeks the tally had risen to forty. There followed a brief respite in the first fortnight of September and then the outbreak resumed. By the end of November there had been 435 cases, of whom 27 died. All of the town's sewage emptied into the river and tidal water flowing into the waterworks had resulted in contamination.

29 JULY   **1823** James Jones was before the court, charged with rape, a capital offence. On the evening of 27 March Jones and Sarah Hampton, a 13-year-old, were milking cows. It was then that 'the prisoner succeeded in effecting his base intentions'. But, 'from the simplicity and backwardness of the girl',

Sarah made a poor witness and the judge directed the jury to acquit Jones. Nevertheless, 'His Lordship reprimanded the prisoner in very strong terms.'

1840 The *Brighton Herald* records the fate of two future transportees: 30 JULY

William Middleton, 15, sweep, was indicted for breaking and entering the dwelling house of George Chalk at the parish of St. Peter the Great, otherwise Subdeanery, on the 10th of June, and stealing therein two silk handkerchiefs, one twopenny piece, 1 metal seal, 1 key, 1 seal, 1 steel chain, a ring and some bread, cheese and bacon, the property of George Chalk. The prisoner was sentenced to be transported for life.

Michael Torbutt, 27, millwright, was charged with stealing at Ifield, on the 27th of May, one calico shirt, one pair of stockings, and one cotton handkerchief, the property of John Luther Jupp – Guilty. A former conviction of felony being proved, the prisoner was sentenced to ten years' transportation.

1948 Librarian Joan Woodhouse left the YWCA hostel in Blackheath, telling 31 JULY
her friends that she was going to Barnsley to stay with her father over the bank holiday weekend. But on the Tuesday, when she did not turn up for

Joan Woodhouse in London with friends, *c*. 1948. *(Daily Mirror)*

work, enquiries were made and it was discovered that she had not gone to Barnsley after all. Joan went on the missing persons list. On 10 August her decomposed body was found in a copse in Arundel Park.

Her movements were now traced. Inexplicably, instead of going north she had taken a train to Worthing where she had left her luggage at the railway station. She had gone by bus to Arundel and had found a spot to sunbathe in Box Copse. She was an essentially modest girl, deeply religious, but she had taken off her clothing. Or someone else had done so. There were also some sleeping tablets near the body.

Alan Wade, the local man who found her, was suspected of having murdered her. Even so, despite a protracted police investigation, there was inadequate evidence to incriminate him. The detectives who investigated the case, first Detective Chief Inspector Fred Narborough and then Detective Superintendent Reginald Spooner, reached different conclusions about Wade's guilt. Professor Keith Simpson, the eminent pathologist, was also of the view that Joan had been murdered.

Joan Woodhouse's father and aunts continued to pursue the case. Because of their efforts and those of the private detective they hired, Littlehampton magistrates heard the case against Wade in September 1950, but after five days they could find insufficient evidence to commit him. Joan Woodhouse's death – be it murder or suicide – remains unsolved.

(Alan Wade is not the real name of the man suspected of murdering Joan Woodhouse.)

AUGUST

Examples of 'penny dreadfuls' which so worried some parents.
(Author's collection)

1 AUGUST **1815** Blacksmith Jesse Attree and old Thomas Howard, labourer, were over at Seaford on estate business. After a few drinks Attree confessed all that he and others were up to. It was only a little drunken boasting but it led to Attree and another man from Firle being transported. They and half a dozen others had been engaged regularly in poaching and a little light pilfering on Lord Gage's estate where they were all employed. For months they had raided their employer's pigeon house at Firle Place, selling the birds for pigeon shoots or to hotels in Brighton. On other occasions they made night-time trips into the grounds and fished in the pond, taking 'eels out of the garden pond, one of which weighed a pound'. Another evening 'they got over the Iron Gate at the head of the Pond into the Garden and searched the frames for Cucumbers and . . . took out five or six Cucumbers'. There were poaching expeditions, too, all on his lordship's land.

After learning this from a man he had known all his life, Howard told the gamekeeper what was happening. Why? Possibly because he was old; perhaps because he hoped for some coal for the winter or blankets or a little extra flour. And because the law required proof, even in that harsh and bitter age, Howard was asked to join the group in their illegal activities so that his statement could eventually be used as cast-iron proof at the Assizes.

The dovecote at Firle.
(Tony Spencer)

And so to 'the Calendar of Persons in Lewes House of Correction to be brought before the Court of General Quarter Sessions on 20th October, 1815',

which included Jesse Attree and others, 'charged . . . with having lately broken open and entered the Pigeon House of the Right Honourable Lord Viscount Gage at the Parish of Firle and feloniously stole Twelve Pigeons'.

Attree and 20-year-old William Kennard were further charged with the theft of three and a half dozen pigeons. Found guilty, both men were sentenced to seven years' transportation. On the expiry of his punishment Attree returned to Firle and resumed his work as one of Lord Gage's blacksmiths. In his lordship's eyes justice had been done.

1870 Two boys, Hall and Joy, were indicted for breaking into a church at Hollingdean and stealing an alms box. There was no evidence against Joy except that he had been seen with the other boy. Hall, now 18 years of age, pleaded guilty. In the past he had been convicted of several minor offences, had spent three years in a reformatory and had been whipped. Now about to be sentenced, he wept bitterly, saying that Joy had proposed the crime, had taken part in it, and had shared the money. Sentencing him, the judge said that Hall had embarked on a sad career of youthful crime. It was necessary in such a case, he stated, to impose a prison sentence. The penalty for robbing a church could be imprisonment for life but on this occasion, however, he intended to sentence Hall to the shortest period permitted – seven years.

2 August

1886 The pernicious influence of a popular literature – cheap comics which dealt with the exploits of highwaymen, thieves and murderers – was considered at the Assizes. Two apprentice glaziers from Eastbourne, both 14-year-olds, had decided on a criminal career. Equipped with jemmy, crowbar, skeleton keys and two daggers, they took lodgings together and their first victim was their landlord whose coat they stole. Then they took off for Hastings where they were arrested and at Lewes Assizes convicted of theft. The glazier who employed both boys – he happened to be the father of one of them – said that they had always been well behaved but that recently they had been influenced by reading 'penny dreadfuls'. Because of their youth and their past good conduct their sentence was light.

3 August

An example of a 'penny dreadful'. *(Author's collection)*

1818 In a civil action at Lewes Assizes an unnamed music master at Chichester Cathedral was accused of assaulting one of the pupils. He had given the plaintiff what was described as 'a severe flogging' for disobedience. The master would occasionally take his pupils to subscription concerts at places like Arundel and Portsmouth where they would perform

4 August

before enthusiastic audiences. He used to pay all of the travel expenses and would give the choir members a few shillings – a small fortune for any schoolboy – but would legitimately keep the rest of the money collected. This was customary and did not form any part of the plaintiff's case. The master was simply anxious that the boys should not abuse their voices and insisted that they did not go out singing without his permission. In particular he forbade their going out to glee clubs, jolly affairs at which, though respectable, music of a kind not really approved of by the music master was sung. Such places were also smoky and drink was consumed. What might these do to the tender throats of his pupils?

On 4 March the plaintiff had sought out the master and had asked if he might go to a glee club in Chichester that evening; unsurprisingly permission was denied. The next day the master discovered that his pupil had disobeyed him and in consequence gave the boy 'a very severe flogging with a cane which produced several black and blue marks upon his shoulders and other parts of his body'.

In the action the plaintiff's claim was that the master had no right of control over pupils out of school hours. For the defendant it was argued that the punishment was part of the discipline of the school and that the plaintiff had known this was the case. Remarkably, considering attitudes at the time about hierarchies and discipline and the rights of older people to chastise the young without comeback, the jury found for the plaintiff, awarding him £5 in damages.

5 August   1776 The indictment of Ann Cruttenden at Horsham Assizes stated:

> The Jurors for our Lord the King upon their Oath Present That Ann the Wife of Joseph Cruttenden late of the Parish of Brightling in the County of Sussex Butcher not having the fear of God before her Eyes but being moved and seduced by the instigation of the Devil on the fifteenth day of June in the Sixteenth year of the Reign of our Sovereign Lord George the third now King of Great Britain & with force and Arms at the Parish aforesaid in the County aforesaid in and upon the said Joseph Cruttenden her Husband in the peace of God and our said Lord the King then and there being feloniously Traitorously Wilfully and of her malice aforethought did make an Assault And that she the said Ann with a certain Knife of the Value of two pence which she the said Ann in her right hand then and there had and held in and upon the right side of the neck of him the said Joseph then and there feloniously Traitorously Wilfully and of her Malice aforethought did strike and thrust giving to him the said Joseph in and upon the right side of the neck of him the said Joseph one Mortal Wound of the breadth of two inches and of the Depth of half an inch of which said Mortal Wound he the said Joseph then and there instantly Died And so the Jurors aforesaid upon their Oath aforesaid do say that she the said Ann him the said Joseph in the manner and form aforesaid then and there feloniously Traitorously Wilfully and of her Malice aforethought did kill and murder against the peace of our said Lord the King his Crown and Dignity.

Ann Cruttenden was found guilty of the murder of her husband and was sentenced 'to be Drawn on a Hurdle and Burned with fire until she be dead on Thursday next'. Ann was 80 years of age, her husband 43. They had been married for eight years.

Of course, executions had to be paid for out of the public purse. In the Cruttenden case Peter Potter, a carpenter, submitted a bill for 'putting up the post for the woman to be burnt on, making a slip board to stand Doing the slide and putting on hurdell for her to ride on and boord for the back and side for ditto; time, nails and board . . . £1 10 shillings'. The gaoler also requested 15 shillings for 'wood and faggots'.

1788 Tom Tyne fought Earl on a stage erected near the stand on Brighton racecourse. 'The town of Brighthelmstone was literally drained of its company,' Pierce Egan reported, 'and the race stand was crowded to excess with nobility and gentry; and among whom was his Royal Highness, the Prince of Wales.' Earl, tall and very strong, was the favourite, and after several

Burning at the stake. *(Courtesy of the Neil Storey Archive)*

6 August

brutally contested rounds was thought to be on the point of winning when Tyne delivered a powerful blow to his opponent's head. Earl reeled backwards, falling against one of the ring posts, and immediately died. 'The Prince', Egan wrote, 'declared that he would never witness another battle. His Royal Highness with great humanity and consideration settled an annuity on Mrs Earl and family.' There is evidence that while Mrs Earl received the promised money the prince did not totally give up his trips to boxing matches. The inquest heard that before the fight Earl had been involved as a supporter at the parliamentary election at Covent Garden, and had been drunk for most of the time. 'It was the opinion of the professional men, that the vessels being so overcharged with blood, that his instantaneous death proceeded from the above cause.'

7 AUGUST   **1939** A bomber aircraft crashed in the sea off Beachy Head. There was a trail of wreckage stretching over 150yd leading to the cliff edge. The pilot and two crew were killed, as was a woman out walking along the cliffs. An inquest jury returned a verdict of 'Accidental Death'.

8 AUGUST   **1920** At last a glimmer of hope on the racecourses. The previous week, after deplorable scenes at the Salisbury meeting a few weeks earlier, some racegoers had vowed that they would never again attend a meeting there and some apprehension had been felt before the meetings at Goodwood, Lewes and Brighton. But all three meetings had gone off with no major disturbance from the racecourse gangs who normally attended these great events. Extra police had attended Goodwood, armed with 'the most serviceable ash clubs'. Those bookmakers who refused to pay protection money to the gangs brought in protectors and at Lewes there were sufficient police to ensure a peaceful meeting. Brighton had always been the most profitable scene for the gangs but again there was a strong police presence. Those villains who did turn up and misbehaved were rounded up and many of them faced prison sentences.

But the peace on the racecourses was illusory. The glimmer of hope soon faded. The gangs, never totally deterred, continued to employ force as well as bribery of police and racecourse officials.

9 AUGUST   **1932** Arthur Wallace, a fruiterer by day, was a thief by night. At Chichester he stole jewellery worth £374 (£16,000 at today's value). On other occasions he broke into jewellers' shops in Havant and Pitsea, escaping with a total haul of £938 (£40,000 today).

Described as a 'persistent and clever criminal', when his case came up at the Assizes his counsel asked the court to take into consideration that in 1910, when he had been serving a sentence in Dartmoor, he had saved the life of a warder who was being threatened by six prisoners with spades. Such assistance seems to have little impressed the judge who sentenced Wallace to five years.

10 AUGUST   **1815** James West, aged 18, convicted of feloniously stealing a silver watch worth 40s, the property of Henry Peters of Wiston, was sentenced to transportation for the term of his natural life.

1817 'The tribe of BLACK LEGS, who are generally in the secret, anticipating the event of these Races, did not honour the turf with their accustomed visit; but the LIGHT FINGERED corps were in full attendance,' announces the *Sussex Advertiser* in fine declamatory style. 'On Wednesday they had a grand field day and practised their various manoeuvres, for the most part successfully. Several persons had their pockets picked of their watches, and others of their money, to the facility of which the tragic conflict between MR PUNCH, his consort JUDY and the DEVIL, in no small degree contributed, by fixing the attention of the crowd which the exhibition occasionally collected. A smart looking boy, only 14 years old (no doubt from London), was detected by Mr. Joshua Mantell, in picking the pocket of Edward Collbran, a butcher, of Southover. This young offender was fully committed for trial at the Assizes. Four one pound bank notes were found upon him, and to account for the possession of the same, he said the notes were the produce of oranges and lemons which he had sold; but this and other of his assertions were proved to be falsehoods.'

11 August

1893 The rackety life of two alcoholic tramps was described at the Assizes. Joe Taylor, a labourer, was tried for the murder of Emily Maria Twiggs, his common-law wife, at South Heighton. In the afternoon, after drinking heavily at Newhaven, they were on the road to Denton. Twiggs, incapable, kept falling down while Taylor shouted at her and from time to time struck her. He was heard to threaten her, saying, 'I'll kick your head off if you don't get up.' He took her up the slope of the Downs and some time later a scream was heard. Shortly afterwards Taylor was heard to call out, 'If I come back to you, I'll cut your throat.' The following morning Taylor told a witness that his wife was on the top of the hill and that she had not spoken since the previous night. He said that he did not know if she was dead. After a search Emily's body was found. She had suffered appalling violence. Taylor later said that he had not killed her and suggested that it might have been men she had gone with up on the Downs. The jury returned a verdict of manslaughter and passed a sentence of fourteen years' penal servitude on Taylor.

12 August

1885 Concern about the sanitary condition of Newhaven, a town of 3,700 inhabitants, had been voiced over the years. The town surveyor's report only confirmed what had been for so long apparent. He had inspected 100 houses and reported that the majority of them were 'faulty as regards their sanitary arrangements. . . . The drains are foul and the traps ineffectual to prevent the emission of sewer gas. Some of these are filled up with flannel rags and others with earth . . . I find the cesspits without covers and some in a state of fermentation and they smell very offensively.'

The old main channel to the west of the island is 'so bad during hot weather that people living in the vicinity are often obliged to shut the windows and doors of their houses and men employed in the shipbuilding yards have been compelled sometimes to leave work on account of the offensive smells'.

A measure of the serious health hazard may be gleaned from the statistic that 25 per cent of children in Newhaven did not reach their fifth year.

13 August

14 August **1868** A local 'cunning man' was called in to work his charms in Cuckfield where a woman had been confined to her bed for several months. As there was no obvious reason for her illness her friends concluded that she was bewitched and the 'cunning man' promised that he would rid her of the evil spirit which plagued her. He told the bedfast woman that it was important to work the charm in the greatest secrecy and at a particular hour. Having studied his book of necromancy and having consulted the planets, he had concluded that the best time for his ministrations would be midnight of the day preceding the Sabbath. Preparations went ahead: new pins and a pair of coal tongs were secretly purchased. All was made ready and on the day, just before midnight, the woman's friends assembled at her house to witness the driving away of the imp the bewitcher had placed over the woman. The 'cunning man' performed certain magic ceremonies, placed the pins in position, burnt incense, and for an hour recited a series of incantations. But after all that somehow he failed to produce a strong enough spell, and the witch 'has still the dominant power, the woman remaining in the same state as before'.

15 August **1916** In the afternoon a seamstress at Lewes workhouse went to the sitting room and found the bodies of the Master, Frederick Newton Bryan, 47, and 16-year-old Vinnie Rushworth, the institution bookkeeper, in their chairs. Two cups, which had contained several samples of café au lait, were on the table along with a bottle of cyanide of potassium and a bowl of bread.

At about midday Bryan had asked one of the staff for a jug of hot water. He said that he and Vinnie were going to try a sample of café au lait, which presumably they had not previously tasted. According to one of the domestics, only two days earlier Newton had warned her that a jug in the cupboard contained rat poison. Dr Fawcett, the workhouse officer, said the couple had died of cyanide poisoning. Miss Rushworth, he said, was pregnant. Bryan's wife was unaware of any liaison between her husband and Miss Rushworth. Days later an inquest jury found that 'Bryan committed suicide and persuaded Miss Rushworth to do so too'. The Coroner said that this amounted to a verdict of murder against Bryan.

Vinnie Rushworth.
(*Sussex Express*)

16 August **1864** At 3 a.m. Hastings police officer Sergeant Jones called in at the Duke of York in Union Street, a regular haunt of prostitutes, for the second time in a few hours. There had been complaints about the noise of music and singing, and he cautioned the landlord again. Even that was not enough. Jones had to return yet again at 5 a.m. Two of the girls he had seen on his first visit left at 4.45 and the other three at 5.30 a.m. All were prostitutes. The defendant, William Ralph, was found guilty of permitting persons of a notoriously bad character to assemble in his house and was fined £1 with 12s costs.

17 August **1857** In his diary John Coker Egerton writes: 'At 1 (ought to have been at 12) the funeral of the late farmer Noakes. Smell very offensive; ought to have been buried on Saturday. I away to another funeral, of a woman named Relf a pauper. The style of the two very different. Really the pauper funeral hardly decent; but I suppose it wd not do to offer any premium to pauperism in any way whatever.' The woman who died in the workhouse was 22 years of age. Let it not be thought that Egerton was other than a decent, caring man but he opposed the encouragement of dependency.

1820 Daniel Hartford, a horse thief who was to be executed the following day, called the prison chaplain to his cell, asking permission to see all of his fellow convicts so that he might warn them of the folly of their ways. Hartford was allowed his wish and exhorted the prisoners to mend their ways and to learn before it was too late. Avoid temptations, he urged them, avoid idleness and drunkenness, the profanation of the Lord's Day and keeping bad company. At his execution on Horsham Common, just as the horse-drawn cart moved from under him, he called out, 'Oh Lord, have mercy.' The spectators were few, we are told, 'not exceeding 200, and a great part consisted of women and children'.

18 AUGUST

1912 At about 8 a.m. a screaming woman, her neck bleeding, stood at the top of the steps of the Enys Road house in Eastbourne where smoke billowed from the upstairs windows. When the firemen and police arrived they found five bodies in the house. Three were very young children. There was also a man and a woman in her twenties. The man, who had left a note, had shot the others before committing suicide.

19 AUGUST

Edith Money, top left, her sister Florence Paler and Money/Murray (though in Eastbourne he was known as Mackie) with two versions of his signature. Merstham tunnel is also pictured. *(News of the World)*

The murderer was identified as a Scotsman, Robert Hicks Murray, said to be a well-connected Army officer. Weeks earlier he had brought his wife Edith and their child from London to spend the summer at Eastbourne. He was frequently absent on military duties. On the afternoon of Saturday 17 August he murdered them. On Sunday evening he brought Florence Paler, with her two children, to the house and on Monday he had shot the two children but failed to kill Florence. Murray had then shot himself.

At the inquest a most curious tale emerged. Florence Paler had lived with Murray in Clapham, London, since 1907. They had never married but they had two children. In June 1910 Florence and Murray were visited by Florence's sister, Edith Paler. This was the first time that Murray and Edith met but two months later they married in secret. From then on Murray maintained two houses. Later Florence discovered the marriage and seems to have reluctantly accepted it.

In August 1912, while Edith and her child resided at Enys Road, Florence and her two children stayed in other lodgings in the town. Neither woman was aware of her sister's presence. When Murray brought Florence and the two children to Enys Road on the Sunday, they were forbidden to go into one of the rooms, in which the bodies of Edith and her daughter lay.

But the oddest feature of the case is that Murray was not an Army officer, Neither was his father a barrister nor his brother an Army officer as he had claimed. And despite his pretended accent he was not Scottish. Both women had thought him all of these things. His real name was Robert Henry Money and he had made no profit from the women. In fact he spent all he had on them. He had owned a dairy in Kingston upon Thames which he had sold in 1906 and he had some property he rented, but perhaps he was running out of money. His motives are not clear.

In 1905 his sister, Sophia Money, had been thrown from a train in Merstham tunnel. She had a gag in her mouth. Her murderer was never found. Was Mackie/Murray/Money responsible for this killing?

20 AUGUST **1920** Young Willie Weller and his mother, on holiday in Eastbourne, went for a picnic on the Crumbles. And while Mrs Weller sat out of the wind 13-year-old Willie explored the beach until he tripped over a black-stockinged foot sticking out of the shingle. The spot where the boy had tripped was in a dip about 25yd from the railway track. The police were called to the body of a girl, buried under a thin shroud of shingle. There was a mask of blood over her hideously mutilated face. Both lower and upper jaws were fractured and several teeth were broken away. Under the chin a triangular wound appeared to have been made with an instrument which had penetrated the roof of the mouth. Her left eye was severely damaged and along the right ear was a long, incised wound. There were no signs of rape or attempted rape.

The doctor believed that the girl had been sitting down when she received the first head wounds from a fist. Then a stone had been picked up and thrown on to her head. He thought that the ferrule of a walking stick could have caused some of the lacerations.

Police photographs of Billy Gray and Jack Field. *(Private collection)*

On 4 February 1921 Jack Field (19) and Billy Gray (28) were hanged together at Wandsworth. But what did happen on the Crumbles that chilly August afternoon? Why was 17-year-old Irene Munro killed by these men whom she believed to be her friends? Robbery? She had only about £2 in her purse; enough for a few glasses of decent beer and the odd packet of Turkish fags. And maybe a little left over to repay some petty debts. Sex? There was no sign of any attempt to interfere with her sexually. The motive for this brutal murder, so callous, so devoid of human feeling, still mystifies. Was it planned? Did Jack Field, carrying his father's walking stick, know, when he set off that afternoon, that he would take part in murder? Had Billy Gray, dull-witted and vicious, decided in advance that he and his pal were going to kill Irene, a girl they had met only a couple of days earlier? They never said.

21 AUGUST   **1822** According to *The Times*, 'The treading-mill recently erected at Lewes House of Correction is daily effecting a diminution of crime, particularly of vagrancy in the county.' Hard labour, even though on the treadmill it might be totally unproductive, was an official element in the aim to reform prisoners. Hard work, separation from all other prisoners and silence were the keys to improving the idle, the dissolute and the inherently criminal though many of those who found themselves behind the walls at Horsham, Lewes and Petworth were people made destitute from lack of work, totally desperate from lack of food, homeless because of their inability to pay rent. No matter, the decent landless labourer, guilty perhaps of doing no more than steal a sack of flour to feed himself and his family, took his place on the treadmill alongside the professional sneak-thief, the footpad and the pimp. And whoever worked on the remorseless conveyor belt found it harsh, exhausting and cruel labour.

22 AUGUST   **1809** A letter of some outrage comes from Newhaven: 'Not a day has passed for more than a week, without an enemy's cruiser being in sight of this place; and there are often three or four large luggers which have taken several vessels. Yesterday evening three privateers were in sight and as the Oporto fleet passed in the night without convoy there is no doubt that there will be many missing as the privateers might capture as many as they could manage. I saw one of the privateers this morning capture a galliot and a schooner with which she bore away to leeward. Twenty sail of vessels are now in sight, and we have not observed a British cruiser for a considerable time.' The nation which had so recently destroyed the fleets of France and Spain expected something better.

23 AUGUST   **1789** 'A much-respected nobleman the other day, in speaking of the late burglary and robbery in the house of Mrs Shelley, remarked, that such is the police of this county, and the activity of its Magistrates, that offences of the above description are seldom if ever committed here with impunity.' In view of the crime rate it is difficult to believe either the remarks of the 'much-respected nobleman' or the reason for their inclusion in the *Sussex Advertiser*. The item, referring to the 'county where Justice *never sleeps*', continues: 'Indeed, a Sussex Gibbet hath taught many a *London Rogue* fatally the truth of this observation.'

24 AUGUST   **1884** Dr John Goldsmith was moved to write to the press about the deplorable riots which had occurred in recent days in Worthing. He had no doubt about where the responsibility for the disorder lay. It was the fault of the Salvation Army who had in the past year established themselves in the town. Earlier in the year, when they paraded on Sundays, there had been violent scenes

Head's Shop Montague St Salvation Army Riot a. Elliot

which stopped only when the Salvationists agreed no longer to march on Sundays. But on Sunday 17 August they had resumed their public parade and as expected there was a renewal of the disorder which spilt over into other days. Late at night on Monday the mob had attacked the Montague Street shop of ironmonger George Head, a senior member of the Salvation Army. The shop windows were broken and then the door was forced open. The rioters poured inside but were repulsed by Mr Head, armed with a spade. Outside, a boy was shot in the face and another man in the wrist. The following day the magistrates fined several of the rioters and decided to call in soldiers to help restore order. These measures did not resolve matters. But in the eyes of Dr Goldsmith all this was the fault of the wretched Salvationists.

The damage to George Head's shop in Montague Street, Worthing. *(West Sussex Library Service)*

1861 Clayton tunnel, 1¼ miles long and 5 miles up the line from Brighton, was the scene of the worst of the early railway accidents. The driver of a London Victoria-bound train, mistaking a signalman's flag at the entrance to the tunnel and fearing trouble ahead, brought his train to a halt and then put it in reverse. While it was still in the tunnel a following train ran into the rear; 23 people were killed and 175 were injured.

25 August

One witness described the awfulness of the scene. There was, he said, 'a mingled mass of dead and dying men, women and children buried beneath the heaps of the broken carriages, with the engine and tenders to the top of and pressing down on the whole, the steam and boiling water at the same time pouring over the unhappy people. . . . The bodies of men, women and children lying together in an almost indistinguishable mass, some, although not dead, being frightfully mutilated and blackened by the pressure, presenting a ghastly appearance, sickening even to those whose duties called them to alleviate their sufferings.'

Another passenger gave his version of the scene. 'The yells and shrieks of the people were awful. Not only of those who were injured, but the rest of the passengers of the two trains, whose alarm, increased by the darkness, was intense. People . . . yelled and shrieked and put up prayers, believing that they should never see daylight again. Their fears increased the actual horror of the situation. They imagined that every moment other trains . . . would run into them and render their doom certain. For some ten minutes we remained in darkness; then lights were hung up against the sides of the tunnel and the scene that revealed itself was terrifying. There, in the background, I could dimly perceive a heap of carriages more or less in fragments which seemed to have been piled one upon the other. I never witnessed such a scene in my life.'

26 AUGUST   1810 William Treble, alias Elbert, alias Thurston, 60, condemned to death for forgery, hanged himself with his handkerchief in his cell at Horsham. In several letters he left behind he indicated his dread of dying in front of a gaping mob.

27 AUGUST   1862 John Lee appeared before Brighton magistrates on a charge of passing a forged Bank of England note, printed on one of the sheets stolen from Messrs Portal in Hampshire. The note had been passed in a draper's shop in North Street. The shop assistant, George Starr, was asked if he had any recollection of the person who handed him the note.

> *Witness:* I cannot identify the prisoner as being that person.
> *Questioner:* Did you see him write anything on the back of it?
> *Witness:* He wrote a name and address.
> *Questioner:* How long was he in your presence?
> *Witness:* About 20 minutes.
> *Questioner:* Now, you say you cannot recollect sufficient of the person who gave you the note to identify the prisoner as that man. Can you say that he is not the man?
> *Witness:* I think him not to be the man.

At this point the police decided not to pursue the matter further in view of this witness's negative response. Lee then produced a character witness who stated that he had known the prisoner for the last twenty years. He was a jeweller with whom he had had extensive dealings and during the whole of the twenty years he had never experienced anything with which to reproach him. Lee was discharged and the police presumably were left with some feelings of embarrassment.

28 AUGUST   1868 The surgeon first saw Lily Jones, only 2 years 8 months old, on a day on which, not for the first time, she had been beaten by her parents. Her body was bruised all over, some of the marks recent, others not so. Her eyes and her nose were swollen and her ear lobes torn. There were lacerations on the elbows and ankles as though she had been tied.

Further investigation revealed that Lily, the daughter of Francis Thomas Jones, a Hastings lodging-house keeper, was a sickly child who because of some deformity of the legs found walking difficult. There were witnesses who attested that she was frequently beaten with a cane and that her parents had tried to have her admitted to the workhouse. Some spoke of the child's hands being tied behind her back after which she was pushed up the stairs, stumbling as she went on her little deformed legs. There were stories that when Lily soiled her bed she was put straight into a cold bath by her mother and then caned. Sometimes she was scrubbed all over with a stiff brush, so vigorously that the skin was torn.

On the day in question she had soiled her bed and was visited with the usual punishment by her mother. Then her father returned home and he beat her with the cane for several minutes. In court the following year, when he faced charges of beating and assaulting Lily, there were witnesses still to be found who swore to Jones being 'a very good sort of fellow' and 'a kind, good, amiable sort of man'. And after all, might not a parent chastise his child, asked defence counsel. It was only a matter of excess. In any case, he said, the jury must bear in mind that Jones was being charged with the caning on one particular day and that all references to other beatings were irrelevant, especially as there was no proof as to who had administered these. The fact that Lily had died in October was not related to the charges that Jones now faced.

However, the jury found Jones guilty. 'You treated Lily with a brutality which, in all probability, you would not have shown had she been a strong and healthy child,' the judge told him, passing a sentence of twelve months' imprisonment.

1944 The Officers' Mess at Marsh Green Army Camp near Hartfield was hit by a flying bomb. There were many casualties including the Commanding Officer. A Spitfire pilot had spotted the V1 and in an extraordinarily courageous manoeuvre had deliberately clipped its wing, trying unsuccessfully to change its flight path and nudge it back over the Channel.

29 August

1833 Two workmen at Hove had an astonishing escape when at about 7 p.m. the Anthaeum, the forerunner of the Crystal Palace, collapsed. This most wonderful building, all delicate iron and glass, simply smashed to the ground the day before it was to be officially opened. First, the top of the dome came crashing down and then the ribs, 'one after another, like a pack of cards, accompanied by a sound resembling the continued firing of cannon'.

30 August

'The millions of sparks produced by so many pieces of iron striking against each other,' says the *Brighton Guardian*, 'made it appear as if the dome had fallen in a bed of flames.' Later, when it was deemed fit to enter, the newspaper reported: 'The ground within is not strewed but actually seems made of iron; there is no walking but upon ribs and sash bars.'

The Anthaeum was the dream of the botanist, Henry Phillips, whose aim it was to create a vast, glass building – its dome larger than those of St Paul's and St Peter's, Rome – where the inhabitants of Brighton would stroll along gravel paths or sit in secluded arbours. In this wonderfully light and elegant building, flowers, exotic trees and shrubs from all over the world would flourish; alien creepers and the fronds of great palms would offer cover from the summer sun. The overall effect would be soft-shadowed, green-hued. The Anthaeum would attract visitors throughout the year, for in winter

An aquatint of the period showing the dome of the nearly completed Anthaeum.
(East Sussex Record Office)

furnaces would push out high temperatures, up to 90 degrees, to promote the extravagant flora. Springing from the ground as a perfect hemisphere, the Anthaeum was to be 164ft in diameter and 64ft high. The structure was to be surmounted by a cupola which was to extend its overall height to more than 80ft. The circumference of this extraordinary building was 492ft.

But there was a technical fault. Engineers and architects had disagreed about the necessity of a central supporting column and at the last minute it had been removed.

'Its destruction must prove a national loss,' mourned the *Brighton Guardian*. So there was no Anthaeum, no inspiring structure which, so it was claimed, would be the envy of the world. But sometimes, in an exceptionally dry season, on the lawns of Palmeira Square, the fading outline of what has been called 'the ruins of a Steam Age dream' can be discerned from the air, just the last faint hint of something special.

31 AUGUST **1910** An inquest was held in Brighton on George Bullock, a holidaymaker from Harlesden, who drowned while bathing in a rough sea. The Beach Inspector stated that if he had had the authority he would have stopped any bathing at the time but it was left entirely to the discretion of bathing-machine proprietors and the wishes of bathers. Returning a verdict of 'Death from Drowning' the jury recommended that the Beach Inspector should have control over bathing-machines as he had over boats in rough weather.

SEPTEMBER

William Calcraft, Britain's longest-serving executioner, hanged more than 400 people in a career spanning forty-five years from 1825. Some hanged by the inept Calcraft, who often used too short a rope, failed to die immediately from a broken neck and instead slowly strangled. On such occasions he was known to jump on the back of the struggling wretch in an attempt to cut short the death agonies. Calcraft officiated at the execution of the infamous Mary Ann Geering. Apparently not especially interested in his trade, he preferred his garden, his pet rabbits and his pony. He was said to be particularly fond of children. *(Author's collection)*

1 SEPTEMBER **1819** John Piper, a 45-year-old burglar, did not treat the occasion of his execution at Horsham before 2,000 people with the respect it deserved, according to the *Sussex Weekly Advertiser*, which was outraged at 'the improper way which he entertained of the awful situation in which he appeared. On the arrival of the cart under the fatal tree, the Revd Mr. Noyce, the clergyman in attendance, ascended it and began to pray, requesting the unhappy man to join him; but this, Piper refused to do, saying he was a murdered man. He went on to observe that there was no law for a poor man and referred to a case at our last Assizes wherein one prisoner was condemned to death and another, charged with a similar crime, was sentenced to two months' imprisonment.' Piper went on to say that the man who arrested him had committed perjury for he had never threatened him with a pistol. 'He was now again entreated to offer up his prayers to his offended God, but in vain, as he said their entreaties would be of no use,' says the astonished journalist. 'A more hardened offender never suffered the ignominy of a gallows.'

2 SEPTEMBER **1829** At the Winter Assizes at Lewes Edward James was charged with the manslaughter of Mary Ann Allcorn, described as 'a girl of the town'. They had had a quarrel, presumably about payment, and James had struck her several times. She had fallen, striking her head a fatal blow against railings. Found guilty, James was sentenced to seven years' transportation.

3 SEPTEMBER **1798** There was more grim news for the readers of the *Sussex Advertiser*:

> On last Wednesday se'nnight in the evening, the following melancholy accident happened at Petworth in this County. As the coachman of the Earl of Egremont was watering a pair of horses in a pond in the park during the storm, one of them took fright at a flash of lightning, and plunged from him into the water beyond his depth. When the coachman perceived that he was unable to swim, and attributing the cause to his being curbed, followed him on the other horse in order to remove the impediment, but in the attempt he fell into the water and was unfortunately drowned with the beast he had endeavoured to save. The other horse swam and recovered the land without injury. Lord Egremont has repeatedly cautioned his servants against watering horses at the above pond, in consequence of a similar accident which happened there some years ago.

4 SEPTEMBER **1819** While a seventy-strong band of smugglers was unloading a considerable amount of contraband spirits and silks at Jew's Gut, near Rye, they were approached by three men, Haisel, Gurr and Chapman, all of them customs officers. Eighteen months later, when two of the officers were charged with 'conspiracy to aid, assist and abet certain smugglers in the landing of uncustomed goods', conflicting accounts of what occurred were heard at Lewes Assizes, and it was odd that it was four smugglers, present that evening, who were called for the prosecution.

Were the smugglers boldly approached and asked for a share of the haul? Did they ask for as many as sixty tubs of spirits in return for not raising the alarm? Did they then settle for twenty-two tubs and take these off with them, leaving the smugglers to finish their work? Was this believable? Were sworn-in members of the Preventive Service open to bribery? Sadly, there had been such cases. But were these three guilty of accepting contraband goods in return for keeping quiet?

In court, the defence asked the jury to believe that the smugglers were being vindictive simply because Haisel and Gurr – Chapman was not charged with any offence – had been so active in their attempts to suppress smuggling. And why, the court was asked, had eighteen months elapsed before the matter was brought to light? Was it solely that the smugglers were maliciously inclined towards their natural enemies? And how could three customs officers have prevented seventy smugglers from landing their goods? On the night in question the defendants, far from cooperating with the smugglers, had fired their pistols to warn *Severn*, the nearby boat of the Preventive Service. And men from *Severn* appeared in the witness box to assure the court that they had heard the pistols fired. They were certain, when they arrived on the scene, that the officers were carrying out their duties appropriately.

The jury, however, found the defendants guilty. Presumably they knew more than readers of the case nearly two hundred years later.

1921 A passenger on the 7.30 train from Brighton to Victoria met with a fatal accident when he was struck on the head by an iron bar which crashed through the carriage window. It had apparently become detached from the engine.   **5 September**

1785 Another entry comes from the diary of John Burgess: 'Wet Great part and very remarkable high wind it is said to be the hihest wind ever remembered don a great deal of Dammage to the Buildings and shipping blowed down a hovel at whillands Great deal of Dammage to the standing corn and likewise to the Hops tore down ye poles very much weat harvest is nearly over about hear.'   **6 September**

1807 'A bowel complaint has of late been very rife here and in many instances proved fatal. Upwards of thirty children belonging to soldiers in our barracks, have been carried off by it in a short space of time.' Yet again the *Sussex Advertiser*, speaking of the barracks at Seaford, makes modern readers aware of how much medical treatment has changed.   **7 September**

1760   **8 September**

John Dutton, Surgeon, at Lindfield, Sussex, after his many Years very great Success in the Inoculation of the Small Pox (as the happy Recovery from that of the ways most dangerous Distemper, of the many Hundreds that have been under his Care during his long Practice, sufficiently evidenceth) gives Notice, That he will be ready to receive Patients at his Houses in Hartfield (which are enlarged and compleatly fitted up for that Purpose) from the last Week in September to the last Week in November, and from the Beginning of February to the Middle of April, for five Guineas each Patient, all Necessaries included.

All Persons who intend to come under his Care are desired to give him timely Notice, that a proper Regimen, &c. may be directed previous to the Operation.

He also waits upon, and operates away inoculates Persons at their own Habitations; and takes in Patients who fail in the natural Way, at any Time of the Year, upon reasonable Terms.

Note, He wants a Man Servant who hath had the Small Pox, and been bred to Husbandry Business.

9 September 1815 Nearing the end of harvest time, Farmer Leggett had found twenty or thirty women on his land. They normally came to glean after the harvest was all gathered in, but as yet the work was not finished. This was not the first time this had occurred; on previous occasions the women had come into the fields before 'the proper and lawful time' and the farmer had had to insist that they keep away until the harvesters had completed their work. This time, however, the women refused to budge, but finally, although the majority of the intruders had gone away, Mrs Pledger had refused to leave. At this point Leggett had raised his horsewhip and struck her three or four blows. For this assault he was fined 40s.

10 September 1940 The war came to Colgate when German bombs were dropped on the village. Four people, the district nurse and three firemen, died. The post office was hit but the family had taken refuge outside the house. The following day a fourth bomb exploded without loss of life.

11 September 1922 At Brighton Police Court George Langham, a bookmaker's clerk, and James Ford, a fruit commission agent, both from London, were committed for trial at the Assizes, charged with inflicting grievous bodily harm on John Phillips during Race Week. It was alleged that after demanding money from Phillips in Chatfields Hotel in Brighton the accused men attacked him outside, Ford slashing his face with a razor and Langham kicking and punching him.

In court the defence denied that the prisoners were connected with any racecourse gang. The suggestion was that fly-weight boxer Langham – real name, Angelo Gianicoli – was a member of the notorious Sabini gang from Clerkenwell's Little Italy, although he did agree that he was an honorary steward of the Bookmakers Protection Association whose leading figure was Darby Sabini. Witnesses swore that neither man was present at any affray outside the Chatfields Hotel. At the Assizes in the following December both men were found not guilty.

This affair was another minor chapter in the great saga of the feuding racecourse gangs – the Sabinis, the Cortesis, the Leeds outfit and the Brummagem mob – in their struggle for supremacy, turning up at racecourses armed with axes, hammers, revolvers, coshes, knuckledusters and any other weapon likely to cause maximum damage to the opposition and to any bookmakers who resisted their offers of 'protection'. At the time this case was being heard the Cortesis were being prosecuted in another court for shooting members of the Sabini gang.

1790 'A woman at Cold Waltham, having formed an improper connection with one of the river diggers, resolved on robbing her house, and decamping with him to the Ouse Navigation. For this purpose she admitted the fellow at midnight into the house, who held her husband in bed, while she packed up the valuables and the money. They threatened to kill the poor man if he alarmed the neighbourhood; but this he ventured to do when they were gone. They were soon overtaken, brought back, and being tied together, were three or four times dragged through a horse pond. This discipline so effectually cooled the lady's affection for her paramour, that she begged her husband to forgive her and take her again, which he good-naturedly did on her promise to behave well.'

The *Sussex Advertiser* likes this story and does not moralise. Presumably local justice was thought enough on this occasion, but one wonders if the wife remained true to her promise.

12 September

1930 The acting stewards of the Kempton Park Second Summer Meeting met to receive the result of the examination of Don Pat, winner of the Bedfont High-weight Handicap. After interviewing the owner and the trainer they referred the case to the stewards of the Jockey Club. After further investigation they concluded that a drug had been administered to the horse before the race. Don Pat was disqualified for this race and for all future races under their rules and was warned off Newmarket Heath course by trainer C. Chapman of Manor Farm, Lavant.

13 September

1848 One of those present when 56-year-old Richard Geering, a farm labourer from Guestling, was placed in his coffin the day after his death noticed that the 'skin was very black and much decayed and skin came off the back of the neck as it was placed in the coffin'. Yet he thought little of this. Neither did anyone else. And they attached little importance to George Geering's death in the following December, for though he was only 21, young people did die. And even the death of 26-year-old James in March of the next year failed to rouse any suspicions. But when Benjamin fell ill his comment to the doctor seems to have been significant. 'My father and both brothers were first taken like me,' the 20-year-old said, 'and vomited just the same kind of stuff.' Benjamin survived but his illness and his comment led to questions being asked and the bodies of the three were exhumed. As a result, Mary Ann Geering, wife and mother, was arrested and charged with three murders and one attempted murder.

At her trial the court heard of her frequent arguments over money; of how she had benefited from the Guestling Burial Friendly Society, which paid out sums of money to members in times of sickness and death; of how she had pawned some of the family's clothing. When Richard was buried she asked for an extra large plot of ground so that all the family might be buried together. Three members of the family ended up there, Benjamin had a narrow escape and there were five

14 September

other brothers and a sister. Did Guestling's serial killer murder for money or was there something else which urged her on? Did she take some kind of perverse pleasure in ministering to the sick men as they lay violently ill in their beds?

Some 4,000 people attended her public hanging at Lewes in August 1849.

15 SEPTEMBER   **1837** 'Philadelphia Martin, aged 37, (on bail) was indicted with fraudulently obtaining by means of false pretences, on the 28th July last, at Ticehurst, four pounds of mutton, the property of John Standen and Thomas Standen and on the 28th August last, eight pounds weight of mutton and one pound weight of suet, the property of John Standen and Thomas Standen. The prisoner pleaded guilty. The witness gave her a good character for former conduct and said that she has a family of eight children, seven of whom are under twelve years of age. The court sentenced her to be imprisoned for the first offence for one week and for the second a fortnight in solitary confinement.'

This matter-of-fact account from the *Sussex Agricultural Express* says nothing about any reasons why Philadelphia Martin might have committed her offence.

16 SEPTEMBER   **1935** There was widespread havoc when one of the worst storms in memory swept the county. Newspaper headlines announced it as the 'Worst Gale of the Century' and, until 1987, so it was. Winds of up to 80mph were accompanied by torrential rain. Not a town or village escaped damage. In the Suffolk House Hotel at Littlehampton a young married woman was killed when a chimney stack collapsed and fell through the roof on to her. At Bognor Timothy White's windows were blown in and at Felpham the roof of a dance hall was ripped off. At Selsey the mountainous seas destroyed bathing huts. Bungalows and caravans at West Beach near Medmerry Hill were wrecked. 'Bosham', one resident said, 'is a place of destruction.' Further east, at Lancing, boats were thrown on to the main road and everywhere roads were blocked by fallen trees and telegraph poles. At Seaford there was a scene of absolute desolation. The whole length of the parade and roadway was strewn with the wreckage of seats, shelters, beach huts and whole flagstones. Portions of the roof of Holy Trinity church at Worthing were sheered off. Burgess Hill also suffered, the gale taking off the roof of a furniture store, while at Hassocks the boat deck on the roof of the Downs Hotel was completely destroyed.

17 SEPTEMBER   **1810** 'The unfortunate convict, Wilson, who was executed on Saturday the 8th inst. at Horsham for a burglary in the shop of Mr. Gill, watchmaker, at Rye, wrote a letter a few days prior to his execution to Mr. Gill, informing him in the most solemn manner, that he had given three of the stolen watches, all new ones, to a Corporal of the regiment to which he belonged; two to Privates, and that two others were hid in a wall at Winchelsea; he also stated that an accomplice named Hodges had all the rest of the stolen property with which he deserted soon after the commission of the robbery.'

Note the use of the word 'unfortunate' in this *Sussex Advertiser* report. There is a sympathy here for a man who seems to have repented of his crime. It is when criminals remain stubborn to the end, refusing to go to the gallows quietly for the theft of a bolt of linen or a sheep, that this newspaper becomes resentful.

1833 '. . . about 10 o'clock, the inhabitants of Chichester and its neighbourhood, to an extent of several miles, experienced the shock of an earthquake. Although the agitation of the earth, and the rumbling sound which accompanied it, continued but for a moment, it was sensibly felt by almost every individual and created a great degree of alarm; and we regret that a poor man, named Marshall who was digging at the time in a chalk pit near Cocking, was killed by the falling in of a quantity of chalk, supposed to have been loosened by the shock.' **18 SEPTEMBER**

1829 William Brazier, 18, was sentenced to death after being found guilty at Lewes Assizes. He had stolen £100 from John King at Chillington. King, a labourer, had kept his fortune in a chest of drawers which, in his absence, was broken into by Brazier. How King amassed such a sum – worth £6,000 today – is impossible to say. **19 SEPTEMBER**

1808 At about 10 p.m. Mr Baker, landlord of the Angel at Midhurst, noticed that Farmer Chalcroft, one of his customers 'apparently in liquor', was riding home to Fernhurst and being followed by two suspicious local characters, Hall and Boxall, one of whom had recently been released from gaol. Calling on one of his post-chaise drivers for help, Baker, armed with a cudgel from a wood pile, set off down the road to ensure that no ill befell Chalcroft. Shortly the farmer's horse stopped and voices were raised, and at this point Baker and his ally rushed to Chalcroft's aid. They managed to secure Hall but Boxall made his escape over the fields. Baker immediately applied to a magistrate for a warrant and Boxall was taken in his bed at 3 a.m. **20 SEPTEMBER**

1938 Expecting the outbreak of war at any time, local authorities found themselves with new and unexpected responsibilities. Hailsham Rural Council members discussed the problem of where to store 40,000 gas masks which had been delivered. The Council's Air Raid Precautions organiser, General Nation, had offered the use of his squash court for a few days pending the finding of better accommodation. It was finally decided that the only satisfactory place for the gas masks was the now disused Isolation Hospital. After this, arrangements were made for the distribution of the masks to every household. **21 SEPTEMBER**

1851 James Wellerd, keeper of Hastings Gaol, records in his diary: 'Georgiana Stevens charged with Disorderly conduct Fasting [fastening] in the Matron upstairs and com downstairs in order to make har eskape ordered that har allowance should be reducte to one pound of Bread per diem for 3 days.' **22 SEPTEMBER**

Georgiana gave the keeper considerable trouble. Earlier in the year her bread allowance was reduced for talking to boys in the street, presumably from the windows of the cell. Twice in June she appears to have had tantrums, breaking her pot on one occasion and windows on another. She was punished twice in November for again breaking pots as well as a bowl and a spoon. Accused of larceny she came up for trial at the Assizes and was transported for seven years 'to such part beyond the seas as Her Majesty's Privy Council shall order and direct'. She was just 16 years old.

Hastings Gaol, c. 1830, with its tower, is in the centre of the picture. The keeper and his family lived on the ground floor and the prisoners on the first and second floors. In front of the building are the stocks. *(Hastings Reference Library)*

23 SEPTEMBER **1798** Seaman John Hanning, who killed one of the press gang at Newhaven, was discovered hanging with a handkerchief round his neck from the bars of his cell by the keeper of Lewes House of Correction. On the day before, Hanning asked another prisoner to write two letters for him, one to his sister and another to a young woman in Dover, in which he stated that he would never see them again and left them his few possessions – a watch, some silver spoons and his clothes. He was buried at the crossroads near St John's Church, 'but the stake, commonly used on such occasions, was dispensed with'.

24 SEPTEMBER **1934** The body of a man washed up on the beach at Seaford was missing its head and legs. Over each collarbone was a surgical incision, made most probably by a doctor. So delicate was the work that it could not have been done by an amateur. Beneath the left incision was a pad of cotton wool; in the right incision a piece of silk had been tied round a blood vessel. It was believed that the man was dead before the incisions were made and before he went into the sea. It was estimated that the body had been in the sea for at least two months, most likely after being thrown overboard from a ship.

25 SEPTEMBER **1899** The inquest on the death of Dr John Dick of Eastbourne was reported in the local gazette. On the night of 14 September a patient, Mrs Eliza Geer, went to the surgery where the doctor made up a bottle of medicine for her. The following morning Mrs Geer took a tablespoonful of the medicine in water and became so ill that another doctor was sent for. Later in the day Dr Dick called on Mrs Geer who told him that his medicine had made her very ill. She told him that she thought it had poisoned her. The doctor, resenting what Mrs Geer had said, replied, 'You could understand a man who drinks poisoning people but not the man who was always sober. To prove to you that it is not poison, I'll take some myself.' The doctor then drank some of the medicine, admitting, 'It

is nasty but it's not poison.' To prove the point Dick took another dose of the medicine. He then went home but when his sister opened the door she found him foaming at the mouth. He fell against the door but had enough strength to ask for a stomach pump which he operated himself. Then five local doctors arrived at the house in quick succession. They found Dr Dick in a serious condition, obviously suffering from strychnine poisoning. He was desperately anxious that no one should think that he had put poison in Mrs Geer's medicine deliberately and implored his colleagues to find out what had happened. Their conclusion was that a genuine error had occurred and that the doctor had intended to put chloroform water in the medicine but had instead picked up a similar bottle which contained strychnine but had no warning 'Poison' label. After rallying for some hours the doctor had a relapse and died. At the inquest the following day a verdict of 'Death by Misadventure from Strychnine Poisoning' was returned.

1771 Jack Upperton held up the post-boy carrying mail from Arundel to Steyning at 6 p.m.. He escaped with 'one bagg of letters called the Steyning bagg' which contained bills valued at £120. He was caught and hanged. There were the usual bills for dispatching him into the next world and for displaying his remains on the gibbet at Burpham. The smith submitted his bill for 'a new set of irons . . . £5'. He was required to measure the condemned man for his gibbet-cage before the execution. In this instance there were additional expenses for 'carrying John Upperton from Horsham to Burpham now down there to be hung in chains and paid for guards to the place £3'. As a warning to others, Upperton's body, coated in pitch, hung in its cage near the site of his crime. **26 September**

1939 A gamekeeper in Pondtail Wood at Albourne near Hurstpierpoint found a woman's partially concealed body in a ditch. So badly decomposed was the corpse that when the pathologist attempted to lift it the head fell off. There were severe injuries to the skull. Various clues led to the identification of the woman – a brooch; the dated stub of a cinema ticket; a handkerchief with a laundry mark; a letter in a handbag addressed to 'Anne'. **27 September**

At last, after five weeks, Anne Cook had been found. She had been reported missing from the Brighton convalescent home where she worked. The police had already talked to the staff and one had actually been to see them to volunteer further information. This was Charlie Cowell, a night orderly at the home. He had told the police that he had arranged to meet Anne at The Level. They were going to the circus. But when Anne had turned up she told him she needed 15s for an urgent train journey. She would not tell him where she was going, Cowell said, but he lent her the money. He never saw her again.

Cowell seemed too anxious to talk to the police and this aroused suspicion. And then there was the witness who before the body was found had seen a man come out of the wood looking very shifty. When the witness was asked for a description it matched Cowell.

Cowell was found guilty of the murder of Anne Cook whom he had taken to the wood on the night she disappeared. They had taken a bottle of wine with them. At some point he had lost his temper: perhaps she had rejected his advances. In any event he attacked her, possibly hitting her first with the wine bottle, although in his statement he said that he had 'attacked her with this lump of wood. I could see she was fair knocked out. I carried her further into the bushes. There was a little ditch. I left her there.'

After the event he had gone back to the wood on several occasions. Was it out of morbid curiosity? Or did he fear that someone might stumble on the body? Whatever it was that led him back to the wood helped put the noose around his neck. And in the same way it was foolish of him to go to the police before the body was found. This had made them highly suspicious of him. It all led Charlie Cowell to the gallows.

28 September **1889** Another entry comes from the Alfriston school log book: 'Mrs Carter, wife of Henry Thomas Carter, attended before the Board and thanked them for remitting the School Fees of her children. . . . Mrs Carter stated that her husband was now in receipt of 14/- per week and two boys out at work, one earning 5/- and the other 5/6 and six attending school one of which she had paid for and the other five remitted. The Board resolved to remit for a period of 3 months the fees payable in respect of the three elder children on condition that the parent pays the fees for the three youngest and that the whole of them attend school.'

29 September **1938** There were more plans for the possibility of war. It was announced that it was officially planned to billet many thousands of London refugees in Brighton almost immediately. Unless international circumstances altered, schoolchildren with their teachers would start to arrive the next day. Each child would bring rations for forty-eight hours and an allowance of 10s 6d (£21 today) would be paid for one child and 8s 6d for more than one. From this sum householders who took in the evacuees would be expected to provide food and care for the children. Brighton Education Committee had prepared a letter which would be sent to parents of all elementary schoolchildren in the next couple of days saying that 'though it is fervently hoped by all those who have dealings with young children that the horrors of war will be spared them, it is thought advisable to notify you at this time of the arrangements which will be made in schools in the event of the declaration of war'. As it was, another year was to elapse before the outbreak of war and Brighton would prove not to be the safest place to which to send evacuees.

30 September **1811** Private Feal was a deserter from the German Artillery, one of the units forming part of the British Army, and he along with another soldier was arrested. They were being taken under escort to their barracks and stopped at Hailsham and put up for the night at a public house. After supper Feal said that he felt cold and asked if he might go to bed. One of the escorts took him upstairs, satisfied that he could not escape, but no sooner had he left the room than there was a gunshot. The escorts' loaded muskets had been left in the bedroom.

Feal was found with a musket on his chest and his brains scattered about the room. He had 'placed the muzzle behind his under-jaw, where the ball entered, and having passed through the back part of his head, penetrated the ceiling, and made its way through the roof of the house'.

OCTOBER

Lewes Gaol. *(Courtesy of Lewes Reference Library)*

1 OCTOBER **1837** Jemmy Botting, England's first salaried public executioner, died at Hastings. At Newgate between 1817 and 1819 he hanged twenty-five men and two women, including the Cato Street Conspirators who had planned to assassinate the members of the Cabinet. At Derby in 1817 he hanged the three 'Pentrich Martyrs', found guilty of High Treason after the crushing of an attempted armed rising of poor labourers. After the hanging the corpses were decapitated by a masked man, after which Botting held the heads aloft in turn, shouting out 'Behold the head of a traitor.'

Botting was a reviled figure, hated for his apparent enjoyment of his work, frequently jeered at and threatened in the street, but he took this in his stride. 'Nay, I never quarrel with my customers,' he is supposed to have said. One of these 'customers' was Faulkener, who had name-called him in public in the winter of 1817, and was later found guilty of rape. Three months later Botting dispatched him at Horsham.

Jemmy Botting holds up the head of one of the Pentrich Martyrs from an original pamphlet. *(Derbyshire Record Office)*

Botting eventually retired because of ill health, living on a 5s a week pension from the City and Corporation of London. Paralysed in his last years and described as 'a gruesome old cripple', he was confined to a wheelchair, but still he retained a morbid taste for accounts of the last moments of men and women at the gallows.

1881 An inquest was held at the Elephant's Head coffee tavern, East Grinstead, on the body of Mary Ellen Goldsworthy, an infant found dead in a shed the day before. Richard Goldsworthy, the child's father, was a travelling hawker. The family had reached East Grinstead in the evening. The landlord of the Railway Inn half-promised them shelter for the night but when they turned up at 11 p.m. they were told there was no accommodation and were turned out into the street. There was no common lodging house in East Grinstead but they were directed to a shed in a cricket field where they slept, Mary Ellen lying between Richard and his wife. At daybreak they found the baby was dead and took it to the police station. Goldsworthy admitted to having drunk heavily throughout the previous day but said that he knew what he was doing; in any case, he said, his wife, Mary Elizabeth Goldsworthy, had been sober. She told the court that the child was 'very convulsive at times, and not at all a strong child'. The jury returned a verdict 'that the deceased came by its death by being accidentally overlaid by its mother and suffocated'. A juryman called attention to the pressing need of a lodging house for the accommodation of the poorer classes, 'numbers of whom were continually sleeping in all kinds of places rather than go to the Workhouse'.

1881 Letters to the press complained of the appalling conditions in which hop-pickers in Kent and Sussex lived from August until October. More than one writer pointed out the social and moral effects of the situation. Why, they asked, were government reports ignored? Why did local authority inspectors pay no attention to what was before their eyes? Why was the 'crying scandal', the 'serious evil', allowed to continue?

Often the pickers were accommodated in barns and provided with straw and hurdles to create walls to provide a modicum of privacy, but sometimes such partitioning was inadequate. Often the straw was dirty; barns, used for cattle in winter, were not always cleaned before the arrival of the pickers. At times up to fifty people, strangers to each other, lived in overcrowded conditions in these hopper-houses. Here they lived, cheek by jowl, with no water supply, no sanitary arrangements, no fireplaces for drying wet clothing and for cooking. There were dangers of fire, too: more than one child had burnt to death after knocking over a candle and igniting the straw. There were outbreaks of cholera and smallpox. 'The least careful of the growers', says one writer, 'declare that the hop-pickers are so bad that no attempt need to be made to better the accommodation for their reception.' Increasingly, respectable families stayed away from the gardens, their places taken by a 'low class of people'.

1747 The meeting of smugglers from Sussex, Kent, Hampshire and Dorset was of major importance in the history of south coast smuggling. A huge consignment of contraband tea from France, already paid for by the smugglers, had been impounded and now at the gathering in Charlton Forest near Goodwood they planned to retrieve it from the custom house at Poole. Their enterprise was successful, demonstrating the power and arrogance of the smuggling gangs, but it was to lead to the brutal murder of two old men, and

Smugglers breaking into Poole Custom House. *(Author's collection)*

this in turn was to result in the authorities' renewed determination to reduce the might of the gangs.

Two years later John Raisse, one of the smugglers, now a witness for the prosecution, was questioned at the Old Bailey about the raid on the custom house:

Court: Do you know anything of its being broken open?

Raisse: It was broken open soon after Michaelmas. I do not know the day of the month. It was a year ago last October. There was tea taken out of it.

Court: Give us an account of what you know about it.

Raisse: I was not at the first meeting. The first time I was with them about it was in Charlton Forest, belonging to the Duke of Richmond. . . We set our hands to a piece of paper to go and break open the Poole Custom House and take out the goods.

Two days later, at 11 p.m., thirty armed men mounted guard in the area leading to the customs house, while another thirty, with axes and crowbars, forced their way into the building, smashing locks, wrenching off bolts and hammering down the doors. They made off with 30cwt of tea, worth at today's value £65,000. Each man carried 27 pound bags of tea.

During their triumphant journey home, with no fear of capture, some of the smugglers stopped for refreshments at Fordingbridge where the locals turned out to see them. One of the smugglers, Jack Diamond from Chichester, looked into the crowd and spotted the shoemaker, Daniel Chater, a man he had harvested with some time past. He shook the old man by the hand and gave him a small bag of tea. This was the first step towards Chater's murder for he boasted of his encounter with the smuggler. When the authorities arrested Diamond some weeks later they insisted that Chater become a prosecution witness at the trial.

In the cold February which followed, Chater, accompanied by an equally old man, William Galley, as escort and both unarmed, set off for Stanstead to hand over a document concerning the matter to a magistrate. But they were intercepted by smugglers who tortured them mercilessly over several days. Galley was buried, possibly alive, at Harting Coombe. Chater, suffering longer, was thrown down Harris's Well in Lady Holt Park and stones were thrown down after him to ensure he was finished off. And it was from this point, when the bodies were found, that the authorities became more purposeful in their efforts to stamp on the great smuggling gangs.

1914 At the beginning of the First World War there was no conscription. All the soldiers were regulars, many of them believing that they would be home by Christmas. Instead these men and others after them found themselves involved in the most brutal war ever fought.

5 OCTOBER

A CALL TO ARMS!

4th (Home Service) BATTALION

ROYAL SUSSEX REGIMENT.

This Regiment is now being raised at Horsham to form a Reserve to the 4th Battalion Royal Sussex Regiment, which has been accepted for Foreign Service. A recruit (subject to the conditions stated below) can decide whether he will enlist for Foreign or Home Service.

CONDITIONS.

TERM.—Duration of the War, or not exceeding 4 years.

AGE.—(a) Foreign Service, 19-35 } Height 5ft. 2in ; Chest 33in.
(b) Home Service, 17-35 }
Ex-Sergeants up to age of 50 years; Ex-Corporals up to age of 45 years.

PAY.—7s. per week (exclusive of board and lodging).

ALLOWANCES (for upkeep of Kit).—1s. 2d. per week.

SEPARATION ALLOWANCES.

Wife, 9s. a week.
Wife and 1 child, 10s. 11d. per week.
Wife and 2 children, 12s. 10d. ,,
Wife and 3 children, 14s. 9d. ,,

Wife and 4 children, 16s. 9d. per week.
Each additional child, 2s. per week.
Each Motherless child, 3s. per week.
A child means a boy up to 14 years and a girl up to 16 years

Enlist at once—delay is dangerous. Apply at nearest Police Station or at THE DEPOT, THE DRILL HALL, HORSHAM.

Hon. Recruiting Officer for this District

Who will enlist men and give all information:

J. A. MINCHIN, Esq.
"WANTLEY," HENFIELD.

HORSHAM OCT? 1914

1930 At Brighton magistrates' court Beatrix Renwick, a young actress, appeared for a second time on charges of false pretences, relating to her obtaining twenty bottles of champagne, three bottles of whisky, three bottles of gin, cigars, and other articles valued at £20 19s (£850 in today's money). Two weeks earlier she had made her first appearance before the magistrates but as the case was not finished she was asked to return to court the following day. However, she failed to surrender to her bail. She had absconded and was arrested at Gretna Green in the company of a man. It was their intention to marry at the black-smith's forge at Gretna, so she said, but she was immediately returned to Brighton via the Carlisle magistrates' court.

6 OCTOBER

A Call to Arms.
(*East Sussex Record Office*)

The defence declared that this was simply a youthful escapade. It was just that matters had gone wrong. All the girl had wanted to do was entertain some of her friends and give them a good time. But why was she staying at a hotel in Brighton under the name of Chris Wren, the daughter, so she claimed, of a barrister? And why did she tell Mrs Corps, the proprietress, that she had recently married a very wealthy man? And then, having had Mrs Corps provide huge quantity of food, and Leonard Green, another hotel proprietor, having been prevailed upon to provide liquor and cigarettes, she had disappeared, bills and rent unpaid.

On arrest she had admitted to the policeman that she was not married. 'I am on my beam ends,' she told him. 'I have been let down by a man.' At least it was true that her father was a barrister. In court, Renwick pleaded not guilty to all charges. She was sentenced to one month's imprisonment with hard labour.

7 OCTOBER   **1791** William Sherlock, a 'profane swearer', was found guilty at Petworth Quarter Sessions of pulling down and destroying the stocks at Cowfold. He was sentenced to one month's hard labour in the Petworth House of Correction. In the same year a Jevington man of the same name, a 'great reprobate', faced charges at Horsham of swearing 'upwards of a hundred oaths'. Was this the same man, spreading his fame across the whole of Sussex?

8 OCTOBER   **1872** A report by Captain Montgomerie to the Chichester Quarter Sessions stated that the Western Division of Sussex had been 'most severely visited' with foot and mouth disease during the past quarter. Affected were 5,467 cattle, 16,690 sheep and 1,105 pigs, a total of 23,262 animals, of which 300 died. There were also twenty-three cases of pleuro-pneumonia in the Petworth, Chichester and Horsham divisions. Of these, nine cattle died.

9 OCTOBER   **1936** The younger man's body, fully dressed, lay across the bed; he had been strangled with a rope. The second man lay with his head against the gas fire, but he was still alive. A suicide note was found in the room. At the subsequent inquest and trial a curious tale was unravelled of events at the flat in Brunswick Terrace in Hove.

Arthur Peake, 43, described as a former sports promoter, employed Arthur Noyce, 20, as his chauffeur. On the night of 8 October they had played several games of draughts and then Noyce had told Peake that he was going to see a girl in Staffordshire and ask her to marry him. According to Peake, there had been no quarrel between the two men about this. Peake said that he had gone out of the room to make a telephone call. When he came back Noyce was dead, the rope around his neck.

Believing that he would be accused of murder – and this is Peake's explanation – he decided to commit suicide and wrote a last note. 'God forgive my wife for what she has done to this boy and his poor mother. May some terrible curse follow my wife, for her warped mind has been the cause of this and her cruelty to me has caused me to take my own life . . . my wife will be pleased . . . I have been slowly murdered by my wife and this poor boy is another victim.' Peake had then taken tablets but they had had no effect. When he awoke in the morning he had tried to gas himself.

The suicide note is intriguing. What had his wife done to the 'poor boy' and his 'poor mother'? Peake had told witnesses that, on the night before the tragedy, he had told 'Jim' (Noyce) about some trouble he had had with his wife, who had accused him of being the young man's father. 'Jim', Peake said, had taken this news very badly. 'I know what I am going to do,' the distressed young man had said. Was Peake saying that Noyce had hinted at suicide?

His wife's story was all lies, all fanciful, Peake said. The idea that Noyce was his son was absurd. But why then in court did the receptionist of a Leicester Square hotel say that when Peake and Noyce stayed there for six weeks the preceding winter Peake had told her that 'Jim' was his son? And then there was Paul Hanson, an actor, who had a quarrel with Noyce at a party in Brighton. He had knocked Noyce to the ground and Peake had knelt down, the tears streaming down his face, and had begged him not to hurt 'his son'.

As for forensic evidence, the eminent pathologist Sir Bernard Spilsbury and two other medical experts for the prosecution found the marks on Noyce's neck inconsistent with suicidal strangulation.

Peake was found guilty and sentenced to death but later reprieved and sent to Broadmoor. But his motive? Did he fear that he was to lose his chauffeur to a girl in Staffordshire? Was Noyce more than his chauffeur, more than a son? And had Noyce, aware of signs of insanity in his employer, decided to leave him?

1912 At about 9 a.m., in response to a call from the Chief Constable, Detective Chief Inspector Elias Bower of Scotland Yard arrived in Eastbourne to take over the investigation of the previous evening's murder.   **10 OCTOBER**

Sometime after 7 p.m. on 9 October Inspector Walls of the Eastbourne Borough Police was called to 6 South Cliff Avenue where a man was crouching on the portico above the front door, obviously preparing to enter the house by a bedroom window. When Walls arrived he called up to the man who turned towards him and fired a shot, from which almost instantly the policeman died. The gunman fled, firing his gun once more though not hitting anyone. He left behind him a trilby hat and two spent cartridge cases.

In the first hours of his investigation Bower, described by his colleagues as 'a rough diamond . . . one of the old-time dicks', made no headway until, late in the afternoon and quite out of the blue, he had a visitor. Dr Edgar Power, young and elegant, had come from London and said he knew the name of the murderer. It was John Williams, a professional burglar, living in the same house as Power. That morning, the doctor said, he had received a postcard from Williams, posted at Eastbourne the previous evening. 'If you will save my life,' it had read, 'come down to 4 Tideswell Road, Eastbourne, and bring some cash with you. Urgent.' Power had travelled to Eastbourne, had gone to the address where

Detective Chief Inspector Elias Bower.
(Private collection)

John Williams and
Florence Seymour.
(Daily Mirror)

Williams and his heavily pregnant lover, Florence Seymour, were staying and
had given Williams money. Williams had now gone to London by rail, Power
told the Chief Inspector, and he intended to go back to London with Florence
later in the day. But, and this was most important, Power was due to meet
Williams the following day at Moorgate station. In consequence, Williams was
arrested there and charged with murder. He became known as 'the hooded
man' because, on arrival at Eastbourne station, Bower insisted that he put a
blanket over his head.

Power helped the police by persuading Florence to show him where Williams had buried the murder weapon on the beach. He also talked her into making a statement to the police.

The trial was notable as the first occasion on which photographic ballistics evidence was presented to a jury. Robert Churchill, an expert witness, proved that the fatal bullet had similar rifling to the bullets he tested in Williams's revolver. While not conclusive, this evidence was influential as far as the jury was concerned. Even though in court Florence retracted her statement, Power's testimony was all-important. The jury returned its verdict in thirty minutes.

Williams saw Florence and their child the day before he hanged at Lewes. 'Now,' he said, handing the baby a crust of prison bread, 'don't say your father never gave you anything.' The son of a minister, Williams was really George Mackay, the black sheep of the family, who had served several prison terms. He had burgled a number of Eastbourne houses that summer.

As for Edgar Power, he was not really a doctor. Nor indeed was he really Edgar Power. He was a conman, Duncan Brady, ex-public schoolboy, ex-medical student, failed businessman, ex-convict and a friend of criminals. It is thought he was in love with Florence and he had recently had a quarrel in which Williams had threatened to kill him. This apparently determined him to give up Williams to the police.

1842 James Wellerd, keeper of Hastings Gaol, records in his diary: 'Catherine Banks, No. 72, having been found guilty of purloining different articles in the prison is ordered by the Visiting Justice to be kept on Bread and water for 7 days.' No. 72 was in fact a girl aged 10 years who at the later Quarter Sessions was sentenced to three months' hard labour, the last week of each month in solitary confinement. **11 OCTOBER**

1884 The Salvation Army paraded in Worthing but so did their opponents, the hooligan 'Skeleton Army', on this occasion 500 strong. Because of the history of violence when the Salvationists paraded, there was a large police presence. 'The hooting and howling', says *The Times*, 'was, as usual, disgraceful.' After progressing along a number of streets the Salvationists were escorted back to their 'barracks'. The 'Skeleton Army' then had its own parade through the streets, flying its black banner with the skeleton emblem. In the afternoon 300 Skeletons marched to Shoreham, breaking through the toll gate without paying. Failing to break into the Salvation Army 'barracks' in West Street they had to satisfy themselves with stone-throwing and window-breaking. **12 OCTOBER**

Later in the week twenty-one men, arrested for the Shoreham incident, appeared at Steyning magistrates' court. While he admitted that he had no sympathy for the Salvation Army, the Chairman, Mr H.P. Crofts, said that peaceful and inoffensive citizens were not to be disturbed in this manner. The men were fined. At Worthing court several men were also fined for assaulting Salvationists.

An attempt by the local authority to restrict the Salvation Army from conducting their usual musical processions was contained in Clause 169 of the

Local Improvement Act which read: 'No procession shall take place on Sunday in any street or public place in the Borough, accompanied by any instrumental music, fireworks, discharging a cannon, firearms, or other disturbing noise, provided that the foregoing prohibition should not apply to any of her Majesty's Navy, military, or volunteer forces.' It was this clause which was at the root of the struggle.

13 OCTOBER **1810** A soldier of the 37th Regiment, quartered in the Lewes barracks, went into a field to help himself to some turnips. Someone, never identified, fired a gun at him, the shot passing through his kidneys and liver. He died the following day.

14 OCTOBER **1789** 'Work in ye shop part of ye day & Went to Hurt to Mr Rendfield to dinner he Buried his Child at our place this after noon a Gearl about 8 munts old.' John Burgess, the Ditchling leather worker, knew enough about losing babies. Three of his children had died in as many years.

15 OCTOBER **1787** The *Sussex Advertiser* was strongly against the new-fangled business of inoculation and equally opposed to women who intervene in medical matters:

> The inhabitants of the town of Brighthelmston in general can but applaud their parish officers for their late vigilance in endeavouring to suppress the practice of inoculating in the town for so dangerous and fatal a disease as that of smallpox which it seems again threatened its baleful influence. The disease appeared in one or two families in the town about ten weeks ago, and an old woman from the country began to inoculate for it, till the officers interfered and threatened her with an indictment if she did not immediately quit the place. This injunction she prudently thought proper to comply with, and very happily for the inhabitants, at this season of the year, the contagion made no further progress. But it is said that notwithstanding the officers' leniency towards this first female intruder in the rights of the medical gentlemen, they are determined to carry the law into its full force against the next similar offender.

16 OCTOBER **1839** Isaac Foster, schoolmaster and unpaid constable of Barcombe, Hamsey and Newick, hearing of the theft of a pullet, immediately suspected William Heasman of Barcombe. Dissatisfied with Heasman's protestations of innocence, Foster insisted on searching his cottage. In the kitchen the constable found crocks of salted mutton and suet, a piece of boiled meat and the remains of a mutton pudding. How could an unemployed man like Heasman afford meat in such quantity? He was arrested and taken to Lewes Gaol for questioning. Heasman, who had a wife, four children under 10 and an old mother, knew that he would be found guilty and transported and he would be unlikely to see any of them again. In turning 'approver' and earning immunity, he implicated several others in his offences.

Over the next two weeks Heasman made fourteen statements, confessing to fifteen thefts of sheep, though it is certain that the full tally of his offences was never conceded. In November 1839 the half-dozen 'Barcombe Gang of sheepstealers', all save one unemployed farm labourers, went on trial at Lewes Quarter Sessions. One, John Jenner, pleaded guilty to four offences, presumably in the expectation that he would be leniently treated. The others pleaded 'not guilty'.

A search of James Towner's house had led to the discovery of a piece of mutton. But Towner said that he was frightened of Heasman. 'If he knew of anyone saying anything against him or trying to hurt him,' Towner later told the court, 'he would hurt them in any kind of way by poisoning their Hog if they had one or destroy their Bees for he would have his revenge.'

Four men were found 'not guilty', but Towner and Jenner, both family men, were sentenced to transportation. Jenner ended up in New South Wales but Towner served his time in the hulks at Gosport, from where he was released in 1845.

1795 'As a chimney sweeper's boy was ascending a flue belonging to the country house of Mr Molineux of Lewes, he stuck by the way, and was so tightly jammed in that it was found necessary to cut away the chimney in order to extricate him from his perilous situation.' The *Sussex Advertiser* seems little concerned that other children stuck up chimneys had not been so fortunate. **17 OCTOBER**

1957 Detective Sergeant Trevor Heath of Brighton CID was arrested for trying to extort £50 from a known criminal. Days later came the arrests of Detective Inspector John Hammersley, second in charge of CID, along with Anthony Lyons, manager of Sherry's Bar, and the Chief Constable himself, Charles Ridge. Some weeks later Sammy Bellson, bookmaker and club owner, was arrested. All five were charged with conspiring 'to obstruct the course of public justice in that Heath, Hammersley and Ridge acted contrary to their public duty as police officers in relation to the administration of the law'. **18 OCTOBER**

A chimney boy, c. 1840. (*Author's collection*)

Among the witnesses for the prosecution at the Central Criminal Court in February 1958 were a housebreaker/pimp, an abortionist and a receiver of stolen goods. They gave accounts of charges against them being dropped in return for money. The dealer in stolen goods had been told not to receive anything stolen in Brighton but he could deal in items stolen outside the town. Police warned him against certain 'iffy' goods.

Hammersley and Heath were each sentenced to five years' imprisonment. Mr Justice Donovan observed, 'Neither of you had that professional and moral leadership which both of you should have had and were entitled to expect from the Chief Constable of Brighton, now acquitted.' Bellson received three years. Lyons and Ridge were acquitted. However, now within a year or two of retirement, Ridge was immediately dismissed by the Watch Committee which stated that he had been negligent in the discharge of his duty.

19 OCTOBER **1841** The Revd Richard Burnett, chaplain at Lewes House of Correction, presented a report to the newly formed Constabulary Committee. The report is full of detail about conditions in the prison; it contains shrewd and humane observations alongside detailed statistical tables of the kinds of offences that prisoners had committed. Burnett points out that the arrival of navvies working on the London to Brighton railway line introduced serious problems for people in the localities where the men worked. He writes:

> These stupendous works, here and elsewhere, have raised up and daily accumulate in the country, a very extraordinary body of men; to which, in my humble opinion, too much attention cannot be directed, whether by the moralist or the political economist. Drawn together from all parts by thousands – most of them men of prodigious strength, violent passions, and ignorant to a fearful and almost incredible degree – separated from the kindly influence of family and friends and from the usage of civilised life – having no home but the public house by day, and a barn or shed or temporary hut, in which several are packed together by night – having no other pastime, after their hard toil, than drunkenness and fighting, for which their large earnings furnish them but too abundant stimulus – enjoying little or nothing of a Sabbath either in body or soul; as appears from most with whom I have conversed – and all this carried on for 5, 6 and more years, with a large proportion of the number – they are literally a mass of heathens, in the bosom of a Christian land.

In an attempt to explain to the Committee 'the attitude of the criminal classes', Burnett included three interviews with prisoners. One of his interviewees, a burglar, told him:

> When we committed the robbery at —, we took a loaded pistol with us; we sold all the silver to a man with a dog-cart. When we broke into — we brought a loaded gun and M— loaded another which we got there and held it ready. He said, 'Mind, if anybody comes, my life is as sweet

as theirs.' About the time the New Police was talked of, he said to me: 'If these police come we shall be done, for if we steal anything we can't carry it home.' After we attacked the toll-house at — with bats and masked, — who was taken and afterwards transported for it, sent us word that unless we did something for him, he would split and betray us. So we had to break into a mill. All the flour we took we sold for 4 guineas which went to get him a counsel.

1850 The newspapers of the time were never hesitant in describing in the most disapproving terms those charged of serious crimes, often before they were found guilty. Three members of the Isaacs gang, active in Sussex and Surrey, appeared before the magistrates at Guildford for the murder of a clergyman in Surrey, and the local press had no hesitation in implying their guilt from their features. The gang had committed violent burglaries at Kirdford, Upper Dicker and Uckfield. From time to time gang members lived in tents on Copthorne Common. They were men who led brutal lives, a shiftless crew, a gallery of reckless rogues, each seeming to match his neighbour in viciousness. They had little fear, less shame. 20 OCTOBER

Richard Trowler, alias Hiram Smith, at 25 years of age had 'the slight, active figure of the accomplished burglar with a cast of countenance at once cunning, cowardly and cruel'. Son of a transportee, a pot boy in a pub at the age of 18, Trowler had taken up with a band of tramping hawkers, those habitual rural nomads, not quite traditional vagrants, but men who might do occasional odd jobs and commit occasional crimes. At this trial, to save his skin, he appeared as a prosecution witness. 'Hiram Smith', we read, 'is about the middle height with narrow contracted shoulders and a stooping figure. His face is extremely forbidding in expression, the features having that sharp prominent character which marks the rogue while the doubtful and hesitating glance of the eye indicates a disposition at once cunning and irresolute.'

Only four years older than Hiram Smith, Levi Harwood at 29 was an even more fearsome-looking character. 'Levi Harwood is a ruffianly looking man, square built and evidently possessing considerable physical strength. His features are coarse and rugged and his face betrays the mastery of violent passions. He looks like one of those idle fellows, half-hostlers, half anything else, who are seen loitering about country inns and waiting for any job that may turn up for them.'

The third man is hardly more appealing. 'James Jones is also about the middle size, his features flat and repulsive and his whole physiognomy expressive of a life of depravity and crime. Both he and Levi Harwood look like bold determined fellows, capable of carrying through any deed of violence they may once have undertaken.'

Levi Harwood and James Jones were hanged for the murder of the Revd Mr Hollest at Frimley.

1891 In the evening there was a serious disturbance at Eastbourne. The Salvationists there were accompanied on their Wednesday evening march by thousands of people, many of them members of the so-called 'Skeleton Army'. 21 OCTOBER

Eastbourne Salvation Army band, 1891. *(Eastbourne Citadel Centenary Brochure)*

With their usual bully-boy tactics they jeered the Salvationists, who marched as ever at a deliberately snail-like pace as they prayed and sang and exhorted bystanders to mend their ways. On this occasion the 'Skeletons' attacked the parade, destroying instruments and tearing up banners. Innocent people were knocked over in the rush and several were hurt. The Salvationists finally escaped and found refuge in the Citadel while the violent mob outside bayed, throwing stones and breaking windows. Bandsman Walter Guy, then 19 years old, recalled how the Salvationists were regularly received in those days when they marched through the town. 'The cursing and swearing, boos, hoots, whistles, coupled with flour, rotten eggs, fish gut, rotten fruit and vegetables, and many more dirty things were thrown at us.'

It was suggested that the cause of the disturbance was that General Bramwell Booth, founder of the Salvation Army, had been present at the Citadel earlier in the day but it did not require his presence to initiate attacks against his followers. Earlier in the year Mayor William Epps Morrison, had declared that the Council would do all in its power 'to put down the Salvation

Army business which was opposed altogether to the spirit of town religion'. The Salvation Army in the eyes of many represented 'the rough world'. Why were they in Eastbourne? The Army's work was among the slums, so they claimed, and there were no slums in Eastbourne. And it was not simply the Mayor or councillors who resented the Salvationists' presence. Some otherwise respectable working men resented them. They had no wish to be associated with the reformed down-at-heel drunks, the born-again former

The storming of the Eastbourne Citadel. (*Eastbourne Citadel Centenary Brochure*)

Salvationists released from Lewes Gaol. *(Eastbourne Citadel Centenary Brochure)*

louts and layabouts, this world's flotsam and jetsam redeemed, the lowest orders, the feckless, the least prepossessing elements of society, all of them now saved. The Council, said the Mayor, would call on the support of the Skeleton Army to help it if need be.

Earlier that year Captain Bob Bell and four band members had been found guilty of 'marching with music' and fined £5 with the alternative of one month's imprisonment, which they served. Over the years sixteen members of the Eastbourne Citadel were imprisoned, either for singing in the streets or 'marching with music'.

22 OCTOBER **1850** *The Times* intones sombrely: 'There is a criminal population dispersed throughout the land – a caste apart which daily and hourly recruits its ranks from all that is most idle, dissolute and unprincipled among us.'

1841 'For several weeks past,' says the *Brighton Guardian*, 'an enquiry of the most searching character has been carrying on by the Magistrates of the Lewes Bench and the police under the direction of Superintendent Fagan into the circumstances of the death of a woman named Smith, an itinerant dealer in tapes, laces, children's trinkets etc., who was pursuing her vocation at Ringmer on the 2nd June 1838, upwards of three years ago, and was next day found drowned in a pond near the Rectory. An open verdict of "found drowned" was returned. It had long been suspected that there had been some foul play in this mysterious affair and certain facts having come to the knowledge of the police, a man named General Washer, aged about 60 years of age, was apprehended on Monday, the 11th inst., on a charge of having murdered the poor woman.'

General Washer was a farm labourer who was arrested but later discharged. Three other village lads who, late in the evening, had had 'connexion' with Hannah Smith who had been drinking all day, were brought to trial. They were investigated and in March 1842 were found guilty of stealing her property, but the conclusion was that, still drunk, she had staggered into the pond after they had left her.

Ringmer Rectory, drawn by John Harding.
(*John Harding*)

J.P.H.

24 OCTOBER   **1933** Chichester magistrates heard the story of Rex, the lion on the loose, a danger to all and a ravening beast which had already killed a sheep at Clymping. When a van conveying wild animals from Butlin's Zoo at Skegness to Bognor Zoo arrived at its destination, the driver discovered that there was a damaged crate with no animal in it. Campers in the area had abandoned their tents and had sought more secure accommodation. Some locals spoke of having rifles at the ready. Mothers and fathers had feared for their children, their dogs, their cats.

But finally the matter came to court. There was no escaped lion. There never had been an escaped lion. But the savaged sheep? The story was disentangled months later at the Assizes when Billy Butlin and his manager were acquitted of setting up a publicity stunt. A local reporter, Alan Proctor from Bognor, sensing a good story, had persuaded a farmer from Pagham, John Wensley, to put a sheep's carcass, suitably mauled, in the bottom of a hedge. It made good copy. Both men were fined for creating a public nuisance.

25 OCTOBER   **1830** One of the Earl of Sheffield's servants picked up an unsealed letter in the park and handed it on to the coachman. The coachman, having read it, gave it to the steward, who in turn handed the letter to his lordship. It read: 'Please, my lord, I don't wish to hurt you. This is the case all the world over. If you don't get rid of your foreign steward, and the farmer, and bailiff, in a few days time – less than a month – we will burn him up, and you along with him. My writing is bad, but my firing is good, my lord.'

Three weeks later Thomas Brown, a 17-year-old labourer, was taken into custody. He was obviously terrified for this was a capital offence. He blurted out to the constable that he was sorry for what he had done. Somebody else had persuaded him to do it. On the way to Lewes Gaol in a cart, the boy told another constable that if he had not been persuaded he would not have been 'in this mess'. He said it was all the fault of the Millers, Young Will and Old Will. The young Miller was the worst, Brown said, because Lord Sheffield had always been good to him and he had no reason to threaten him. Old Will, on the other hand, had been dismissed by Lord Sheffield and he was resentful. They had asked him to write the letter because neither of them could write.

At Brown's trial witnesses came forward to say that he had always had a good character. Possibly it was this which saved him from hanging: instead, he was transported for life.

26 OCTOBER   **1942** In the early hours of the afternoon a single German bomber, its guns firing, flew over Eastbourne from west to east. It dropped four high-explosive bombs, one of them, a direct hit, killing three adults and a 14-year-old boy in Willoughby Crescent. In their home in Seaside a mother and her two children, a 10-year-old girl and a 5-year-old boy, were also killed. A bus driver was another victim of the raid. Twenty nine other people were injured, seven of them, including a 15-year-old girl and a 13-year-old boy, fatally. This was not the town's worst air raid but it was perhaps typical of the random nature in which civilian populations were visited with death.

1858 Georgiana Noldrett, 'a rather handsome looking' 18-year-old, left her
home in Chichester to stay with her aunt in Southwick. Her aunt soon concluded
that the girl was pregnant but Georgiana explained that she was suffering from
dropsy. After some days and a bout of illness Georgiana told her aunt that she
intended to go home. Her aunt offered to send for a doctor but Georgiana rejected
the idea and said she would return to Chichester the following day. After breakfast
Georgiana left in a horse and cart but her appearance had worried the old woman
who sent for the police. The body of a full-term baby girl was found in the water-
closet. There was a tightly drawn ribbon round the baby's neck, two deep cuts on
the throat, a bruise on the head and seventeen cuts on the body. Dr Fuller who
examined the body was unable to say if the infant had ever had an independent
existence and therefore there was no legal proof that she had been born alive.
The defence argued that the injuries were the result of 'an unhappy young
creature' delivering her own child. The jury returned a verdict of guilty to a
misdemeanour 'in concealing the birth of the child'. Georgiana was sentenced
to fifteen months' imprisonment with hard labour.

1795 Another sad tale comes from the *Sussex Advertiser*: 'As a poor man was
driving his cart from Brighton to Shoreham under the Cliffe, at the time the
tide was making, the rise of water rendered the road . . . near Copperas Gap, so
difficult, that he mistook it and was, with his horse, unfortunately drowned. The
body was soon afterwards found and carried into Portslade Church to be owned.
Later the body of a man much mangled, having no head, and the calves of his
legs apparently eaten off, was driven on shore by the tide, a little eastward of the
town of Brighthelmston. It was taken up and buried on the beach.'

1823 As the hearing into the bankruptcy of Mr Andrews of Brighton proceeded,
the reasons for his financial difficulties were revealed. When his wife had gone on a
fortnight's visit to relations in Pulborough, he had been visited at his Edward Street
home by a succession of women, 'with whom he had shared his bed, and who, of
course, had possessed some claims on his generosity'. There were perhaps ten or
a dozen of these visitors though Mr Andrews was never specific on this. The ladies
were not common prostitutes, he said, but he could not say whether they were
married or not. He assured the court that they were all very fine women. Andrews
told how they used sometimes to throw gravel up at his bedroom window and how
he would go down and let them in. He could not remember if he burnt a rushlight
in his window as a kind of signal of his availability. The servant usually made his
bed though there were occasions when he made it himself so that she would not
realise that two persons had slept in it. As for payment, he was never very liberal:
they seem to have been satisfied with trifling sums. When Andrews had moved
from Edward Street to West Street, some of the women used to call upon him for
money and he was generous then because he was afraid that his wife might hear
what he had been up to. Finally he admitted that he frequently gave the women
two or three sovereigns at a time and over the period as much as £100, equivalent
to £6,000 today.

1823 Here, the *Sussex Advertiser* illustrates that hooliganism is restricted
neither to the present century nor to poorer people:

Captain Molineux and several others figured in another disturbance when on leaving the York Hotel in the Steine between 2 and 3 a.m., and finding an empty fly belonging to a man of the name of Vaughan they shoved it over and broke the glass frame, and assaulted the man with sticks and knocked in the crown of his hat kicking him at the same time. They got away but Vaughan followed them and, meeting with a watchman, gave them in charge. The Captain retorted by giving Vaughan in charge, and both parties agreed to go to the town hall to settle the matter. On the way thither Capt Molineux swore he would knock the watchman down if he suffered the fly man to speak. When they got about opposite the bottom of Church Street Capt Molineux and his party ran away and effected their escape, the watchman being unfortunately unprovided with a rattle.

31 OCTOBER **1928** Marie Jacquin, a 21-year-old French girl, called on Edwin Paxton and demanded £10,000 from him, threatening him with a loaded revolver. This bizarre event was later unravelled at the Assizes.

Paxton, a single man, lived alone in a flat in Bexhill. The previous year Jacquin, working in Bexhill as a governess, had attracted his attention by throwing a note in his car inviting him to go out with her. Perhaps he treated it as a joke but they did meet on a regular basis. According to the court report 'friendly relations started' and in September 1927 Jacquin went to live in the flat as Paxton's housekeeper. In the following February she returned to France. In March Jacquin returned to Bexhill but not to the flat. Paxton paid for her to stay in digs. In July Paxton gave her £1,000 in return for her promise not to molest or annoy him and to go back to France. What had been happening? There is a vagueness about what exactly occurred during this period, which the judge commented on in the later court case.

When she turned up yet again at Paxton's flat he had let her in. They talked for a while, then she had asked him, 'Do you know why I am here?' 'No,' he had answered. 'Well, you will know in about five minutes' time.' At which point she opened the flat door and introduced a Frenchman. Now she took out the revolver. 'If you do not pay me £10,000 in ten minutes I will shoot you,' she told him. Did she think that Paxton had that amount of cash in the flat? After three hours of apparent bargaining with no progress being made, Paxton said that he must go down to his car in the street and put it in the garage. The three of them went down into the street where Paxton seized his chance and dashed off to the police station.

When Jacquin was arrested she claimed that the gun was not hers. Paxton had put it in her hand when they were in the street, she said. They had had an argument when she went to the flat. She said he had asked her to bring him £3,000 worth of cocaine from France.

Marie Jacquin was found guilty of demanding £10,000 with menaces and sentenced to a surprisingly light twelve months' imprisonment with hard labour. It is as strange a case to us as it was to the judge who commented as he passed sentence: 'I cannot help feeling that there was a vein of silliness and theatricality at the back of this proceeding which justifies me in taking a more lenient course.' Was he implying that there was something about Paxton's part in the matter which was also suspect?

NOVEMBER

Hastings Police, 1854. *(Hastings Reference Library)*

1 NOVEMBER   **1764** Thomas Turner writes in his diary: 'I this day heard the melancholy news of the death of my old acquaintance and worthy friend John Lang, who died a-Monday last of the smallpox under inoculation; a very sober and worthy young man, but from a bad constitution had the smallpox excessively full, which proved mortal.'

2 NOVEMBER   **1795** The *Sussex Advertiser*, like most newspapers of the period, always welcomed items about the gruesome and the bizarre. And if both qualities were present so much the better. 'About 7 o'clock on Saturday morning the garden wall of Mr Osborn of Poynings was blown down by the high wind and unfortunately just as a poor woman named Marshall was passing it she was buried in the ruins and dug out with her back broken. She survived only a few hours and then expired in great agony.'

3 NOVEMBER   **1899** On a wild night of rain and wind Westhampnett Place, an elegant Elizabethan building, then in use as a workhouse, went up in flames. There were 115 men and women sleeping in, and of these more than half, 'mostly poor people of the feeblest condition', were in the infirmaries. The Master and the Matron, alerted to the situation, organised the escape. Two nurses cleared the female dormitories. Many of the aged inmates were terrified of using the fire escape in the gale-force wind and had to be helped every step of the way down to the ground. In the women's infirmary some patients, bedfast and wrapped in blankets, were carried down the fire escape. One of the able-bodied inmates, William Waller, recalled: 'I jumps out of bed and gets the boys up.' He led them through the men's infirmary and took them to the ground by the recently installed fire escape at the front of the building. He then returned to help the escape of the women in the infirmary. There was one casualty; a frail old man collapsed and died.

But while the patients were ushered to safety, there was insufficient manpower to save the building from the flames. When the fire brigade arrived from Chichester the water tanks ran out of water. In the previous year the

After the fire at Westhampnett. *(West Sussex Record Office)*

Guardians had decided, in the interest of the ratepayers, not to connect the water supply to the mains. One witness recalled the wretched scene. 'It was a sorrowful sight to see the poor creatures being carried to conveyances, some of them saying, "I shall never see the Caroline Ward again."' Very evidently some had a sincere affection for Westhampnett Place but it never reopened as a workhouse. Grossly underinsured, it could not be rebuilt.

1830 At Brede farm labourers decided to take action against Mr Abel, one of the overseers of the poor. He was intensely disliked by many of the poor, because in fulfilling his obligations to the ratepayers he frequently escorted paupers not born in the parish over the parish boundary. He used the parish cart for their few belongings but once over the boundary, his work was over, the rate burden reduced, and the paupers were now abandoned, left often in parishes which would also move them on.

4 November

The following day the Brede men met local farmers and the vicar at the Red Lion where two resolutions were agreed. The first promised substantial increases in wages, a promise never realised. The second resolution read: 'The poor are determined to take the present overseer, Mr Abell [sic], out of the parish to any adjoining parish and to use him with civility.' Abel was placed in the cart with exaggerated ceremony and escorted out of the parish by a crowd of jeering labourers. Other parishes meted out similar treatment to their overseers.

1817 The Brighton Town Commissioners had posted public notices warning inhabitants not to celebrate the anniversary of the Gunpowder Plot with fireworks. This seems to have had no effect because in the evening a crowd assembled in the Steine and set off their crackers. The High Constable, John Williams – in effect the police chief – took some of the ringleaders into custody. In the course of the evening there was a struggle between the mob and the High Constable's men over a burning tar barrel which was finally extinguished. Now thoroughly roused, the crowd made its way to Williams's house and his windows were smashed and it seemed that even greater violence would follow. At this point several companies of the 21st Regiment of Fusiliers came on the scene, bayonets fixed. Then the Riot Act was read out and suddenly peace prevailed. But by now the damage had been done. Some few had received injuries in the struggle, but none so seriously as John Rowles, who had been discharging his duties as a peace officer. Quite accidentally a bayonet had pierced and passed through his body, just above the hip. Rowles died from the wound. The authorities were held responsible for what had happened. They, after all, had called in the military. John Williams and two others appeared at Horsham Assizes, charged with 'Wilful Murder'. Fortunately they were found not guilty.

5 November

1779 It is odd that in such a naturally boisterous age, the *Sussex Advertiser* should seem to disapprove of the Bonfire Night proceedings:

6 November

Last Tuesday evening proving wet, the anniversary of The Powder Plot was commemorated in the Cliffe, on Wednesday evening, when some mischievous person fixed a lighted squib to the waistcoat of a lad named Fowle, whereby he was so dreadfully burnt, that he now lies in a distressing, if not dangerous state.

On the same evening a number of lighted squibs were cowardly thrown at a poor, defenceless servant girl, who in consequence had her gown (which she could ill afford the loss of) burnt from her back, and her person placed under such alarm and fear that she was for some hours after in hysteric fits.

7 NOVEMBER

1887 The Master of Alfriston school notes in the logbook that 'Several children are absent this morning from illness among whom may be mentioned – Maud, Ernest and Minnie Whymark, Kate and Wm Norman, Alice Gatland, Arthur Cole, Charley Pettitt, Ellen Marchant, Ruth Russell and Edith Teague. The illness consists of a "breaking out" upon the face and head.'

8 NOVEMBER

1933 Only days after they met, Albert Probert from Hove and Fred Parker, a Dover man, both of them in their twenties, took lodgings in Portslade. Neither man was in employment and they spent the next few days touting sweepstake draw tickets round the locality. On the night of 13 November they broke into 80-year-old Joseph Bedford's junk shop and emptied two cash boxes, one of which held silver and coppers and the other farthings. What they stole would be worth £250 today. Parker was armed with a revolver which, he always maintained, he thought was unloaded. Probert carried a tyre lever. In the course of the robbery the old man was savagely battered almost beyond recognition.

The execution of Parker and Probert at Wandsworth. (*Illustrated Police News*)

Straight after the robbery the two men went off to Worthing, finding rather better digs. The next morning they bought new suits. Call it a hunch but a policeman on duty felt instinctively uneasy about the two men when he saw them in the High Street. Perhaps it was the very newness of their clothes which alerted him. After all, in the Depression most young men could not afford to buy new clothing.

The two men were taken to the police station for questioning. In Parker's pockets the police found twenty-seven farthings. Strange, because even then farthings were of little value. Parker was weak, and under pressure he admitted that in the course of a shop robbery in Portslade they had knocked out an old man. At that moment he was unaware that Joseph Bedford had just died in Hove hospital. From this point the fate of Parker and Probert was sealed. Although Probert came out with an ingenious alibi at the last moment, the jury at the Assizes were not convinced about his story. Both men were hanged at Wandsworth on 4 May 1934.

1872 George Dadswell, a 25-year-old labourer, was brought before the   9 NOVEMBER
magistrates charged with 'attempting to destroy himself by laying himself
across the metals of the Railway at Jarvis Brook, Rotherfield, on 7th
November, 1872'. At the next Assizes he was sentenced to one month's hard
labour.

1883 David Laurence held two significant positions in his community.   10 NOVEMBER
He was the Assistant Overseer of the Poor, and Treasurer of Winchelsea
Corporation. Only a man of the greatest integrity would be entrusted with
such posts but David's father was one of the two Overseers of the Poor and
it seems that there was a family tradition of public service. And he was
such a reliable man, a carpenter, a craftsman, married with two young
children. But at the inquest on his death surprising facts emerged.

The auditor had arranged the annual examination at Rye of the
financial records of all of the associated parishes on Friday 9 November.
Shortly after noon George Laurence, the father of David, in company
with the other overseer, called at David's house. The idea was that they
would go to Rye together. But David was not at home and his wife was
equally puzzled as to his whereabouts. After searching for him in vain,
the two older men decided to leave for Rye without him. They took with
them the books, which they found in David's house, hoping that he
would catch them up later.

At Rye, however, there was bad news. The auditor detected a shortfall of
£100 in the accounts, an amount equivalent today to about £6,000. But in
David's absence there was no point in the auditor pursuing the matter. The
two overseers returned to Winchelsea, no doubt persuading themselves that
there must be some explanation for the missing money and for the missing
David. His father found him in the garden shed, hanging from the rafters. The
jury came to the kindest possible conclusion that 'not being of sound mind he
killed himself by hanging'.

But why did a decent, hardworking man like David Laurence, that least likely
of men to commit a theft, resort to such a crime? The question seems not to
have been answered.

1877 Thomas Geering in *Our Sussex Parish* writes of the gale which blew   11 NOVEMBER
down Windo'or windmill near Wilmington: 'Twice I have seen her in
flames and for that the last time. She will never now be rebuilt. The latter
mishap was brought about by a strong sou'wester in the night. The break
failing in its grip, away went mill and all to destruction. I opened my eyes
at about 6 a.m. to see one of my oldest acquaintances expire in flames,
leaving only a lifeless lump to mark the spot where all my days I had
seen the sweeps swing round in merry mood.' Although Geering offers no

precise date, the storm of the night of 11/12 November is recorded in the national and local newspapers. 'Experienced sailors', according to *The Times*, 'describe the violence of the storm as something altogether exceptional; certainly we have not for years had anything like it on this part of the [south] coast.'

12 NOVEMBER   **1909** A painter, Charles Cohen, faced charges of abducting Amelia Kapinsky, a 16-year-old Russian, taking her with him to Blackpool to work as a prostitute. The girl had thought that they were going to London but once on the train he told her their true destination.

At one point, at Preston she thought, they got out of the train and found a tall German to whom Cohen had previously introduced her in Brighton and another man called Stephens. Here Cohen left the three who went on to Blackpool where Amelia was taken to meet a middle-aged man. Stephens told her that if she stayed with this man she would be given a present. She was then seduced and afterwards worked as a prostitute, handing over £10 to £15 each week to Stephens. After she refused to steal from one of her clients she was beaten by Stephens and so she ran away from Blackpool. Cohen, who had a previous conviction for a similar offence, was sentenced to eighteen months' imprisonment with hard labour.

13 NOVEMBER   **1825** In the course of his *Rural Rides* through the southern counties William Cobbett, the radical journalist and polemicist, met a young farm worker at Rogate. Like many unmarried young men he had found it hard to find work because farmers, anxious not to raise the Poor Rate too high, preferred to employ married men with families. So it was that many young men found themselves out of work, existing on handouts from the Overseers of the Poor. Cobbett writes: 'Here, in this part of Sussex, they give a single man seven pence a day, that is to say, enough to buy two pounds and a quarter of bread for six days in the week, and as he does not work on Sunday, there is no seven pence allowed for the Sunday, and of course nothing to eat . . . the poor creature here has seven pence a day for six days in the week to find him food, clothes, washing and lodging!'

14 NOVEMBER   **1790** 'A fellow named Tyler who lodged at the George Inn, Burpham, found means to steal thereout a quantity of plate, belonging to the landlord; and some money from the pockets of two men who were sleeping in a room adjoining to his apartment, and got off undiscovered; but not content with this booty, he, a few hours after, stole a horse, the property of Mr c. Elliot of Arundel; but having the folly and assurance to call up a saddler about three o'clock the next morning to purchase a saddle for his stolen horse, he was by means thereof detected and secured. He was fully committed to Horsham Gaol to take his trial at the next assizes.'

Another example from the *Sussex Advertiser* of a less than bright criminal.

The George Inn,
Burpham.
(Alan Skinner)

1821 The celebrated surgeon and palaeontologist, Gideon Mantell from Lewes, wrote in his journal: 'Was called to a most distressing accident at Chailey Mill. A poor boy by some accident got his clothes entangled by an upright post that was rapidly revolving; the lad in consequence was whirled round with great velocity, and his legs were dashed against a beam; the consequence was a separation of the left tibia from its articulation at the knee joint and the laceration of the whole muscles of that leg: on the right side the femur was knocked away from its epiphysis, and projected between the muscles of the ham; but in both instances the joint of the knees remained perfect and uninjured. It was considered absolutely necessary to amputate the left leg above the knee: the right femur was reduced and kept in its place by appropriate compresses; but the constitutional shock was so great that the boy died the next day.'

15 NOVEMBER

Dr Gideon
Algernon Mantell.
(SCM)

This, of course, was in the days before anaesthetics.

1918 Only days after the armistice was declared an inquest jury at Eastbourne considered the death in a local military hospital of Private Hugh Hamill, who had been hit by the propeller of an aircraft he was preparing for take-off. He

16 NOVEMBER

was just about to spin the propeller when, seemingly of its own volition, it turned and hit him with such force that it disintegrated. After the accident the aircraft was checked but there were no indications of electrical or mechanical faults. The jury found that the accident, which could not be explained, was unavoidable.

17 NOVEMBER 1838 'Sir, I am requested by the Guardians of this Union to report to the Poor Law Commissioners that they have admitted into the workhouse the eldest child of Jonathan Carpenter, a pauper belonging to the parish of Eastbourne. It appears that Carpenter only earns 12 shillings a week and he has himself, wife and seven children to maintain. The Guardians, feeling that it was absolutely impossible that the whole of this family could be supported by the parent, have adopted the course above mentioned.'

18 NOVEMBER 1839 'Stunt said that himself, John Wood and Marchant went to Hawkhurst to the house of Mr. Lavender where they took out a square of glass, unfastened the window, and got in. They took a great many articles, and among them a desk, a gun, a cloak, and about 12oz. of silver. They brought them all to Jack Wood's and in a few days they started with them for Brighton. Wood carried the gun and offered it for sale as he went along at a blacksmith's shop on Meckham [Magham] Down. They then went on to Brighton and pawned it. The silver was sold and Wood said it went to London that night.'

Here the *Brighton Guardian* is describing a quite slick operation. The gang had transport for heavy items, a place to hide their haul for a few days and knew where to get rid of what they had stolen.

19 NOVEMBER 1836 A violent rainstorm swept the county, resulting in widespread damage. One witness records, 'Buildings were unroofed, trees torn up by their roots, barns, churches and many other structures blown down.' On this occasion the roof of Hailsham church was blown away leaving just bare rafters.

20 NOVEMBER 1797 'Yesterday se'nnight a poor woman named Putland, of Jevington, dropt down in a fit, whilst pursuing a pig, which had got into her garden, and instantly expired.' Brief but graphic – another triumph for the *Sussex Advertiser*.

21 NOVEMBER 1884 The Master of Rottingdean junior school has a sad entry for his logbook: 'On Wednesday the teacher received information that the boy SEALE had died the night before in the hospital from Diphtheria. This is the 4th death in that family in 12 days.' Children at every school throughout the period suffered from bronchitis, scarlet fever, measles, ague, typhoid fever, chicken pox, ringworm, mumps, whooping cough, chilblains, carbuncles, boils, smallpox and sometimes 'breaking out' on the face.

22 NOVEMBER 1935 At a hearing before Worthing magistrates, George Smith, 32, a bricklayer of no fixed abode, was charged with attacking a school teacher, referred to as

Miss X, on the downs near Chanctonbury Ring in October. At the next Assizes Smith was found guilty and it was revealed that he had a long criminal record for larceny, housebreaking and assault on a woman. He received the maximum sentence for this offence – two years' hard labour. The judge regretted that the sentence was totally inadequate.

1860 *The Lancet* published a letter from an unnamed gentleman who had   23 NOVEMBER
two months earlier bought a house 'in one of those fine eastern terraces facing the sea at Kemp Town, Brighton'. Shortly after moving in he became 'annoyed by a foul effluvia from the drains and soon afterwards the cook was prostrated with fever, and confined to her bed during a space of ten days. My children and servants sickened in succession and were attacked with headache, sickness and febrile derangements, clearly attributable to poisonous atmospheric agency. Examination showed that the drainage of the house was wretchedly imperfect. My youngest child did not, unhappily, escape so lightly as the rest of my household, and I have just brought her back to London, suffering from a most severe form of diphtheria which, I need not tell your readers, arises almost invariably from bad drainage.'

The writer had no luck when he approached the town council. There was no officer responsible for public health matters and the town council had done nothing to remedy the objectionable state of the drainage, even though it had been urged to do so on many occasions. Even the Board of Health in London, though aware of Brighton's drainage problems, had no jurisdiction over the town council.

The writer quoted a recent report by the Registrar General which said 'the mortality in many of the towns has been excessively high, and this has been notably the case in Brighton. To take one instance, the deaths (386) exceeded the births (377) in St Peter's, Brighton.' The report added that 'the inhabitants of this sub-district are chiefly artisans, mechanics and the labouring poor. In many of their dwellings, a very insufficient supply of water has been available to them, owing to the dryness of the weather in the first portion of the quarter, the water in the wells in use having been very low. There is no effectual drainage attached to their dwellings, and the cesspool system is in general use.'

1845 At 3 a.m. Thomas Denyer, the head gamekeeper on the Barkfold   24 NOVEMBER
Estate at Kirdford, woke up one of his assistants, William Puttick, to tell him there were poachers about. He had heard shots. The two men went down to Jacksland where they came across four men in the wood. 'Go to work,' one of them called out. 'There are only two of them.' Nevertheless, when the keepers approached them the men retreated into a meadow where there was a scuffle. A shot was fired. Denyer was struck so severely with the rifle of another of the gang that it smashed. Denyer now feared that his life was in danger and fired at one of his assailants, Ben Remnant. The next day Remnant, a confirmed poacher, died of his injuries, but before he did so he confessed that if his gun had not jammed he would have shot Denyer.

At the inquest the jury found Denyer guilty of manslaughter, a verdict which was reversed at the Assizes the following March.

25 NOVEMBER **1872** John Coker Egerton, rector of Burwash, writes in his diary: 'Poor Mrs J. Sinden died last night of typhus fever, a victim I believe, to cesspools, drains and bad smells.'

26 NOVEMBER **1871** At about 1 o'clock on a bright moonlit night brothers James and Daniel Deadman, both of them gamekeepers on Blackdown Mount, encountered five poachers armed with rifles. They were first alerted to the poachers' presence when they heard a shot over towards Little Skirmer's Coppice and they went to investigate. They heard voices and another shot and saw the flash of a gun.

A poaching affray. *(Courtesy of the Neil Storey Archive)*

THE FIGHT.

Then there was a set-to when one of the poachers, Sherlock, tackled Daniel Deadman and another poacher, Chandler, struggled with James. During the scuffle the other poachers came on the scene and in the dark one of them, Stoxold, aimed a blow at Sherlock. 'Don't hit me, mate,' Sherlock called out and Stoxold then turned his attention to Daniel, hitting him on the head with the barrel of his rifle. He followed this up with a similar blow to James's head, seriously injuring him. At this point the poachers ran off.

But Stoxold could not keep his night's escapade to himself. Within hours he was relating his tale in the Three Horse Shoes, his local at Lickfold, not far from the scene of the crime. This inevitably led to a prosecution and a sentence of eighteen months' hard labour for Stoxold and twelve months for each of his companions.

1843 For three hours each morning the Eastbourne Self-Supporting Schools taught boys aged around 8 years old reading, writing and arithmetic. In the afternoons they were set to work on plots of approximately 5 acres for every twenty boys. The following schedules offered an example of how the field work was organised:

27 November

Week commencing November 27th, 1843
Monday: Drilling wheat, carrying dung and potatoes with the heifer, one load of each a mile; one cow stall-fed with turnips, mangel wurzel, and straw; one cow and a heifer stall-fed with turnips and straw.

Tuesday: Drilling wheat, carrying dung and potatoes with the heifer, one load of each a mile; one cow stall-fed with turnips, mangel wurzel, and straw; one cow and a heifer stall-fed with turnips and straw.

Wednesday: Drilling wheat, carrying dung with the heifer, one load of each a mile; one cow stall-fed with turnips, potatoes, mangel wurzel, and straw; one cow and a heifer stall-fed with turnips and straw.

Thursday: Drilling wheat, collecting street scrapings, putting 100 gallons of liquid manure to the Italian rye grass, 4 rods; one load of each a mile; one cow stall-fed with turnips, mangel wurzel, and straw; one cow and a heifer stall-fed with turnips and straw.

Friday: Drilling wheat, carrying 18 loads of dung on to the land with the heifer, and laying two lumps in each load, putting 36 gallons of liquid manure to the rye, 2 rods; one cow stall-fed with turnips, potatoes, mangel wurzel, and straw; one cow and a heifer stall-fed with turnips and straw.

Week commencing December 4th, 1843
Monday: 15 boys to the school; digging the oats stubble, and some picking off the roots and hoeing before the boys on the same ground.

Tuesday: Boys digging up the mangel wurzel, some cutting the tops from them, and some carrying them to the pigs and sows, small ones picking stones.

Wednesday: Boys emptying the tanks from the pigsties, some digging the ground for tares, some sowing of tares, and some picking off the roots.

Thursday: A wet day thrashing [sic] wheat over a barrel, and some platting [sic] straws to make hats, mats or baskets.

Friday: Boys getting up to the mangel wurzel, some carrying to the heap to heal them up for the spring, small ones picking off the weeds.

Saturday: Getting up turnips for the cows on Sunday, emptying the portable pails, cleaning out the pigsties, school, and round the building.

28 NOVEMBER

Ye Olde Smugglers Inne, Alfriston. This was once Alfriston's largest private house, belonging to the butcher, Stanton Collins. *(Tony Spencer)*

1831 The *Sussex Advertiser* says that 'The desperate gang of thieves who have so long with impunity infested Alfriston and its neighbourhood are likely, most of them, to be brought to justice. Some men are in custody on a charge of being connected with a gang, one of whom was arrested on passing through Lewes on Saturday night. It is said that some important disclosures have been made, the particulars of which for the ends of justice it may be prudent at present to withhold from the public.'

The gang member arrested in Lewes was Stanton Collins, the Alfriston butcher who for several years had led his younger drinking companions on minor lawbreaking escapades. Collins was transported after his trial for the

theft of three sacks of barley. Other members of the gang were responsible for poaching, sheep stealing, arson and vandalism. One of them, Samuel Thorncraft, was hanged for arson. Only one gang member committed a major crime. Lewis Awcott stole jewellery valued in excess of £200 from a travelling jeweller staying at the George public house. He was transported for seven years. The Huggett brothers, James and John, who were later to face charges of assault and robbery, sheep stealing and animal maiming, were transported for life. William Trigwell must have been artful for he was never charged with anything of consequence: on one occasion he was fined £2 for poaching 'on the hill at Litlington'. As for John Reeds, a serial offender, although found guilty through the years on several charges, he somehow managed to escape transportation.

1747 Only weeks earlier *La Nympha Americana*, an 80-gun ship, had been captured by Commodore Walker from the Spanish off Cadiz. In addition to a cargo of velvets and laces it carried £5,000 in cash and quicksilver valued at £30,000, a total today of £5 million. Now it was being brought to London where captain and crew would share some of the prize money. They were in the Channel when a ferocious storm hit them. The 100-strong crew struggled for hours as the Nympha made for the shelter of Beachy Head, but before it reached its safe haven the ship was smashed against the cliffs of Birling Gap.

29 NOVEMBER

Contemporary woodcut of the plundering of the wrecked La Nympha Americana. *(SCM)*

Thirty sailors were immediately lost and the rest struggled to save themselves.

Scores of people from all parts of the area were alerted to the distressed ship's plight, and came not to rescue the beleaguered mariners but to plunder. Despite the unrelenting storm some waded out through the towering waves and climbed up into the ship. Others robbed the corpses thrown up by the waves on to the snow-covered beach. The ship's liquor store was raided and drunken looters carted off whatever they could lay their hands on. Soldiers were sent for to control the crowds and two looters were shot. But even soldiers joined in the mêlée, helping themselves to what they could. It was a shameful episode in Sussex history, when the lives of more than 100 sailors and looters were lost.

30 NOVEMBER   1885 'The weather very wet – the roads are flooded', writes the Master at East Chiltington CE School, who elsewhere records the usual litany of ailments at his school throughout the year. 'Children unable to come. Floods up the Navigation Lane. Many Scholars still away. Some recovering from sickness. Others falling with a rash.' The Master also mentions that the boys have to bring water to their homes from the well and at least one boy was poorly because of this.

DECEMBER

Christmas Day, 1909, in the female ward at Hastings workhouse. Are they listening to a speech by some local dignitary or taking part in a service of worship? At the back of the hall there are quite obviously well-intentioned citizens in attendance. *(Hastings and St Leonards Pictorial Advertiser/Hastings Reference Library)*

1 DECEMBER **1817** The *Sussex Advertiser* records a very common crime, one for which men and women had been executed only a few years earlier: 'At Battle Fair, on Saturday se'nnight, three persons were taken up on suspicion of circulating counterfeit shillings and sixpences of the late coinage, but nothing being found on them to warrant their detention, they were dismissed. The principal and supposed cashier of this little band had contrived to get off before the others were taken up. Similar frauds were attempted but, we believe, without much success at Hastings Fair on the following Tuesday.'

2 DECEMBER **1815** The *Adamant*, out of Malta and carrying an extremely valuable cargo, struggled for hours up the Channel. Huge seas and powerful winds made her progress slow. The hope was that she might make Newhaven but midnight came and passed and the port was still some distance away. In the next few hours, the vessel foundered on the rocks near enough for the townsfolk, undeterred by the continuing storm, to come out to help themselves to whatever they could. And the word was about – had been for hours – so that men and women from all around the district turned up with baskets and sacks and wagons, seeking their share. But in London, in Lloyd's Coffee House, the underwriters – when they heard of their loss, estimated at £100,000 – determined that something must be done to stop the regular wholesale plunder of wrecks. They sent men from the Bow Street office down to Sussex with orders to pursue the matter rigorously. Armed with writs the 'Runners' entered as many as 200 houses. In Horsham and at the Pelham Arms in Seaford they found sheets of copper. Elsewhere, in Blatchington, Alfriston, Bishopstone and Newhaven, they found more evidence of plunder. Some people, learning of the effectiveness of the search, suddenly recalled that they had property from the *Adamant* and informed the officers.

3 DECEMBER **1821** Farmers met at Lewes to discuss the depressed state of agriculture. At Ringmer twenty-five men were out of work and in Burwash, out of a total population of 1,900, there were 400 unemployed. Wadhurst and neighbouring parishes were similarly affected. One farmer said that matters had reached such a pitch that the poor were threatening the overseers, who sometimes felt themselves to be in danger. Mr Ellman, a prominent farmer from Firle, had seen men employed drawing sand and it was a painful sight. One of the men, the leader, worked with a bell about his neck.

4 DECEMBER **1896** Throughout the day a fierce south-westerly wind whipped up massive waves which constantly buffeted the Brighton Chain Pier. The following day the *Sussex Daily News* reported its last hours. 'When the evening closed in yesterday, the old Pier was standing much as it had done for the last few months, its ancient glory of paint and polish considerably faded and a distinct aspect of dilapidation about its head and its two seaward clumps of piles, which appeared to have derived a considerable tilt from the violence of the south-western gales, and it looked as if another good shove on that side would settle its business once and for all.'

The Chain Pier in 1838. *(SCM)*

After the storm. *(SCM)*

Great crowds braved the weather to see the old structure finally brought down at about 10.30 p.m. by the relentless battering of the sea. 'I saw the middle pile go,' one witness said. 'As it went, the chains sank and disappeared from our view. A moment or so afterwards there was a crackling as of breaking timber and the tower of the first pile fell, as if dragged over by the weight of the chains and the span of the chains connecting it with the land sank right down. The light at the Pier-head remained until the last. After the tower on the first pile had fallen, the light went out almost directly – the fall of the tower and the disappearance of the light were almost simultaneous.'

Thousands of huge timbers, half a ton in weight, crashed on to the beach, smashing fishing boats and bathing machines. Some timbers, driven westward, came up against the West Pier, smashing several of its great supporting columns.

Though neglected in recent years, the pier's passing was deeply felt by many in the town. 'The disappearance was spoken of regretfully,' says the *Sussex Daily News*, 'but a general feeling has found expression that, after all, the famous structure came to no ignoble end. It perished grandly in the storm. It refused to die by inches.'

5 December **1879** In the logbook of Alfriston School the Master indicates the inadequacy of the buildings: 'The children have all worked together, since the cold weather set in, in the Infants Room although little could be done for want of space.'

6 December **1831** It was late in the afternoon, getting dark, and Samuel Wickham, a sailor, walking along the beach at Brighton, had his attention drawn by the squawking of seagulls which were pecking busily at a bundle. When Wickham went closer he realised that it was the body of a woman. He did not stay to investigate but went off to find help. It was totally dark when he returned with three other men and together they placed the body on a hurdle and took it to the Wish Barn. Doubtless the men were chastened for they had recovered the body of a female wearing white stays, a slip and black worsted stockings. But the body had no head and the arms had been cut off at the elbows.

The following day the inquest took place. Mr Boorman who lived in Frederick Gardens, knew of a missing girl, Anna Hobbs, who lived with her brother in Union Street in the Lanes. But he could not be sure that it was Anna Hobbs who lay there in her coffin.

Edward Hobbs, the brother of the missing Anna, was confident that the body was that of his sister, an 18-year-old who was rather stout and only about 5ft in height. She had worn black stockings, just like those on the body now before him. Anna had lived with him and his wife, working as the house servant. On the day she went missing there had been a brief and, according to Edward, quite unimportant disagreement between the two women. Unknown to Edward and his wife, who both believed that she had gone on with her domestic tasks, Anna had left the house and had not been seen since. He had tried to find her and had even posted notices asking for information but none had been forthcoming. Another witness, Mark Jefferey, said that he had seen Anna on the day of her disappearance walking along the road towards Shoreham with a soldier.

Anna was not pregnant and her body bore no other visible injuries. It appeared that she had been dismembered with a knife. While the doctors could not say how she had died they were firmly of the opinion that she had not been long in the water.

The jury returned a verdict of 'Wilful Murder' but no murderer was ever found. Could it have been the soldier seen by Jefferey? But where could a soldier have dismembered a body? Soldiers lived in barracks with no privacy. Could the place of Anna's death have been her brother's house? Had an altercation with her sister-in-law have turned to violence? But perhaps it is unfair to point the finger at people unable to defend themselves.

The head was removed to prevent identification but why, in pre-fingerprint days, were the arms taken off? Was it for the convenience of transporting the corpse, just as John Holloway had done only months earlier with his wife Celia's corpse? The echoes of Holloway are strong here: Holloway's trial was due to begin on 15 December.

This is another of Brighton's horrific tally of murders, little known, but certainly potent in its possibilities.

7 December

1931 At the Assizes Mr Justice Rowlatt expressed the wish that it should be absolutely impossible to embezzle funds from a local or government authority without being found out. An accountant with the Bognor Regis Urban District Council had fraudulently converted to his own use £315 (approximately £14,000 today) belonging to the Council. He was sentenced to six months' imprisonment.

8 December

1829 *The Times* seems not unduly saddened to report that 'an incorrigible poacher was committed to Lewes House of Correction. He has managed his concerns so seasonably that his last 11 Christmas dinners have been taken in the same prison.'

9 December

1906 James Berry, 'the humble instrument of the law in Britain in launching 193 souls into eternity', and now in retirement an ardent evangelist, was in Brighton spreading the word. Since giving up his post

as public hangman he looked back to his experiences on the scaffold as a dreadful dream. Despite the care he took to estimate the necessary length of rope, one miscalculation led to the decapitation of a 15st man. Berry was also the hangman involved in the failed execution of John Lee, 'the man they couldn't hang'. While he believed that one of those he hanged was the authentic Jack the Ripper – a Londoner, John Henry Bury, who paid the penalty at Dundee for murdering his wife – Berry no longer had any faith in the effectiveness of hanging. In his present work, which gave him great happiness, he had made a

James Berry.
(Author's collection)

Above: James Berry's business card. *(Author's collection)*

	SCALE SHOWING THE STRIKING FORCE OF FALLING BODIES AT DIFFERENT DISTANCES.										
Distance Falling in Feet Zero	8 Stone	9 Stone	10 Stone	11 Stone	12 Stone	13 Stone	14 Stone	15 Stone	16 Stone	17 Stone	18 Stone
	Cw. Qr. lb.	Cw. Qr. lb.	Cw. Qr. lb.	Cw. Qr. lb.	Cw. Qr. lb.	Cw. Qr. lb.	Cw. Qr. lb.	Cw. Qr. lb.	Cw. Qr. lb.	Cw. Qr. lb.	Cw. Qr. lb.
1 Ft.	8 0 0	9 0 0	10 0 0	11 0 0	12 0 0	13 0 0	14 0 0	15 0 0	16 0 0	17 0 0	18 0 0
2 „	11 1 15	12 2 23	14 0 14	15 2 4	16 3 22	18 1 12	19 3 2	21 0 21	22 2 11	24 0 1	25 1 19
3 „	13 3 16	15 2 15	17 1 14	19 0 12	20 3 11	22 2 9	24 1 8	26 0 7	27 3 5	29 2 4	31 1 2
4 „	16 0 0	18 0 0	20 0 0	22 0 0	24 0 0	26 0 0	28 0 0	30 0 0	32 0 0	34 0 0	36 0 0
5 „	17 2 11	19 3 5	22 0 0	24 0 22	26 1 16	28 2 11	30 3 5	33 0 0	35 0 22	37 0 16	39 2 11
6 „	19 2 11	22 0 5	24 2 0	26 3 22	29 1 16	31 3 11	34 1 5	36 3 0	39 0 22	41 2 16	44 0 11
7 „	21 0 22	23 3 11	26 2 0	29 0 16	31 3 5	34 1 22	37 0 11	39 3 0	42 1 16	45 0 5	47 2 22
8 „	22 2 22	25 2 4	28 1 14	31 0 23	34 0 5	36 3 15	39 2 25	42 2 7	45 1 16	48 0 26	51 0 8
9 „	24 0 11	27 0 12	30 0 14	33 0 23	36 0 16	39 0 18	42 0 19	45 0 21	48 0 22	51 0 23	54 0 25
10 „	25 1 5	28 1 23	31 2 14	34 3 4	37 3 22	41 0 12	44 1 2	47 1 21	50 2 11	53 3 1	56 3 19

Berry's Scale, used to calculate the 'drop'. *(Author's collection)*

considerable number of conversions. He admitted, however, that he found the people of Brighton 'harder to draw' than elsewhere, considering them too much engaged in worldly affairs. At Hailsham, on the other hand, where audiences were much more responsive, a young man whose behaviour had caused his parents much worry had walked to the front to declare his intention to change his ways. 'His sister was so overcome with gladness that she fell prostrate and had to be assisted from the hall.'

10 DECEMBER **1787** The *Sussex Advertiser* publicises the following great day's sport: 'Advertisement – Bull Baiting: there will be a bull baiting on Wednesday, the 26th of December 1787 at Hooe, the best dog to be entitled to a collar, value one guinea, the second dog to be entitled to half a guinea. The bull to be at stake by 10 o'clock in the morning. Dinner on table at one o'clock.'

Original notice of bull baiting. *(Sussex Advertiser)*

11 DECEMBER **1831** Samuel Thorncraft and John Reeds, both young farm labourers, had been drinking for much of the past two days in Levett's beer-shop at Milton Street and at the nearby Royal Oak. Thorncraft was aggrieved at his employer,

MILTON FIRE.

Near Alfriston.

£200.
REWARD.

WHEREAS
On SUNDAY EVENING last,

THE

BARNS

AND RICKS,

At Milton Farm, in the Parish of Arlington,

Were maliciously SET on FIRE.

Whoever will give Information against the Offender or Offenders, so that he or they may be brought to Justice, shall receive TWO HUNDRED POUNDS -REWARD, over and above all other Rewards ; to be paid on Conviction.

F. H. GELL.

LEWES, 12th December, 1831.

BAXTER, PRINTER, LEWES.

Wanted notice offering a £200 reward. *(East Sussex Record Office)*

Charles Ade, of Milton Court Farm and he and Reeds hatched a drunken plan to set fire to the barn. But in court Reeds was to become a prosecution witness. Here is part of the *Sussex Advertiser*'s account of his evidence, saying that Thorncraft had intended to cast the blame on John Ford, another farm labourer:

The prisoner and I went over the green meadow; we went towards Alfriston as far as the ash tree; we then went across to the barn; prisoner told me he had got tinder, matches and candle; we both went in at the stall; I struck the light; he lit the matches and told me to be off. I went away. I saw him put the matches in the peas mow; I went over to the rick settle; prisoner came after me and told me it had caught; we then ran across the green meadow; he told me he had the steel of J. Ford; he said he had got plenty of witnesses to show that it was Ford's steel; we went across the green field; I could not keep up with him so he stopt for me on the causeway. He said then, 'Now we must go back', but we did not but ran across a ploughed field and lay in a hedge. We stopt a minute; he said we must not stop here or they will say it is us.

12 DECEMBER **1925** Edward Dixon, 22, was found guilty of robbery with menaces and sentenced to a gaol term of five years and twenty strokes of the 'cat'.

13 DECEMBER **1844** The following extract comes from an anonymous letter from a farm labourer which was sent to the *Brighton Herald*: 'I am a labouring man with a family of five children. Two of my boys work at wages, 2s 6d each weekly. My own wages is only 5s weekly, in consequence of my not being so strong as my fellow labourers. . . . People in towns are little aware of the petty tyranny existing in villages.' Attached to the letter is 'An Address to the Labourers of Sussex' which includes the following lines:

Let us respectfully ask the three gentlemen whom we maintain in luxury out of our labour viz. the landlord, clergyman, and farmer, not to grind our faces as they hitherto have done. Let us pray them to stretch forth their hands to save us from that squalid poverty towards which we are approaching with gigantic strides. Our condition gets worse every year. . . . There are those who think that bread alone is sufficient to keep a man's strength up who has to labour in the fields. I wish that those that think thus would accompany me on a cold winter's morn, with the bitter biting north wind blowing in his face, with rain, sleet, or snow. Let him work in the fields for five hours, and afterwards sit under a wet cold hedge and eat for his dinner a bit of bread day after day. . . . The difficulty of bringing up a family at this time is extreme.

14 DECEMBER **1869** William Tulloch of Slaugham received an anonymous letter, threatening both to burn down his house and to blow his brains out. This was, the writer said, because he was 'so sharp to the poor'. Henry Tullett, a 20-year-old broom maker, was charged with the offence and in March 1870 he appeared before the Lord Chief Justice at Sussex Assizes. The motive according to the prosecution was that two of Tullett's cousins were in prison after having been caught poaching on Tulloch's land.

In evidence against Tullett, letters he had written while on remand in Lewes Gaol had been compared with the anonymous letter. Mr Chabot, described as 'the celebrated expert', was called as a prosecution witness and was firmly of the view that the characteristics of Tullett's prison letters were identical to those of the threatening letter. The jury were allowed to compare the letters, the judge commenting that they ought to consider the general character of the handwriting – the manner of making letters and words; the use or non-use of capital letters; the spelling; the habit of joining or not joining letters.

Tullett was sentenced to eight months' imprisonment.

1891 Caesar Gurr, a 25-year-old labourer, shot a pheasant on the land of Thomas Thompson and then assaulted the gamekeeper, George Robson. At the Quarter Sessions a letter he had written was produced in which Gurr pleaded guilty, expressing his regrets for what he had done, and promising not to go on Mr Thompson's land again save when he crossed it to go to church. The court took into account the injuries to the gamekeeper and he was sentenced to three months' hard labour.

15 December

1950 A matron at a nursing home in Worthing faced a charge of murder at the Assizes. The court heard evidence that she had placed a pillow over the head of a difficult patient to keep her from screaming. Mr Justice Humphreys, summing up, said that there was not the slightest evidence to suggest that the matron had intended to murder her patient. The jury returned a verdict of manslaughter but added a recommendation for mercy. The judge sentenced her to eleven days' imprisonment, which meant her immediate discharge.

16 December

1787

17 December

By his Majesty's Royal Letters Patent.
LEAKE'S PILULA SALUTARIA
Justly famous for CURING in all its Stages, the VENEREAL DISEASE.
ONE small PILL is a Dose; and the taking of one Box in a recent Case will soon convince the Patient of his speedy Recovery. Nothing can be better contrived, more safe, or more convenient than this Remedy for such as are obliged to go Journies, or to Sea, as it needs no Confinement nor Restraint of Diet; and 60 Years experience (in an extensive Practice) has proved, that it will effect a Cure, when repeated Salivation and all other Methods avail nothing. For the Scurvy, and other chronic Disorders, this Medicine has not its parallel: – Upwards of 40,000 Persons of both Sexes, have been radically cured of the bar of cruel Disorders within of the last Eight Years. Prepared and sold by the sole Proprietor, THOMAS TAYLOR, Member of the Corporation of Surgeons, London. . . .

The original notice regarding the pills. (*Sussex Advertiser*)

The very great Success of these Pills has induced several Wretches to Counterfeit them; in order to prevent the Public being imposed on by such in future, every Box is sealed up with a Stamp, on which, by Favour of the Commissioners is printed, at the Stamp Office, London, 'T. Taylor, No. 9, New Bridge-Street.' – To imitate which is Felony.

It was said at the time that so widespread throughout all classes were syphilis and gonorrhoea that three-quarters of all surgeons in London earned their living from attempting cures. And there was still plenty of room for quacks like the celebrated Taylor.

18 December **1934** At Sussex Assizes Sir Oswald Mosley, leader of the British Union of Fascists, along with three party members, was acquitted of a charge of riotous assembly and assault at Worthing, the so-called 'Munich of the South Coast'. Mosley, whose party had many members locally, including a town councillor, had been speaking on the evening of 8 October at Worthing Pavilion. Outside, a crowd of 300–400, opposed to the Fascist creed, had gathered, shouting, jeering, setting off fireworks and chanting, 'One, two, three, four, five, We want Mosley dead or alive.' When Mosley and his blackshirted bodyguards came out of the pavilion, the crowd surged forward and at this point blows were exchanged. At some point the Fascists felt themselves strong enough to march around the roundabout but then reinforcements arrived for the opposition and Mosley and his companions fled to a café near their headquarters in Warwick Street. The windows of the café were smashed and the crowd outside was threatening but then the blackshirts broke out and more fighting ensued. After a two-day trial the judge declared that it was impossible to assign blame for 'the battle of South Street', and the case was closed.

19 December **1860** An inquest into the death of Martha Ann Greenway was held at the Duke of Cumberland public house, Easebourne. When the servant girl went to church on the Sunday afternoon all had seemed well but on her return neither her master, her mistress nor their two children appeared to be in the house. Perhaps, the girl thought, they had gone to church at Fernhurst. As a result she went off to her mother's house. At 9 p.m. a neighbour heard a child crying and sent for the constable. He searched and found a child in a nearby ditch. It was the Greenways' 8-month-old baby. The constable then forced entry into the rear of the house and found the second child, 2½ years old, asleep in bed. But near the front door he came across the body of Mrs Greenway. Her throat had been cut and another cut starting on the right cheek stretched right down to the breastbone. Yet another knife wound sliced down from the throat to the fourth rib. Two hanks of hair, stiff with blood, were found on the kitchen floor where presumably the first blows had been struck, although there were no signs of a struggle.

But why had one child been abandoned in a ditch? Witnesses recalled that Greenway showed little affection for his younger child. Perhaps it had been his intention to murder it too. The inquest heard that he had been released from

Bethlehem Asylum only on the previous Friday after a ten-week confinement. Two days later Greenway was discovered at Elstead. He was later declared criminally insane.

1943 The Coroner declared at the end of the inquest held at Chichester that he had just heard 'one of the most baffling combination of circumstances which a Coroner could have to investigate'. The jury had returned an open verdict, quite unable to assign any cause to Mrs Madge Knight's death. Weeks earlier, on 18 November, 43-year-old Mrs Knight of Manor Cottage, Aldingbourne, had wakened the house with her screams and was found to have severe burns on her back, from which she died. But how had she been burnt so that the skin had peeled off her back? There was no coal fire in the house; the electric fires were turned off; the likelihood of acid was considered but rejected. And how was it that there was no damage to the bedding or the carpets? It was all most mysterious. Was it poltergeist activity? Was it a case of spontaneous human combustion? These possibilities were considered but no definitive answer was ever reached about Mrs Knight's strange death.

20 December

1830 Edward Bushby, 26, of East Preston was sentenced to death for arson at Lewes Assizes. 'The judge told the prisoner that he had been found guilty upon clear and satisfactory evidence of a crime punishable by the laws of this country with death. The sentence of death was not always carried into full effect; but the offence of arson was of that description, and particularly at the present time was one of so alarming a character, that if not checked, the country would be plunged into ruin and desolation.' The learned judge added, 'I dare not, consistently with my duty to the public, recommend you to His Majesty as an object of mercy.'

21 December

Bushby had worked on George Olliver's Homestead Farm but in this winter of discontent he challenged Olliver over wages. When Olliver refused to raise the wage for threshing corn with a flail and threatened instead to use a threshing machine the two men had a furious row, the farmer telling Bushby that he would never find work on local farms. That night a corn stack on Homestead Farm was set on fire and Bushby was heard to say 'Let it burn' and that he wished Olliver was in the middle of the fire. Almost immediately he was arrested. On 1 January 1831 Bushby was hanged. Olliver received £500 from the government for prosecuting an arsonist. He established a Prosecuting Society with the money.

1770

22 December

To Dr FLUGGER . . . Author of the Lignorum Anti-Scorbutic Drops
Sir,
I should be both guilty of ingratitude to you, and injustice to my fellow-creatures, were I not to make public the surprising CURE my Wife hath received in taking Eight bottles of your Lignorum Anti-Scorbutic Drops. After having been afflicted upwards of sixteen years, with several ulcers in her legs, which, notwithstanding every method that could be thought of was tried, and no cost spared, became more foul and corrupted: insomuch,

To Dr. FLUGGER,
In Prefcot-Street, Goodman's Fields, Author of
the Lignorum Anti-Scorbutic Drops,
SIR,

I SHOULD be both guilty of ingratitude to you, and injuftice to my fellow-creatures, was I not to make public the furprizing Cure my Wife hath received in taking Eight bottles of your Lignorum Anti-fcorbutic Drops.

After having been afflicted upwards of fixteen years, with feveral ulcers in her legs, which, notwithftanding every method that could be thought of was tried, and no coft fpared, became more foul and corrupted; infomuch, that a mortification was haftily enfuing, and a violent Fever had feized her, together with a whole complication of diforders; fo that her life was really miferable, and all relief difpaired of, but by death; till perfuaded by Mr. Shoubridge, the agent for the fale in this town, to try your Drops, which, to the furpize of all who knew her, and much to our comfort, perfected a Cure in a few months; and fhe is now in perfect health, and free from all diforders whatfoever.

Witnef; my hand,
RICHARD COOK,
Cooper.
Horsham, Dec. 22, 1770.

Dr Flugger's advertisement.
(*Sussex Advertiser*)

that a mortification was hastily ensuing and a violent Fever had seized her, together with a whole complication of disorders, so that her life was really miserable, and all relief despaired of, but by death; till persuaded by Mr Shoubridge, the agent for the sale in this town, to try your Drops, which to the surprise of all who knew her, and much to our comfort, perfected a Cure in a few months; and she is now in perfect health, and free from all disorders whatsoever.

Witness my hand
RICHARD COOK, Cooper.
Horsham Dec 22, 1770.

PS The truth of this may be relied upon and can be testified by many of the inhabitants of this town.

And what else could the good doctor not cure? And how might he have persuaded Richard Cook to endorse his Lignorum Anti-Scorbutic Drops?

23 December   1899 The crash just outside Wivelsfield station was the greatest rail disaster since the Clayton tunnel catastrophe thirty-eight years earlier. What had begun as a bright winter's day had suddenly changed and almost the whole county had become enshrouded in a dense, impenetrable fog.

The boat-train en route to Victoria from Newhaven had responded to fog signals and had slowed to a speed of no more than 5 miles an hour. It had just pulled clear of Wivelsfield station when at 6.30 p.m. it was hit in the rear by the Pullman train from Brighton. The engine of the Brighton train overturned and several carriages of the boat-train, telescoping, were derailed, tumbling down the embankment. Two of them caught fire and were almost totally destroyed. Six people were killed and seventeen injured.

24 December   1925 At East Grinstead police court Thomas Jackson, a 75-year-old of no fixed abode, was charged with refusing to do his allotted task at the East Grinstead Workhouse and also with breaking three panes of glass. He had been told at 8 a.m. to wash some floors and this he declined to do. He left the workhouse later in the morning, went down the road, picked up some bricks, returned to the workhouse and smashed the windows. Jackson told the court that he had done this because he wanted to spend Christmas in prison. He was sent to prison for seven days. 'Right, sir,' he said. 'Thank you very much.'

1866 In the early hours of a moonlit Christmas Day two of the keepers on the watch on Colonel Harcourt's land at Buxted heard a gunshot. They separated, going by different paths to where they thought poachers might be. They were aware also that other keepers, all of them armed only with sticks, would be making their way towards the sound. One of them – and it is interesting that in the report none of the keepers is identified by name – suddenly found himself face to face with three men. This keeper was struck with a gunstock and then, as he defended himself against one of the other poachers, he received a blow from a bludgeon (in Sussex they were usually called 'bats') which broke a bone in his arm. Another blow felled him, rendering him unconscious.

Two other keepers came upon the men, demanding to know why they were on private land. There was a brief attempt at an excuse – they were taking a short cut home, the men said – but then a vicious fight took place. One of the keepers was given such a beating that he was off work for more than three months.

At the Assizes three months later three labourers – William Troubridge, a powerfully built man, and the brothers James and George Sams, both described as 'rather good looking young fellows' – were each sentenced to five years' imprisonment.

1941 The Boxing Day dance in the lounge of the Mulberry Hotel, Goring, was limited to guests and ticket-holders. As usual the hotel closed its doors to the members of the public at 10 p.m. Just before midnight there was the sound of a rifle shot and a bullet entered the lounge window, ricocheted off the ceiling and hit William George in the left leg.

Company Sergeant Major Murdoch, who was in the bar at the time, rushed into the lounge and saw a Canadian soldier, Gerard Bertrand, pointing a rifle at a young woman. As Murdoch went towards him Bertrand shouted 'Stop! If you come near me I will shoot you!' Undeterred, Murdoch went forward and struggled with Bertrand. Another shot was fired from the rifle but this time no one was hurt. Eventually Bertrand was overpowered by the CSM and other guests and the rifle was taken from him. In the magazine there were three rounds of .303 ammunition. Now less aggressive, Bertrand said, 'I'm sorry but I wanted a drink.' Later he told PC Anderson, 'I could not get in so I fired up to frighten them.'

Two days later Bertrand told the magistrates he had been on duty on Christmas Day but had Boxing Day off and had gone drinking. By the time he arrived at the Mulberry Hotel he was very drunk. He had been refused entry and, enraged, had gone back to his billet, got his rifle, and returned. Then the fracas had begun. 'Booze let me down. I am very sorry for it all.'

An officer speaking for Bertrand said that he was a very hard worker and had only once before been in trouble. The Chairman of the Bench told Bertrand that the people of this country were grateful to Canada for sending her soldiers here but a great many Canadians were getting out of hand. Bertrand was sent to prison for three months, one on the wounding charge and one month for being drunk in possession of a loaded firearm, the sentences to run concurrently.

27 DECEMBER

1836 The snowstorms that began on Christmas Eve were the worst in thirty years. All along the very edge of the Downs, where these come to a quite abrupt halt on the south-eastern side of Lewes overlooking the Cliffe, high winds had forced the snow into deep drifts, which now overhung the houses of Boulder Row in a continuous wall. As the snow thawed the wall of snow threatened the houses below. Some urged the occupants of the terrace to evacuate their houses temporarily but their warnings went largely unheeded despite increasing falls of icy slabs. Then suddenly came the avalanche.

'A gentleman who witnessed the fall,' the *Sussex Weekly Advertiser* reports, 'described it as a scene of the most awful grandeur. The mass appeared to him

A contemporary
drawing of the
avalanche in 1836.
*(East Sussex Record
Office)*

to strike the houses first at the base, heaving them upwards and then breaking over them like a gigantic wave to dash them bodily into the road; and when the mist of snow, which then enveloped the spot, cleared off, not a vestige of a habitation was to be seen – there was nothing but an enormous mound of pure white.'

After the first hesitant slippage had come a deep-throated thunder which cut out all other sounds. Then came the thuds, the echoing crashes, the collapse of walls as the houses shifted from their foundations and were thrust 35yd and more across the road by tons of falling snow. And then there was a silence. Seven houses at the end of the terrace had been totally destroyed. Inside there were fifteen people, of whom only seven survived.

1950 At Brighton's Bevendean Hospital taxi driver Harold Bath and his daughter, Elsie, were confirmed as having smallpox. Though the disease had long been thought eradicated, the local Health Department had preparations for such an unlikely eventuality. Staff and patients at the hospital as well as their families, were vaccinated. Others came down with the disease. Within a fortnight 5,000 people who had been in contact with those who had fallen ill were traced and vaccinated. The Brighton Health Department bore the burden of a seek-and-find operation throughout the British Isles. **28 December**

Bevendean and Foredown Hospitals were both quarantined, with no one – neither patients nor staff – allowed in or out for thirty-four days. In all, out of twenty-nine confirmed and six unconfirmed cases dealt with there between 29 December and 7 February there were ten deaths. Harold Bath and a 48-year-old domestic worker died at Bevendean. At Dartford, out of nineteen patients, including Elsie Bath, transferred from Bevendean, four died. These included two nurses, and a gardener from Bevendean Hospital whose only contact with patients was to remove a Christmas tree from a ward. Of fourteen cases sent to Portslade two nurses and a domestic worker from Bevendean perished. A laundry worker also died there.

The Brighton smallpox outbreak, with its most terrifying possibilities, came and left in the freezing grimness of the post-Christmas period.

1789 Late at night the Eight Bells at Jevington was surrounded by armed local constables seeking the landlord, James Pettitt, better known as the 'Jevington Jigg', but also known by a variety of aliases such as Gibbs, Williams, Wilson and Morgan. As ever, this notorious character was being sought for some or other felony – smuggling, perhaps, or horse stealing or barn robbing – but on this occasion there were in the house several relatively respectable men and women playing whist, some of whom were alarmed at the prospect of gunfire and violence. The gentlemen went outside to reason with the constables. Their wives were distraught, they said, quite put out at the thought of what might happen. One of the ladies had actually fainted. Might she not be allowed out for fresh air? And what gentleman could deny a lady in such circumstances? But it was Jigg who made his getaway in bonnet and gown. **29 December**

Jigg's house at
Jevington.
(Tony Spencer)

Months later Jigg was less successful, ending up in Horsham Gaol. But at the Assizes his counsel, well paid by his wealthy client, managed to get him acquitted. There were other days and other escapades, more law-breaking and other narrow escapes from justice, until Pettitt was eventually sentenced to death for the theft of a horse. The sentence was commuted and he was transported for life.

30 DECEMBER **1822** For running a brothel at 32 North Steyne Row, John Dann and his wife, along with five women, found themselves in front of the Brighton magistrates. The court heard of 'a most disgusting scene of iniquity'. Ann Wood, 'one of the unfortunates', gave evidence about conditions. There were only two rooms in the house. In one room, men and women, 'all of the lowest order', slept in a common bed on the floor. Upstairs, in the room where Dann, his wife and five children slept, there was similar provision for the girls and their visitors. The girls were paid 10s 6d a week for the board and lodging. Two of the 'fair frail ones' had only recently become prostitutes

but others 'had been longer a prey to distress and infamy'. The three more experienced girls were sent to the treadmill for a month each and the two others were bound over to give evidence when the case came up at the Assizes.

On their way home from searching Dann's brothel the peace officers heard a cry of 'Murder' in Chapel Street. They found a woman struggling with a man named Priest. The woman, Mrs Wilson, claimed that her sister, only 15 years old, was in Priest's house with a man. She had tried to bring her sister away, she said, and Priest had struck her. At this point Priest dashed into the house, locking the door. The officers ran round to the back of the house where they saw two men helping two girls out of a window. The girls were arrested but, 'owing to the humanity of the officers' were not taken to 'that receptacle of filth and all that is disgusting, the so-called black hole'.

The case went to the Quarter Sessions and the Wilson girl was bound over to give evidence. She said that she had no idea that the place was a brothel. Two friends had taken her there for a glass of elder wine. Priest had disappeared and a warrant was issued for his arrest.

1919 The verdict at Midhurst Coroner's Court was that Charles James Brice, a former soldier in the Canadian Army and more recently a lumberjack at Eastham, committed suicide. Brice had been deeply in love with barmaid Amelia Kersey. They had gone for walks and to the cinema together, and they were probably lovers, judging by a letter she sent him, inviting him up to London during her holiday. 'You must get accommodation for us both', she had written, enclosing a wedding ring for him to wear. But something went wrong over the Christmas holiday. Brice was staying at the Angel Hotel where Amelia worked and there had been a falling-out. On the Sunday evening Amelia went to bed shortly after 9 p.m. after arguing with Brice, and barricaded the door with a chest of drawers. And after that there was confusion. Brice, a powerfully built man, forced his way into the bedroom. Shots and screams were heard, and Amelia ran downstairs, blood flowing from wounds to the head, breast and thigh. In the bedroom the Canadian was dead, shot in the chest.

31 DECEMBER

SHOT BARMAID

Amelia Kersey. *(Daily Sketch)*

BIBLIOGRAPHY

Books

Ackerson, John, *History of Brighthelmston*, Brambletye Books, 2005

Albery, William, *A Millennium of Facts in the History of Horsham*, privately published, 1947

Allen, Andrew, *Dictionary of Sussex Folk Medicine*, Countryside Books, 1995

Arscott, David, *East Sussex Events: Death, Disaster, War and Weather*, Phillimore, 2003

Baines, J. Manwaring, *Historic Hastings: A Tapestry of Life*, Cinque Ports Press, 1986

Brent, Colin, *Georgian Lewes*, Colin Brent Books, 1993

Burgess, Donald F., *No Continuing City: the Diary and Letters of John Burgess*, privately published, 1989

Burstow, Henry, *Reminiscences of Horsham*, FCCBS, 1911

Chapman, Brigid, *The Chronicles of the Cliffe*, Book Guild, 2003

Cobbett, William, *Rural Rides*, Macdonald and Janes, 1975

Eddleston, John J., *Murderous Sussex*, Breedon Books, 1997

Egan, Pierce, *Boxiana*, Sherwood, Jones, 1823

Ellison, R.A., *Eastbourne's Great War*, SB Publications, 1999

Firmin, Boys, *An Illustrated Guide to Crowborough*, HPU, 1890

Geering, Thomas, *Our Sussex Parish*, Country Books, 2003

A Gentleman of Chichester, *Smuggling and Smugglers in Sussex: The Genuine History of the Inhuman and Unparallel'd Murders Committed on the Bodies of Mr William Galley, A Custom-House Officer in the Port of Southampton: And Mr Daniel Chater, A Shoemaker of Fordingbridge in Hampshire*, published by B. Dickenson, 1749

Gilbert, Edmund W., *Brighton – Old Ocean's Bauble*, Methuen, 1954

Humphrey, George, *Eastbourne at War*, SB Publications, 1998

Johnson, W. Branch, *The English Prison Hulks*, Phillimore, 1970

Johnson, W.H., *Sussex Disasters*, SB Publications, 1998

——, *Sussex Tales of Mystery and Murder*, Countryside Books, 2002

——, *Sussex Villains*, Countryside Books, 2003

——, *Sussex Murders*, Sutton Publishing, 2005

Kyrke, R.V., *History of East Sussex Constabulary 1840–1967*, privately published, 1967

Longstaff-Tyrrell, Peter, *That Peace in our Time*, Gote House Graphics, 1993

——, *Front Line Sussex: Napoleon Bonaparte to the Cold War*, Sutton Publishing, 2000

——, *The Seaford Mutiny of 1795*, Gote House Publishing, 2001

Marchant, Rex, *Hastings: A History and Celebration of the Town*, Ottakars, 2004

Pratt, Malcolm, *Winchelsea*, privately published, 1998

Robertson, Charles A., *Hailsham and its Environs*, Phillimore, 1982

Royall, Michael, *The Petworth House of Correction*, privately published, 1990

Standing, R.W., *East Preston Workhouse 1791–1869*, privately published, 2000

Surtees, John, Barracks, *Workhouse and Hospital*, Eastbourne Local History Society, 1992

Thomas, Spencer, *West Sussex Events: Four Centuries of Fortune and Misfortune*, Phillimore, 2003

Vaisey, David (ed.), *The Diary of Thomas Turner*, Oxford University Press, 1984

Wells, Roger (ed.), *Victorian Village: The Diaries of the Revd John Coker Egerton*, Alan Sutton, 1992

Windrup, Anthony, *Horsham: An Historical Survey*, Phillimore, 1978

Wojtzak, Helena, *Women of Victorian Sussex*, Hastings Press, 2002

Record Office Papers

The National Archives
ASSI 36/48
MEPO 3/3022
HO 18/69/13r

East Sussex Record Office
SPA 1/6/9
SPA 11/3/4
COR/1/3/12–15
QAC/3/E1/1–6
QAP/2/E4/3

West Sussex Record Office
Add MSS 24, 113
Goodwood MS 155

Derbyshire County Record Office
Folder D1667/Z77

Newspapers and Magazines

Brighton Guardian
Brighton and Hove Herald
Cinque Ports Chronicle
Daily Mirror
Daily Sketch
Daily Telegraph
Eastbourne Chronicle
Eastbourne Citadel Centenary Brochure
Eastbourne Gazette
Hastings and Cinque Ports Iris
Hastings and St Leonards Observer
Hastings and St Leonards Pictorial Advertiser
Illustrated London News
Illustrated Police News
News of the World
Sunday Graphic
Sussex Advertiser
Sussex Agricultural Express

Sussex County Magazine
Sussex Daily News
Sussex Express
Sussex Weekly Advertiser
The Times
West Sussex County Times
West Sussex Gazette

INTERNET

Cruttenden Connections (http://homepage.ntlworld.com/ian.cruttenden1/